AF570717

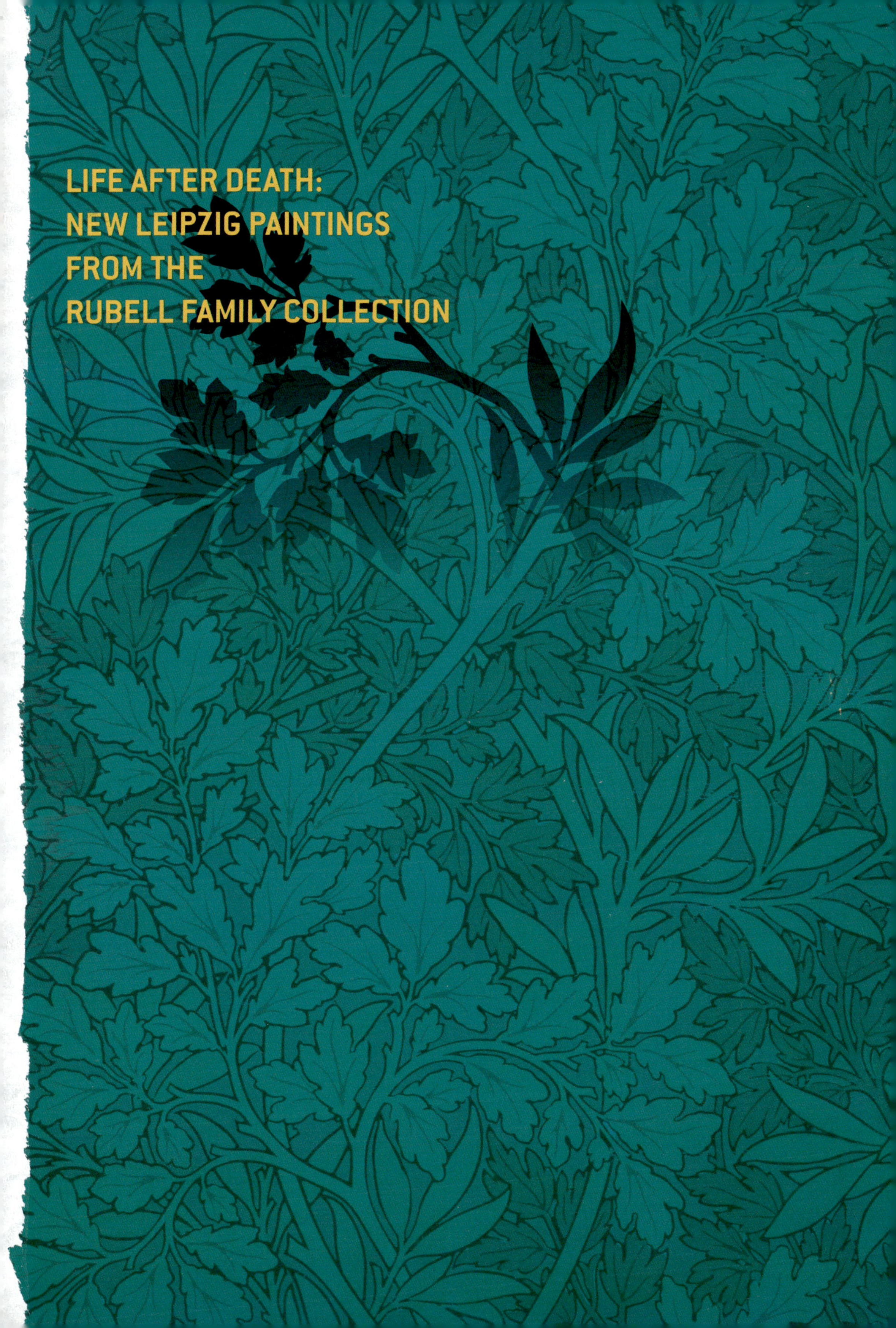

LIFE AFTER DEATH: NEW LEIPZIG PAINTINGS FROM THE RUBELL FAMILY COLLECTION

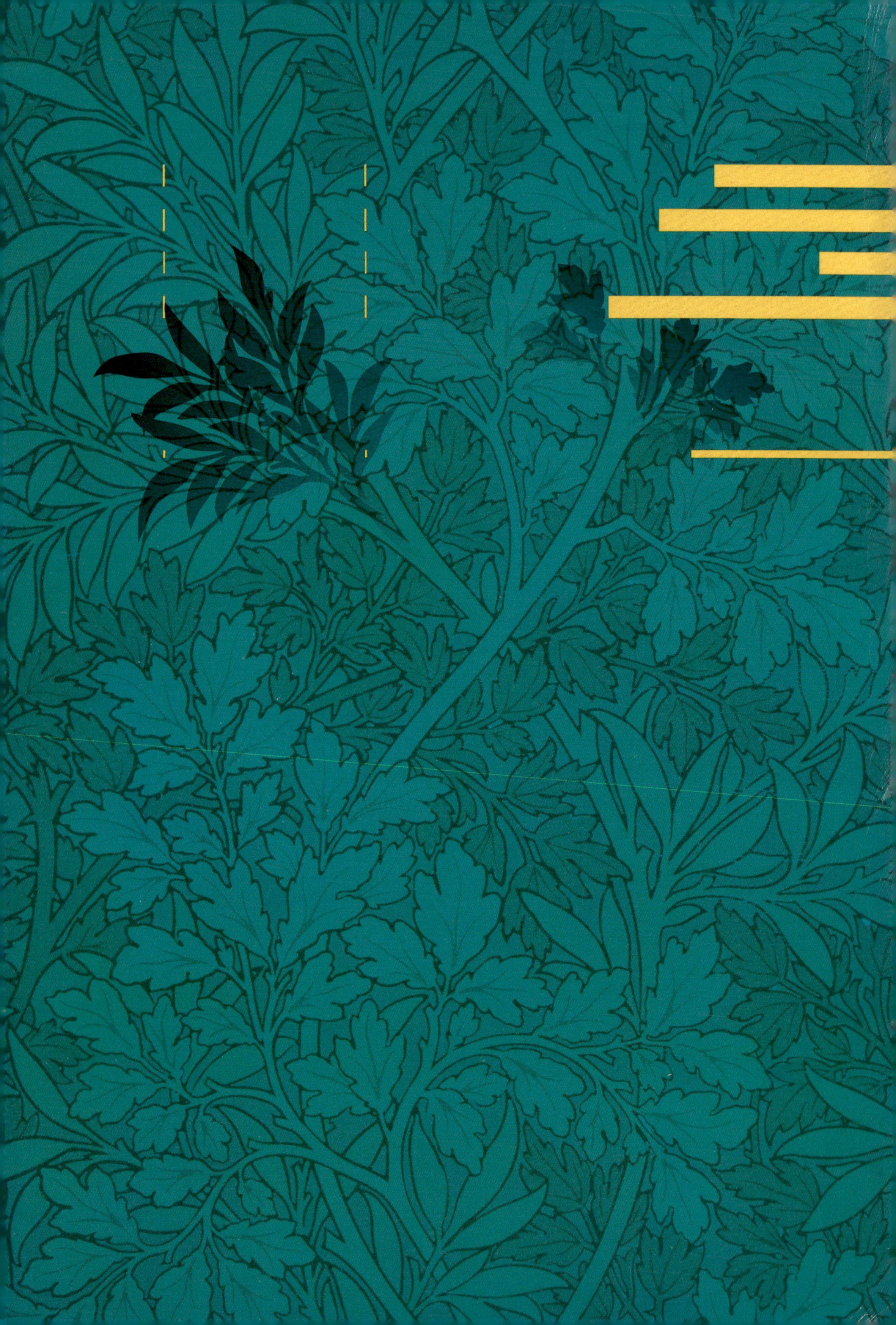

LIFE AFTER DEATH: NEW LEIPZIG PAINTINGS FROM THE RUBELL FAMILY COLLECTION

Mark Coetzee and Laura Steward Heon

December 1, 2004 – February 27, 2005
Rubell Family Collection, Miami, Florida

March 19, 2005 – March 31, 2006
MASS MoCA, North Adams, Massachusetts

April 21 – June 19, 2006
SITE Santa Fe, Santa Fe, New Mexico

September 5 - October 29, 2006
Katzen Arts Center Museum, American University, Washington, District of Columbia

February 16 – June 3, 2007
Frye Art Museum, Seattle, Washington

June 23 – September 30, 2007
Salt Lake Art Center, Salt Lake City, Utah

First published in 2005 by the
Rubell Family Collection
95 NW 29th Street
Wynwood Art District
Miami, Florida 33127
United States of America
Telephone: 305 573 6090
Facsimile: 305 573 6023
Bookstore: 305 573 6033
rubellcollection@mindspring.com
www.rubellfamilycollection.com

and

MASS MoCA
1040 MASS MoCA Way
North Adams, Massachusetts 01247
United States of America
Telephone: 413 664 4481
Facsimile: 413 663 8548
www.massmoca.org

Published in conjunction with the exhibition
Life After Death:
New Leipzig Paintings
from the Rubell Family Collection
organized by MASS MoCA and the Rubell Family Collection
and curated by
Mark Coetzee and Laura Steward Heon

Presented at:
Rubell Family Collection
(95 NW 29th Street, Miami, FL 33127)
December 1, 2004 - February 27, 2005

MASS MoCA
(1040 MASS MoCA Way, North Adams, MA 01247)
March 19, 2005 - March 31, 2006

SITE Santa Fe
(1606 Paseo De Peralta, Santa Fe, NM 87501)
April 21 - June 19, 2006

Katzen Arts Center Museum, American University
(4400 Massachusetts Avenue, Washington, DC 20016)
September 5 - October 29, 2006

Frye Art Museum
(704 Terry Avenue, Seattle, WA 98104)
February 16 - June 3, 2007

Salt Lake Art Center
(20 South West Temple, Salt Lake City, UT 84101)
June 23 - September 30, 2007

Authors: Mark Coetzee and Laura Steward Heon
Photography: Mark Coetzee
Book Design: Jung Kim
Registrars: Larry Smallwood and Juan Valadez
Copy-Editing: Elizabeth Martinez

Color Origination: Color Reflections
Printing and Binding: Imprenta Mariscal

First Edition: December 2005
ISBN: 0-9716341-4-9
Library of Congress Control Number: 20040950348

The type for this book was set in
Conduit and MrsEaves

This book was printed on Coache Creator Matt (150gsm)
with end sheets of Bristol (160gsm)
sewn and case bound in 2.5 mm board
covered with Coache Creator Gloss (150gsm)
with a Matt Film Lamination

Printed in Ecuador

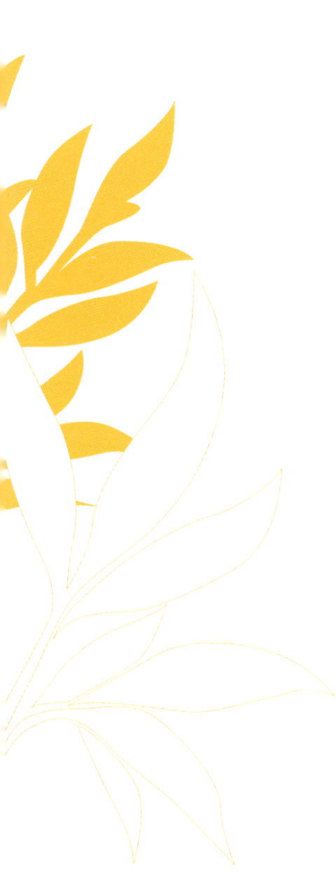

Exhibition Statement

"Life After Death" positions the paintings and drawings in this exhibition in the afterlife – the afterlife of the German Democratic Republic (GDR or East Germany), of social realism, and of painting in general. Traces of the GDR inhabit the grim interiors and muddled social modernist architecture in these paintings. Social realism, once the dominant style behind the Iron Curtain, possesses the figures who rarely make eye contact, keeping their thoughts to themselves. Painting itself (its death is an unlikely event that art critics proclaim every ten years or so) crops up in the emphasis on craft. You can see it in the use of classical gestures, graphite scaling grids, forced perspective, and careful attention to color.

These seven artists chose to study at the Leipzig Art Academy, in the former East Germany, in the decade after the fall of the Berlin Wall in 1989. This was an unlikely decision at a time when the inhabitants of Leipzig were leaving in droves for the West, and when the main currents of art flowed away from painting, toward video, photography, and installation art. The untimely embrace of a shrinking East German city and conventional medium is imprinted on the pictures, but rather than buckling under the weight of place, time, and tradition, they convey something surprising and subjective. The mystery of these pictures, with their out-of-date sources and classical techniques, is their utter and beguiling singularity.

Mark Coetzee and Laura Steward Heon

Tilo Baumgärtel
Tim Eitel
Martin Kobe
Neo Rauch
Christoph Ruckhäberle
David Schnell
Matthias Weischer

Contents

Rubell Family Collection
NORTHERN LIGHT
MASS MoCA
SITE Santa Fe
Katzen Arts Center Museum, American University
Frye Art Museum
Salt Lake Art Center

Though the city of Leipzig boasts its most famous musical son, Bach, as well as one of the oldest art schools in Germany, few considered this a contemporary visual art destination of any reckoning. In the last year or two, however, this consideration has changed dramatically.

When Don and Mera Rubell visited Leipzig in the fall of 2003, the trip proved to be pivotal – not only for the family, which includes son, Jason, and daughter, Jennifer, and their famed Collection, but also for the careers of a group of young artists living and painting in what was the former East Germany. Gallerist Christian Ehrentraut introduced the Rubells to this unique group of painters, and their excitement was so great, they literally bought up entire exhibitions.

Opening the crates upon arrival in Miami, we all joined in Don and Mera's enthusiasm. These collected works from the New Leipzig School were at once thrilling and provocative, and clearly something we needed to share with the public.

It was immediately decided to mount a comprehensive exhibition of these paintings, and the Rubell Family Collection set out to acquire further pieces to complete the project. Fourteen months and 62 pieces later, an exhibition under the title "Northern Light: Leipzig in Miami" opened on December 1, 2004, and ran for three months.

Laura Steward Heon and I had been speaking for many years of doing something together for the MASS MoCA galleries, drawing from the vast resource of art objects that make up the Rubell Family Collection. Countless hours spent perusing the storage rooms, dreaming of one show after another, it wasn't long before we found our next calling: to honor Don and Mera's commitment to these Leipzig artists by delving even deeper into the New Leipzig School and its talented painters. Of course by this stage many collectors, galleries and museums too had developed this almost frenzied interest.

I am grateful to the Rubells for their guidance and constancy, and for always encouraging me to find personal enrichment in my work. As such, Laura and I had the distinct pleasure of throwing ourselves deeply into conversations about this work, free from the usual pressures of trying to fundraise, beg for loans and negotiate the politics that curators seem to spend so much time doing. Slowly, and quite enjoyably, this exhibition and book took form, and "Northern Light" developed into "Life After Death."

We hope your experience with these artworks is as positive and enriching as ours – that they give you pleasure, of course, but that you also consider the issues surrounding their creation: that is, the identity of place, the weight of tradition, the difficulties of realism, and the ongoing debate about painting itself.

Mark Coetzee
Director and Curator

Rubell Family Collection
MASS MoCA
SENSE OF ADVENTURE
SITE Santa Fe
Katzen Arts Center Museum, American University
Frye Art Museum
Salt Lake Art Center

In its now seven years, and until "Life after Death," MASS MoCA had never mounted an exhibition of paintings, nor had we ever presented a show drawn exclusively from a single private collection. We know that our galleries – unusually large, infused with side light, irregular in circulation, nobly impressed by their 120-year history as a working factory – are hospitable to large-scale sculpture, complex multimedia installations, and other physically immersive work. But, up to now, we were unsure they could sustain the weight of tradition and the unrelieved two-dimensionality of conventional painting. And since we don't collect, we have been – how to put it? – liberated from the intricate *pas de deux* that often unfolds between great collectors and the museums that covet the fruits of their labor.

"Life after Death" cut through all that.

Following visits to Leipzig in the fall of 2003, Don and Mera Rubell began assembling what has become the single most important concentration of this still incipient movement, perhaps anywhere outside the *Baumwollspinnerei* (spinning mill) art complex in which the artists still live and work. With a reputation for acquiring and showing precisely the kind of impossible-to-display, hard-to-own work often associated with MASS MoCA's own program – big, direct, hard-hitting art, full of life, and with no fear of wit or drama – this relatively quiet corner of the Rubell's collecting activity was much less well known. And while a small group of other adventuresome collectors were beginning to turn their attention to eastern Europe, the fresh energy and exciting painterly thought emerging from the Leipzig group was still little known to the general public. We very much wanted to show this new work to our audiences, testing our galleries, and the Rubells wanted the paintings to be shown together – simple enough motivating forces, but the result was an exceptionally strong exhibition, and this fine catalogue.

The paintings themselves are as affecting as they are resistant. Never has so much drab brown, grey and green paint resulted in such strangely alluring and surprisingly vivid tonal combinations, or such evocative painterly spaces. Curators Mark Coetzee and Laura Steward Heon recognized that these works could not only hold their own in our unconventional galleries, but that they would also build upon one another to develop a subjective emotional space that derives from the intricate spatial structures of the paintings themselves. Their selections -- and their installation -- rewards multiple visits. But you have to look closely. Matthias Weischer's magisterial *St. Ludgerus*, at first all thick slabs of grim olive-brown, ultimately reveals a spatial impossibility as elusive and delicate as James Turrell's, the dense layers of paint crisply incised by the back of brush, only to be augmented again by the literal, plastic rising of extreme impasto. David Schnell's *Planks (Bretter)* inserts a sweet, Barbizon-like miniature into the forced perspectival depths of a complex space-box that commences with the delicate flowery surfaces of Japanese screen painting, and ends with the thumping, all-over ground notes of Anselm Kiefer. Even after a year of living with these works, we're still finding visual puns, witty art-historical references, and passages of sheer technical bravura that continue to absorb our attention.

Direct, generous and immensely caring of its art and artists, the Rubell Family Collection was an excellent partner. Don and Mera were encouraging and expansive. Mark Coetzee, Curator of the Collection, and Laura Steward Heon of our staff, made for a spirited curatorial tag team. I join the MASS MoCA Foundation in thanking the Rubell Family Collection for its generous loans and sense of adventure that gave us this "Life after Death".

Joe Thompson
Director

Rubell Family Collection
MASS MoCA
SITE Santa Fe
AESTHETIC TRAJECTORIES
Katzen Arts Center Museum, American University
Frye Art Museum
Salt Lake Art Center

This exhibition grew from my many conversations with Mark Coetzee concering some of art's fundamental questions: how does it function? what makes a work successful? and where does our pleasure in it lie? These concerns may seem old- fashioned, but ultimately they are the ones that sustain my personal engagement with art. Our goal here was simply to create an exhibition for the galleries at MASS MoCA from the collection that the Rubell family has built; an exhibition not driven by a theme, but rather by a search for the intersection of our aesthetic trajectories at the time. Our conversations to this end were deeply rewarding, and I will always treasure them.

It thrills me to host "Life After Death" at SITE Santa Fe, as it was the last exhibition I organized before leaving MASS MoCA in March 2005. Having it travel to SITE is personally satisfying and represents a connection between the two institutions that I hope will continue for years to come.

SITE Santa Fe is a dynamic museum, a *Kunsthalle* celebrating its 10th anniversary in 2005. It was founded in tandem with its Biennial exhibition, the only international biennial in the United States, organized by invited curators of international reputation, the majority of whom have gone on to serve as curators for the famed Venice Biennale. This progression is indicative of SITE's place in the international contemporary art world: ahead of the curve. SITE has offered a flexible venue at pivotal moments for many great artists too numerous to list here. Our tradition, as well as our future, lies with artists on the edge.

It has been a pleasure working with our colleagues at MASS MoCA and the Rubell Family Collection. On behalf of SITE's Board and staff, I thank those two institutions for their intelligence, kindness, and professionalism.

Laura Steward Heon
Director and Curator

Rubell Family Collection
MASS MoCA
SITE Santa Fe
Katzen Arts Center Museum, American University
DISTRACTED IN WASHINGTON
Frye Art Museum
Salt Lake Art Center

The American University Art Department has a long tradition of training figurative artists. It began in the 1940s when the Phillips Gallery Art School merged with AU's nascent art program, becoming one of the first schools, along with Cranbrook Academy and the University of Iowa, to offer a graduate degree in studio art. Early faculty members Robert F. Gates, Ben L. Summerford, and William Calfee were committed to the most advanced ideas in contemporary art. Gifts of art from Duncan Phillips and Katherine Dreier formed the core of its excellent teaching collection.

With such parentage, the collection and art department were rooted in post impressionism and American modernists coming of age during WWII. AU taught the kind of figuration where color and light and technical mastery were all-important. There was a decidedly French flavor to its modernism.

As the world split between representation and abstraction, AU became known for its conservative, academic approach to painting in Washington, DC, positioned in opposition to what became known, thanks to a brief visit by Clement Greenberg, as the Washington Color School. In more recent years, AU has become a more diversified art department infused with young blood and again comfortable with the newest styles and genres. But certainly through the eighties and past the time of the collapse of the Berlin Wall and the reunification of East and West Germany, AU was an academic realist counterpart to the social-realist training offered at the Leipzig Art Academy.

It is ironic, or maybe just normal, that we long for what is lost after we work so hard to lose it. Imagine a nostalgia for the German Democratic Republic and social-realist painting concurrent with the rise in our re-appreciation of Adolphe William Bougereau and all that uncomfortable fifties furniture. Will we one day long for a president who takes extended vacations in Crawford, Texas, and can't pronounce nuclear?

Perhaps painting refuses to die just because of this continual process of building and destroying traditions. Call it a cycle of renewal. The academy has always been something for artists to react against, whether it is the French Salon, the followers of Vuillard, or GDR social realism. Artists may need this wall of opposition to test themselves against, to struggle to fashion something new and relevant for their times.

What is so disturbing, and dazzling, about the young artists in "Life After Death: New Leipzig Paintings from the Rubell Family Collection" is how perfectly relevant their art is to our lives in the West today. While the flash and bang of installations and projections are in the museums and art fairs, our time is captured by the empty, achingly beautiful rooms of Matthias Weischer. We feel our contemporary disconnectedness in the crowded scenes of Christoph Ruckhäberle. Who can blame us if we retreat to the confections of Bougereau and other popular distractions?

Jack Rasmussen
Director and Curator

Rubell Family Collection
MASS MoCA
SITE Santa Fe
Katzen Arts Center Museum, American University
Frye Art Museum
A SUSTAINED MOMENT
Salt Lake Art Center

In the discourse of representational art, the title "Life After Death" evokes the many times, from the 19th through the 21st century, and since the invention of photography, that painting has been declared dead or merely beside the point. Photography is a medium and system of representation which is often said to have seized painting's primary historical function: that is, the depiction and representation of the world we live in. Yet we presently find ourselves – not for the first time and no longer unexpectedly – in a sustained moment celebratory of painterly representation. Contemporary artists seem especially eager to explore the rich possibilities of figuration informed by both painting and photography, or better put, painting that is always also about photography.

The Frye Art Museum's focus has long been representational art. We recognize, however, that what we talk about when we talk about representational art is a shifting notion, unstable through time and across cultures. 21st century artists, for example, using the tools and materials of human genomic research, have begun to create new life forms *as art*. These artworks include new strains of transgenic bacteria and living mammals released into the world, creations that are of course not without controversy. The point I want to emphasize here is that when artists are capable of creating artistic *subjects* as well as artistic *objects*, the anchors of any discourse of representational art seem especially up for grabs.

The Frye's mission statement reflects an embrace of the contested and shifting ground of representational art, something we often refer to, both in-house and in exhibitions, as the "R Word."

Through its exhibitions, collections, and programs, the Frye Art Museum engages audiences, challenges perceptions, and encourages dialogue about representational art in all its complexities, past and present. Admission to the Museum will always be free.

Our exhibitions and programs examine this compelling and troubled notion from a variety of perspectives, in historical and contemporary presentations across mediums. All of this is to say that when I first saw "Northern Light: Leipzig in Miami" at the Rubell Family Collection in winter 2004, I was sure this was the right exhibition for the Frye at this moment in its history.

At the core of the founding Frye Collection, formed between 1893 and 1930 by Seattle residents Charles and Emma Frye, is 19th-century German and Austrian painting. These holdings include fine examples of both history paintings – representative of academic high art – and genre paintings – the still lifes, landscapes and domestic scenes long considered low art, even craft, and permissible only in the Academy's late and declining years. Although these paintings have always held interest for art historians, they have gone in and out of favor with general audiences.

In his will Charles Frye provided funds for a free public art museum, which was also to house and showcase his collection. When the Frye Art Museum opened its doors to the public in 1952 this collection was offered to broad audiences for the first time. This was a cultural moment dominated in the United States by American abstract expressionism; the relationship between representational art and abstraction had congealed into a dichotomy still best expressed by critic Clement Greenberg's ascerbic formulation of "avant garde vs. kitsch." This idea of representational art as anti-abstraction – as conservative at best, and nostalgic, even reactionary, at worst – still persists in certain quarters, even as more and more contemporary artists find potential in the exploration of recognizable subject matter in mediums such as painting, photography, video and performance, as well as in less-definable interstices between these mediums.

The Frye Collection is always on view in the Museum galleries and provides a worthy historical counterpoint for viewers of the New Leipzig School's powerful contemporary paintings, and their significant, although not uncontested, contribution to the recent discourse on representational art. We are pleased to be part of the effort to introduce this important art to broader audiences in the United States, while at the same time furthering our investigation of representational art's varied historical strands and contemporary manifestations.

Robin Held
Chief Curator and Director of Exhibitions and Collections

Rubell Family Collection
MASS MoCA
SITE Santa Fe
Katzen Arts Center Museum, American University
Frye Art Museum
Salt Lake Art Center
DIFFERENT NEIGHBORHOODS

In late spring of 2005, a friend who is an artist, advocate and patron of the contemporary arts in Salt Lake City, shared with me images and literature about a powerful and timely exhibition she had recently seen at MASS MoCA. Her enthusiasm for "Life After Death: New Leipzig Paintings from the Rubell Family Collection," especially the paintings of Neo Rauch, was contagious, and motivation enough for me to request that my staff make inquiries regarding the availability of this significant collection. Their findings: the show would travel.

In discussions since, Mark Coetzee stressed the desire of the Rubell family to have this important part of their collection made available to other venues outside of the East Coast of the United States. Like me, the Rubells feel it is vitally important to present the contemporary ideas and compelling images of artists from as many different perspectives and cultures as possible, to as many audiences as possible. Perhaps "the world is flat" as Thomas L. Friedman suggests in his recent book of the same name. Perhaps also the contemporary artists of the world are the bellwether for change and understanding. We are all citizens of a global community, and thus can't afford to be ignorant of distant happenings, in this instance, the art from beyond our norm, from the former East Germany. We cannot lose ourselves in the innocence and naiveté of the hinterlands of Utah or the American West. All of us, living in Leipzig or Salt Lake City, have a neighborhood on which we depend for comfort, compatibility and collective knowledge. But we must share our perspectives with other neighborhoods. Rarely is there the opportunity, amidst the urban sprawl of our region, to see such engaging and personal art that is reflective of a people, a culture, a polity and a country so often misunderstood, distant and seemingly foreign. This is much more than just an exhibition – it is an aesthetic, social and intellectual encounter well worth our participation.

I graciously thank the Rubell family for their generosity in making this collection available to audiences of the American West. And I commend their wisdom in providing this unique opportunity for these courageous artists of the New Leipzig School to have their works shared outside their "neighborhood." To Mark Coetzee, Curator of the Rubell Family Collection, I extend my thanks for his leadership, and for his efforts in getting this work "out west," as requested by the family.

Ric Collier
Director

Life After Death:
New Leipzig Paintings from the Rubell Family Collection

Tilo Baumgärtel Tim Eitel Martin Kobe Neo Rauch Christoph Ruckhäberle David Schnell Matthias Weischer

Neo Rauch
1960 in Leipzig
Lives in Leipzig

Tim Eitel
1971 in Leonberg
Lives in Berlin + Leipzig

David Schnell
1971 in Bergisch Gladbach
Lives in Leipzig

Tilo Baumgärtel
1972 in Leipzig
Lives in Leipzig

Christoph Ruckhäberle
1972 in Pfaffenhofen
Lives in Leipzig

Martin Kobe
1973 in Dresden
Lives in Leipzig

Matthias Weischer
1973 in Elte
Lives in Leipzig

Painting is dead. Long live painting! This is a familiar refrain among curators, critics, and art historians. If painting is dead, then figure painting is moldering, and social realism is completely petrified, and therefore (according to this inverted logic) must be the liveliest painting of all. The disparagement of figure painting, a kind of recurrent matricide among artists and art historians, probably began soon after Zexeus painted his famous grapes with such realism that birds pecked at them. As real as a figure painting might be, it can never be as real as reality and so is doomed to fail if judged by that standard. It has failed miserably by many other standards: too bourgeois, too proletarian, too spiritual, too mundane, too burdened by its history. But failure, and attendant low expectations, is often the precursor of success. In December 2000, a group of five young German artists, all recent graduates of the prestigious Leipzig Art Academy (more properly known as *Hochschule für Grafik und Buchkunst*) in the former German Democratic Republic, organized a small exhibition of figure paintings, landscapes and interiors in Leipzig. Unsurprisingly, the exhibition attracted no notice from the international contemporary art community. From that humble beginning, the "New Leipzig School" has grown to be something of an international phenomenon, and its painters (the original five have become a loose group of twelve or so) are making work that has museums and collectors in its thrall.

This exhibition presents seven artists affiliated with the New Leipzig School. Six of them were students at the Leipzig Art Academy in the decade after the fall of the Berlin Wall in 1989; the seventh, Neo Rauch, studied there in the 1980s and remained at the school as a senior teaching assistant throughout the 1990s, working closely with students. Following their graduation from the school, the younger artists all remained in Leipzig and formed an association called *Galerie LIGA* (the League Gallery) together with the gallerist Christian Ehrentraut and six other students not included in this

This exhibition presents seven artists affiliated with the New Leipzig School.

exhibition. They agreed that they would only show their works as a group for two years, from 2001 to 2003. Rauch also remained in Leipzig, but was not part of *LIGA*.

All of these decisions – to move to Leipzig, to study painting in the 1990s, to form a cooperative, to remain in Leipzig even after some success – are unusual ones, and not necessarily indicative of promising careers. But all of these decisions have had an effect on the works these artists create, works that share thematic and technical concerns. They are first and foremost products of their time and place; that much is evident, but that is not all. Most of the paintings and drawings shown here are figurative: we can easily recognize landscapes, interiors, and people. They are carefully composed and carefully rendered; there are few wild expressionistic brush strokes, no unbridled passion in the pictures. That is not to say that the pictures are not full of feeling -- they are -- but the feeling is deeply subjective and deeply restrained. And though the paintings are not expressionistic, they are, at times, virtuosic: the painterly techniques used here are grounded in centuries of tradition as well as in recent critical debates, and informed by the craft of painting as taught in one of the great traditional academies of art.

the painterly techniques used here are grounded in centuries of tradition as well as in recent critical debates, and informed by the craft of painting as taught in one of the great traditional academies of art.

Critics have struggled to find a way to compare the Leipzig artists with the last crop of German painters to capture the attention of the art world, the German branch of neo-expressionists, known as the *Neue Wilden*, whose star rose and fell during the 1980s. These painters are typified by their de facto leader, Georg Baselitz, in much the same way that Rauch relates to the younger Leipzig artists. Baselitz painted deeply personal, extremely expressive figurative pictures, rooted in earlier German expressionist traditions, as well as psychotic art. In the 1970s, he painted his figures upside down in order to stress the act of painting over his subject matter. The Leipzig painters share a similar concern with creating tension between subject and the act of painting, but that may be the only thing they share. Whereas the *Neue Wilden* were expressionists, it is not too much to call the Leipzig painters "repressionists." Their works show restraint. They withhold. And though they share the *Neue Wilden's*

The Leipzig painters share a similar concern with creating tension between subject and the act of painting...

dedication to the act of painting, their dedication is mediated through academic tradition and near-Greenbergian modernism. The paintings are aggressively flat and airless, kept under tight control, and adamant about technique and repose.

In fact, the emphasis on technique is extreme enough to overtake the subject, in some cases becoming the subject itself. This is perhaps most obvious in the work of Matthias Weischer. His painting *St. Ludgerus* ostensibly depicts two couches and a coffee table, but also offers a catalogue of techniques. For example, he has drawn a black grid on top of the paint in the lower half of his canvas. The grid at first glance resembles a scaling grid used by painters for centuries as a way to scale up their studies – make a drawing, grid it out, and transfer the image square by square to a larger canvas – but in this case the grid is on top of the painting. This canvas is obviously not a study for a much larger one; the point of the grid is to flatten the image, to remind us that we are looking at a painting, not a living room. Another technical anachronism is the faint trace of a figure seated on the couch on the right side. This pentimento has left her feet behind – they dangle from absent legs just above the floor. Painterly games of presence and absence, or masking, are played on the coffee table. There are two wine glasses, one represented in paint, one in bare canvas; the glass vase that holds flowers is painted in, but the flowers themselves are bare canvas. Some objects, like the arms of the couches, are made to turn in space, others, like the lampshade, are utterly flattened. The casement for the window is painted on top of the brown wall, and where there should be glass allowing a view behind the wall, Weischer scrapes away the paint, showing us canvas rather than the street.

In fact, the emphasis on technique is extreme enough to overtake the subject, in some cases becoming the subject itself.

Painterly games of presence and absence, or masking, are played...

Such fancy footwork pertains to centuries of tradition, but what makes it interesting is its relation to the key critical idea of modernist painting, that of "object nature." Articulated most adamantly by the influential critic Clement Greenberg at mid-century, the idea of object nature concerns the essence of painting, in particular abstract painting. Greenberg and his followers insisted that this essence was to be found exclusively in the shape of the canvas, the flatness of the canvas, and its color.

Such fancy footwork pertains to centuries of tradition, but what makes it interesting is its relation to the key critical idea of modernist painting, that of "object nature."

Founded in 1764, is one of the oldest art schools in Germany, It is highly regarded for its tradition of figure painting...

The origin of the technical emphasis may be traced to the Leipzig Art Academy, that entity that brought these seven painters together. Founded in 1764, and one of the oldest art schools in Germany, it is highly regarded for its tradition of figure painting, which, before the reunification of Germany in 1989 and 1990, was bound to state-mandated "social-realist" painting. While academies in the West eschewed figurative painting, and sometimes painting itself, in favor of abstraction and work in new media, photography, video, and installation, the Leipzig Academy produced some of East Germany's most highly regarded figure painters, such as Bernhard Heisig, Wolfgang Mattheuer, and Werner Tübke, as well as Arno Rink and Sieghard Gille, professors at the academy who advised all of the LIGA painters. Its rigorous two-year foundation course consisted primarily of portrait and nude studies. The state-mandated focus on figure painting foreclosed experimentation with subject matter or form, but it left technique free to develop. The legacy of technical experimentation pervades all of the LIGA painters' works.

A strange surrealism and a discordant palette pervade their interiors, cityscapes, and landscapes, which are often populated by disaffected figures.

In addition to their affiliation with the Leipzig Art Academy, the New Leipzig School painters share stylistic concerns, which are shaped in part by the tradition of the school and by East German social realism in general. A strange surrealism and a discordant palette pervade their interiors, cityscapes, and landscapes, which are often populated by disaffected figures. A general feeling of world-weariness and ennui speaks to the East German political situation: these are depictions of places and people that are not prepared to integrate into the brand-new optimistic West. Unready to face the new, they are nostalgic for the old, but more from habit than any affection. In these paintings, we sense the afterlife.

The Leipzig paintings are expressive of the contemporary German neologism *Ostalgie*, a combination of *Ost* (east) and *Nostalgie* (nostalgia), which denotes this longing for the GDR. This strange nostalgia is best known in the United States through the German film *Goodbye Lenin*, which was widely screened here. It tells the story of a young man living in the former GDR in the late 1990s. His mother, an ardent Communist, has just awakened from a coma that she has been in since before the fall of the Berlin Wall. Concerned that the shock of the transformed Germany might kill her, he and his friends go to incredible and comic lengths to replicate East Germany in her little apartment, searching out government-issued pickles, making up fictitious newscasts, and the like.

Neo Rauch's paintings are emblematic of *Ostalgie*. Ten years older than the other Leipzig School artists, Rauch was an assistant to his former professor at the Academy, Arno Rink, and taught several of the younger painters, as noted above. He is by far the most established of the group – some would not even include him as a member – and traces of his strange vision appear in some of the works of these younger artists. In his 2003 painting *Das Neue* (*The New*), three figures who demonstrate no awareness of each other occupy an unusual conglomeration of spaces. The foreground might be a domestic interior, but it dissolves into a horizontal band of bright yellow haze. In the background, some brutish industrial buildings are somehow washed by the sea. One figure in a T-shirt stands in the middle of the scene with his back to us, his legs uncomfortably crossed. A seated woman concentrates on a blue-green lump she is knitting. A speech balloon emerges from the mouth of a professorial figure with a top hat, pointed beard, and cane. He says, in precise lettering "*Das Neue*." *The New* is apparently a bewildering time and place for these refugees of history. They appear to exist in some kind of historical purgatory: the figure in the T-shirt could be Rauch's contemporary, the figure in the top hat must belong to the late 19th or early 20th century, but the woman knitting could come from almost any time from 1950 onward. Similarly, their surroundings give few hints, or give deliberately contradictory hints, about time and place. Rauch has transformed figures proper to social realism with a dreamlike ambiguity that owes more to surrealism.

The New is apparently a bewildering time and place for these refugees of history. They appear to exist in some kind of historical purgatory...

The ghost of social realism in Neo Rauch's and the other artists' works has been sighted (and cited) more than once. That the painters have social realist forebears is not surprising, given the fact that the style was mandated by the GDR for many decades before 1989, and that both Rink and Gille, the primary teachers of these artists, were inculcated in this style. What is more interesting than "repo-realism" (that it has been repossessed, or in Rauch's case, never let go – the term appears in German criticism of these artists) is the repurposing of realism. Where social realism was uplifting, this work gives no direction; where that was unambiguous, this is aggressively vague; where it presented figures striving energetically forward, this offers figures who list. The intense withholding in these pictures invites a different term than "repo-realism." It is repressionism. The stifled emotional tenor of these artists' works links them in a more profound way than does their use of realistic figures, landscapes, and interiors.

The stifled emotional tenor of these artists' works links them in a more profound way than does their use of realistic figures, landscapes, and interiors.

It is this quality that Tim Eitel's work shares with Rauch's. Eitel, the only one of these seven artists to leave Leipzig (for Berlin) makes figures who stand around awkwardly, never belonging to the place they are in, very rarely facing the viewer. But unlike Rauch's, Eitel's figures are definitely our contemporaries, and their activities, such as they are, take place in office parks, museums, and other unsurprising places bereft of surrealism. Painted in watercolor or thin veils of oil, his figures seem to exist by the thinnest of margins. They might float away or fade out at any moment. Eitel takes photographs of places and people that interest him separately and combines them in his compositions, which may contribute to the "not-quite-groundedness" of the figures, even, as in *Verweis,* when he has given near equal emphasis to the shadow cast by the figure, as to the figure itself.

Painted in watercolor or thin veils of oil, his figures seem to exist by the thinnest of margins. They might float away or fade out at any moment.

Occasionally Eitel will cover a large swath of canvas with a simple, regular shape in an uninflected dark color. In *Container*, he covers the right quarter of the canvas with a dark grey bar that echoes the broad hunched back of the figure in the trench coat, as well as the big blue dumpster, set nearly square to the picture plane, on the left. This bar seems to have floated in from a supremitist composition made nearly a century earlier. It flattens the already flat image, just as the scraped windowpane does in Weischer's *St. Ludgerus*. Its flatness locates *Container* on a modernist trajectory, but the emotional tenor, low hum that it is, places it on a different one. The grey bar is the emotional equivalent of the dumpster and the broad back of the figure.

Christoph Ruckhäberle, like Weischer, carries on at least two conversations with the viewer in his works, one about Leipzig and one about painting. And like Eitel's figures, some, but not all of Ruckhäberle's figures, project their desire to be invisible. In his painting *Suite*, a dour woman, nude but for her knee socks and slippers, stands with her arms sternly crossed over her chest in the middle of a drab East German room. The other figures in the room, mostly men in various stages of undress, sit in the corners, looking weak and uncertain, recoiling both from her and from us, the viewers. All of the figures seem like actors because of their precise positions, placed squarely in front of a striped wall that resembles a stage backdrop. A similar theme prevails in *Comedy*. What does this disappointed woman have to do with the dejected men around her? One possibility could be the general feeling of "gender panic" prevailing in Germany after World War II: simply put, there were many more women than men. Of the men who survived the war, a war they failed to win incidentally, many returned home seriously injured. And many German women, like their counterparts in the United States, were not keen to relinquish to their returning husbands the power and independence they gained while working during the war. These paintings may convey unease about a powerful, sexualized woman surrounded by weak, ineffectual men.

Christoph Ruckhäberle... carries on at least two conversations with the viewer in his works, one about Leipzig and one about painting.... some, but not all of Ruckhäberle's figures, project their desire to be invisible.

Like the Weischers, these paintings convey unease about painting. They are intentionally poorly painted: the wallpaper lines wobble down the canvas, precluding any hope of realism, perspective lines are all a little off, causing the planes of floor, rug, and walls to pitch around unconvincingly. All of the figures seem to wear flattened masks. And like Weischer, Ruckhäberle has hung pictures on the walls of his interiors, in this case a reproduction of a woodcut by Matisse that looks more like the famous painting the *Black Square,* painted in 1913 by Kasimir Malevich, the founder of suprematism. By including it here, Ruckhäberle signals that he knows what he is doing, that he is making an informed choice for ham-fisted figure paintings over sleek idea-driven abstractions. He may also be making suggestions about the nature of art in a social revolutionary society. Malevich strove to make a painting without ambiguity, a painting that could be understood and appreciated by workers and intellectuals. For a brief moment in the early days of Communist Russia, this kind of painting was championed by the state, but was soon replaced by social realism – the earnest figurative style celebrating the lives of workers – intended to be uplifting and, above all, unambiguous. It was this kind of painting that the Leipzig Academy was known for under the GDR. You can almost sense nostalgia for painting in these works, as well as the strange nostalgia for the GDR.

You can almost sense nostalgia for painting in these works, as well as the strange nostalgia for the GDR.

Perhaps the most mysterious picture in the exhibition is the only large-scale drawing. *Die Pause* [*The Pause*] was drawn by Tilo Baumgärtel with charcoal on a white sheet, roughly measuring 4 x 8'. In the foreground, two Asians are on the terrace of their apartment in an anonymous urban neighborhood comprised of simple, modern, low-rise apartment buildings. One is making a traditional ink painting on the floor. In an Asian-like script, she writes, "*Die Pause*" in German. Her companion stares out at the rainy afternoon and at the deserted streets and shops, which also have signs in similar script. The poses of the figures are unnatural and ill at ease, as though they were marionettes or mannequins, a quality shared with both Eitel's and Ruckhäberle's figures. A profound stillness, typical of a long lunch break on a rainy day, pervades the cityscape, which Baumgärtel has crisply, even relentlessly, drawn with heavy geometry and sharp angles reminiscent of his classmates David Schnell and Martin Kobe.

The two figures share their apartment with aquariums of cuttlefish. Baumgärtel has taken great care with the eerie light effects peculiar to aquariums – light moving through the water and glass to illuminate the darkened apartment in shadowy, watery pools. This kind of detail bespeaks Baumgärtel's training at the Leipzig Academy's justly famous life-drawing class. Near the center of the picture is a large aquarium with a black cuttlefish, a little too big for his tank, that suddenly releases ink into the water. This is the only action in the whole composition. The black amorphous shape that fails to conceal the fish in the tank is the emotional hub of the drawing, in which everything seems to recoil from examination, to hold its breath until we, the viewers, leave. The black ink cloud, the weird aquarium light, the rainy afternoon, "*Die Pause*" in black script, even the presence of these foreign people in what is presumably a neighborhood of new immigrants, all engender a sensation of dislocation and deep reserve.

everything seems to recoil from examination, to hold its breath until we, the viewers, leave.

Baumgärtel, like Rauch, grew up in the so-called "niche society" of Leipzig, in which one of every 17 people was a spy, forcing everyone to keep their private, imaginative lives utterly separate from their public ones. Ten years younger than Rauch, Baumgärtel was in his late teens when the Iron Curtain was pulled back in 1989. In both artists' oeuvres, a sense of deep interiority engulfs the figures that live in ambiguous, artificial, strangely resistant times and places. The English saying about "living in a fishbowl," does not exist in German, but that is exactly what the artist has evoked. The two Asian figures on their open terrace in this rainy, forbidding place live in a fishbowl just as surely as the cuttlefish does, but without recourse to his ink shroud.

There is no room or air for uneasy figures in the compositions of David Schnell and Martin Kobe. Schnell's landscapes are all painted in one-point perspective, that is, all the lines converge at one point, called the vanishing point, near the center of the picture. This kind of scientific perspective was invented by Fillipo Brunelleschi in the early Renaissance and has been a staple of academic training ever since, but rarely has it been taken to such an extreme. Brunelleschi's hope for scientific perspective was to locate figures and architecture in realistic space, to make rational pictures in which everything was at its proper scale. But Schnell uses perspective the way surrealists Salvador Dali and Giorgio de Chirico did: to place irrational things in rational space. Heavily geometricized bales of hay float above an abandoned East German airstrip. A length of colorful plastic flags – as you might find at a rural fair – are marshaled at crisp angles

Schnell uses perspective the way surrealists Salvador Dali and Giorgio de Chirico did: to place irrational things in rational space.

through a clear Guardi-esque sky. Even in a park, with an empty park bench in the foreground, this is clearly no place for people. Schnell has said his inspiration comes from driving around the environs of Leipzig. More than a third of the population of Leipzig left for West Germany in the decade after the fall of the Wall, and the atmosphere of a "shrinking city" or ghost town is present in these works, as it is in Weischer's empty rooms.

In *Bretter* [*Planks*] we see ourselves trapped in an ailing barn or airplane hangar. The boards are so distressed that they offer little protection from the elements. Rather, they visually function like some kind of incarceration device allowing us to see what is beyond but making us aware we are still trapped inside. We see the landscape through the cracks, a landscape that seems to be overwhelming the structure. At the end of Schnell's beloved one-point perspective vanishing point we see a door, but with no human presence it is impossible to determine scale. We never know if we could walk up to it, and through.

Curiously the canon of one-point perspective that was developed to clearly define and order reality, here, makes us giddy and unsettled.

Kobe takes one-point perspective to its illogical conclusion. Floors seem to hover, walls open up into windows, windows seem to be paintings, ceilings become floor tiles. Like Oz's Dorothy in her hallucinogenic tornado, nothing is grounded. Curiously the canon of one-point perspective that was developed to clearly define and order reality, here, makes us giddy and unsettled. We find ourselves in a place not conducive to supporting human habitation.

From a distance the red paintings seem crisp and new, illustrating the success of the modernist architectural ideal. Come closer though and we see pencil lines, the very structure of a painting, showing through, as in some showcase city building [the Palace of the Republic in Berlin, for example] which had been continually cleaned and polished so much that all the patina has been removed, the carpets threadbare, and only traces of chrome shine are left on the support structure maze. Modernist concepts that were literally concretized as a gesture to a utopian communist ideal, here function simply as some dated futuristic science fiction B-grade film: an idea of the future based in the past.

"Life After Death" positions these paintings and drawings in the afterlife – the afterlife of the German Democratic Republic, of social realism, and of painting in general. Traces of the GDR inhabit the grim interiors and muddled social modernist architecture in these paintings. Social realism possesses the figures who rarely make eye contact, keeping their thoughts to themselves. Painting itself – both classical technique and Greenbergian modernism – is the real subject of the works. The entire project is engulfed by emotional restraint, to the point of repression.

"Life After Death" positions these paintings and drawings in the afterlife – the afterlife of the German Democratic Republic, of social realism, and of painting in general.

These seven artists chose to study at the Leipzig Art Academy, in the former East Germany, in the decade after the fall of the Berlin Wall in 1989. This was an unlikely decision at a time when the inhabitants of Leipzig were leaving in droves for the West, and when the main currents of art flowed away from painting, toward video, photography, and installation art. The untimely embrace of a shrinking East German city and conventional medium is imprinted on the pictures, but rather than buckling under the weight of place, time, and tradition, they convey something surprising and subjective. The mystery of these pictures, with their out-of-date sources and classical techniques, is their utter and beguiling singularity.

Mark Coetzee and Laura Steward Heon

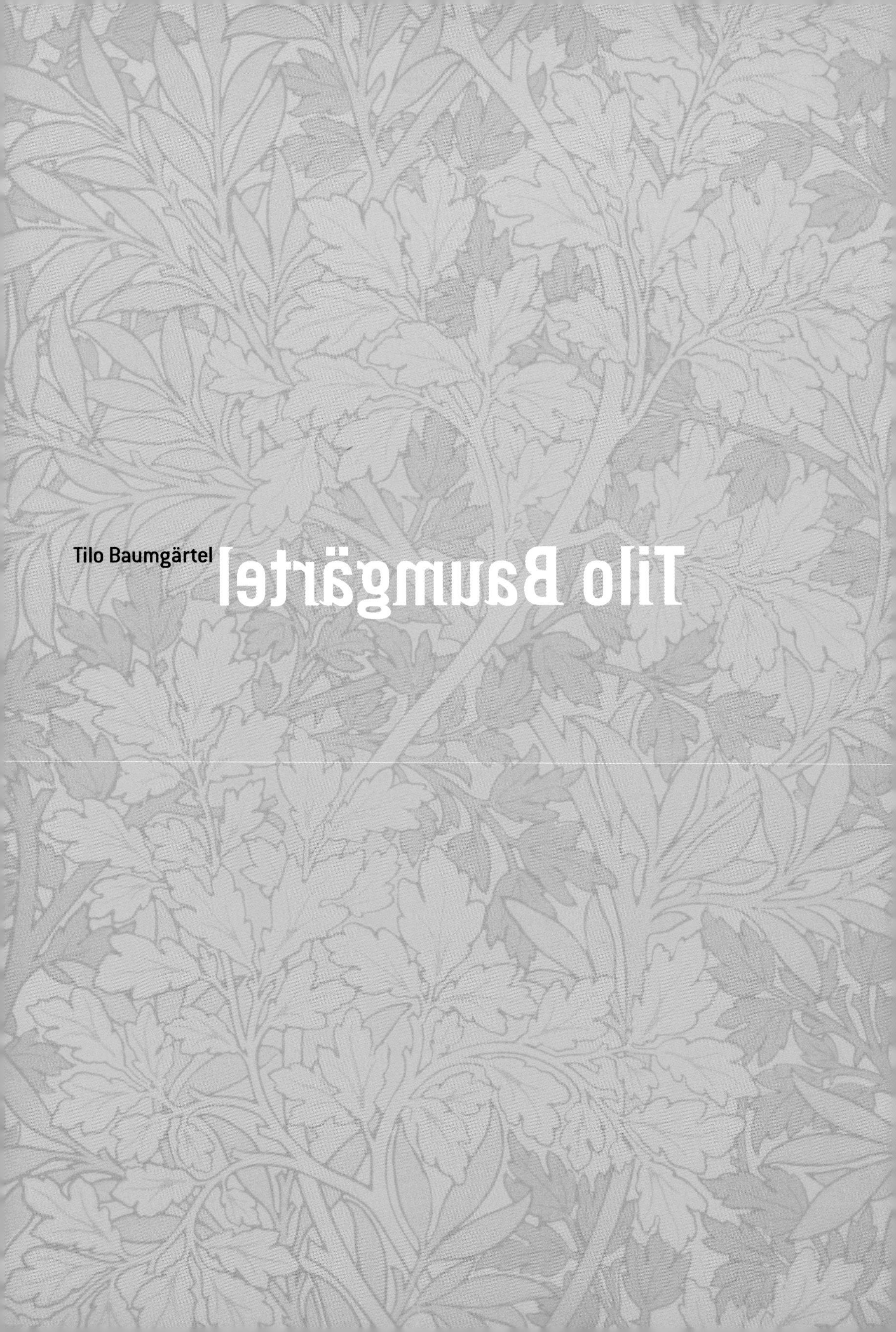

Tilo Baumgärtel

Tilo Baumgärtel

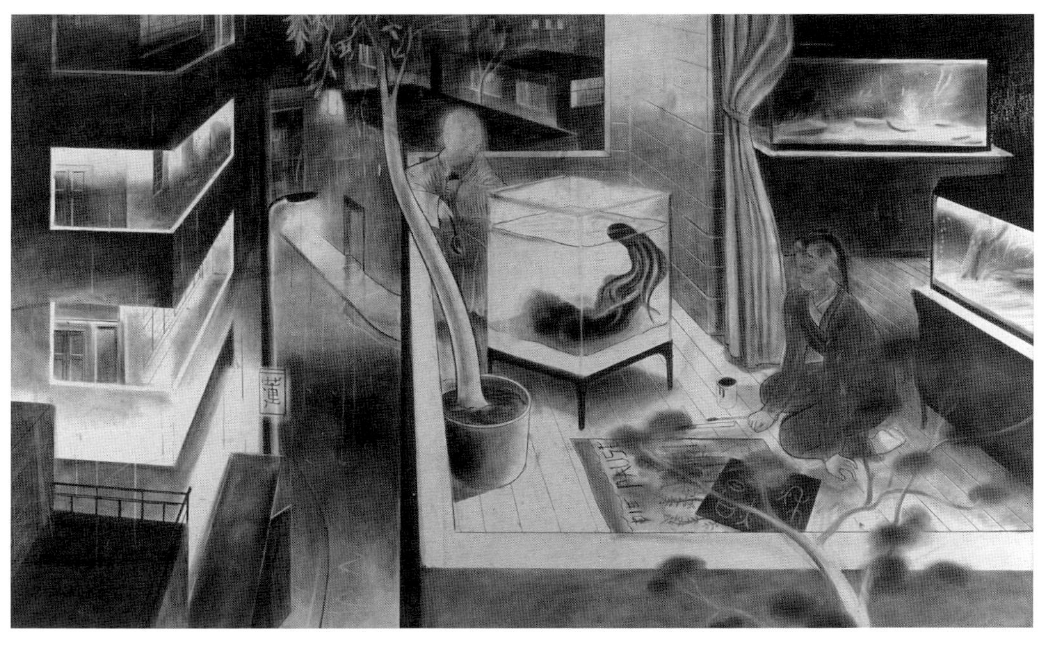

Tilo Baumgärtel
Die Pause (The Pause), 2004, Coal on paper
62 1/2 x 102 in. (158.8 x 259 cm)
TB1

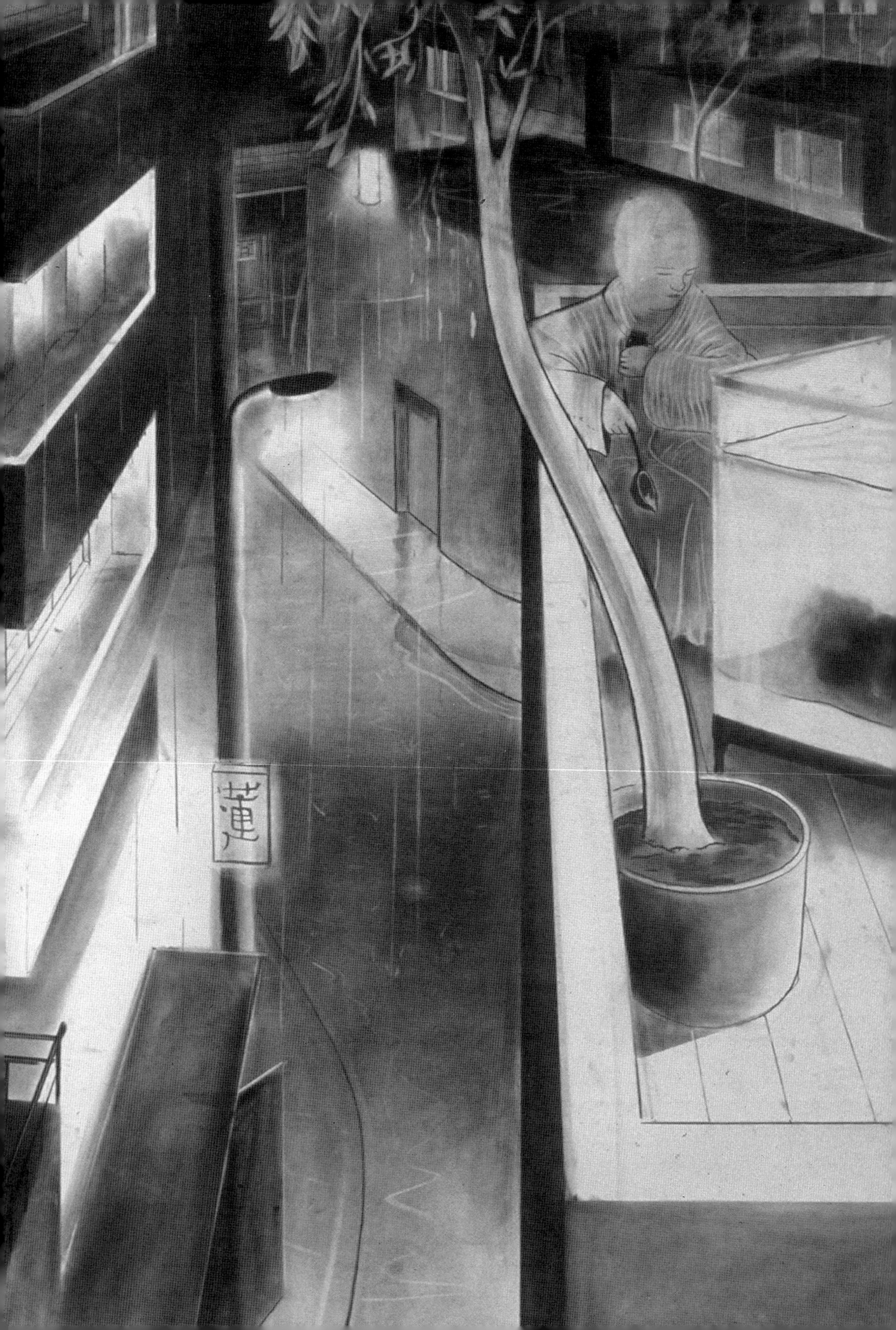
蓮

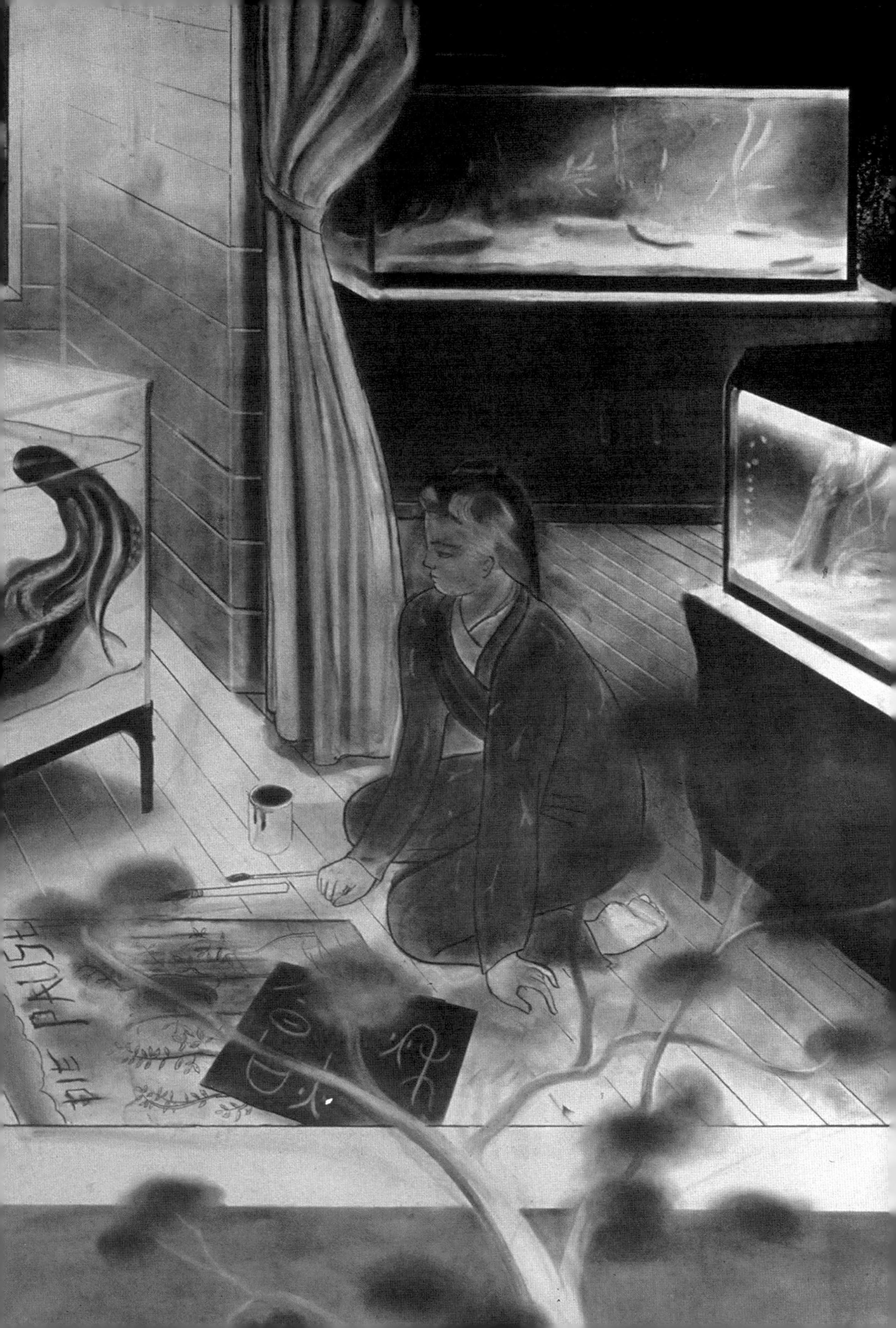
DIE PAUSE

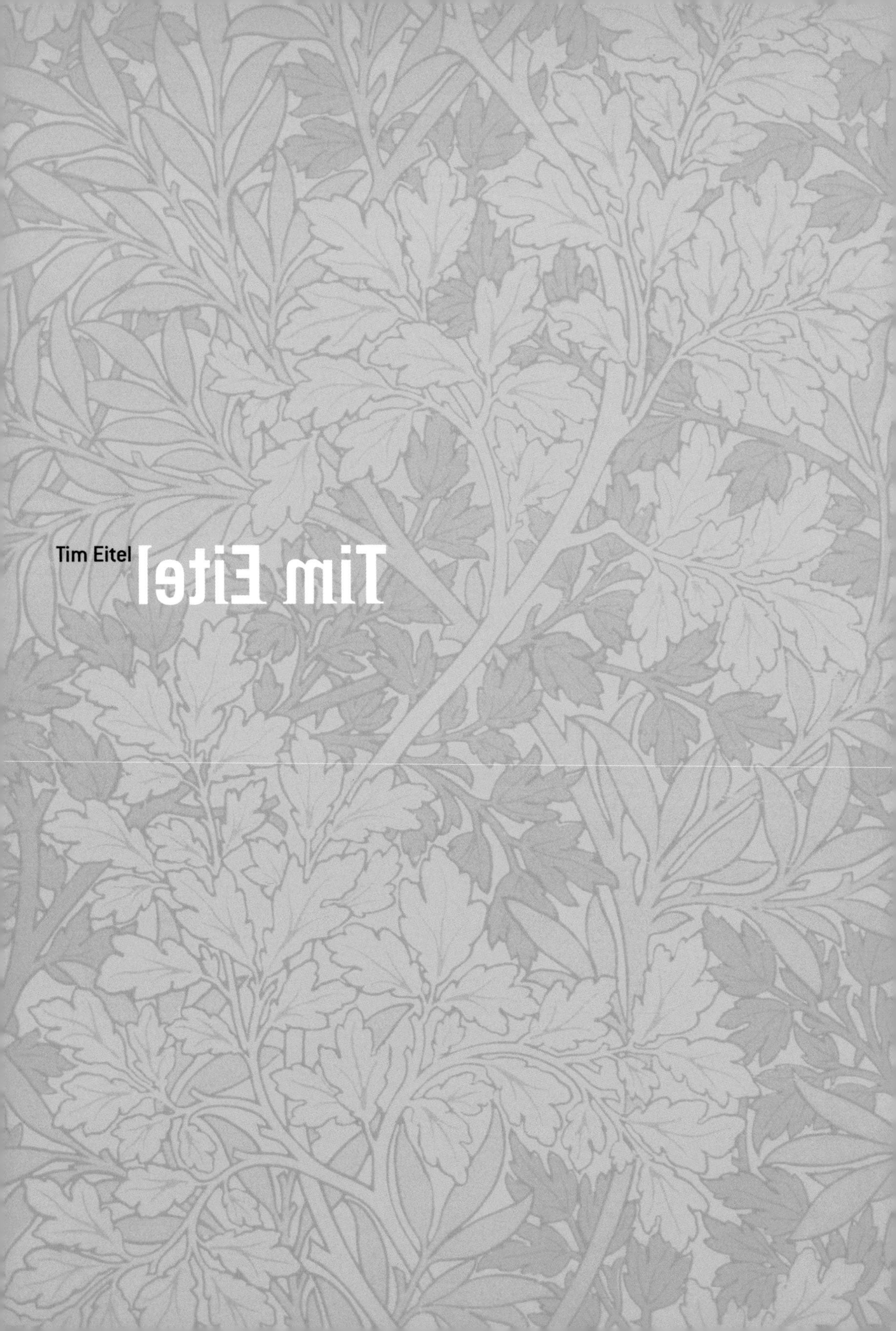
Tim Eitel

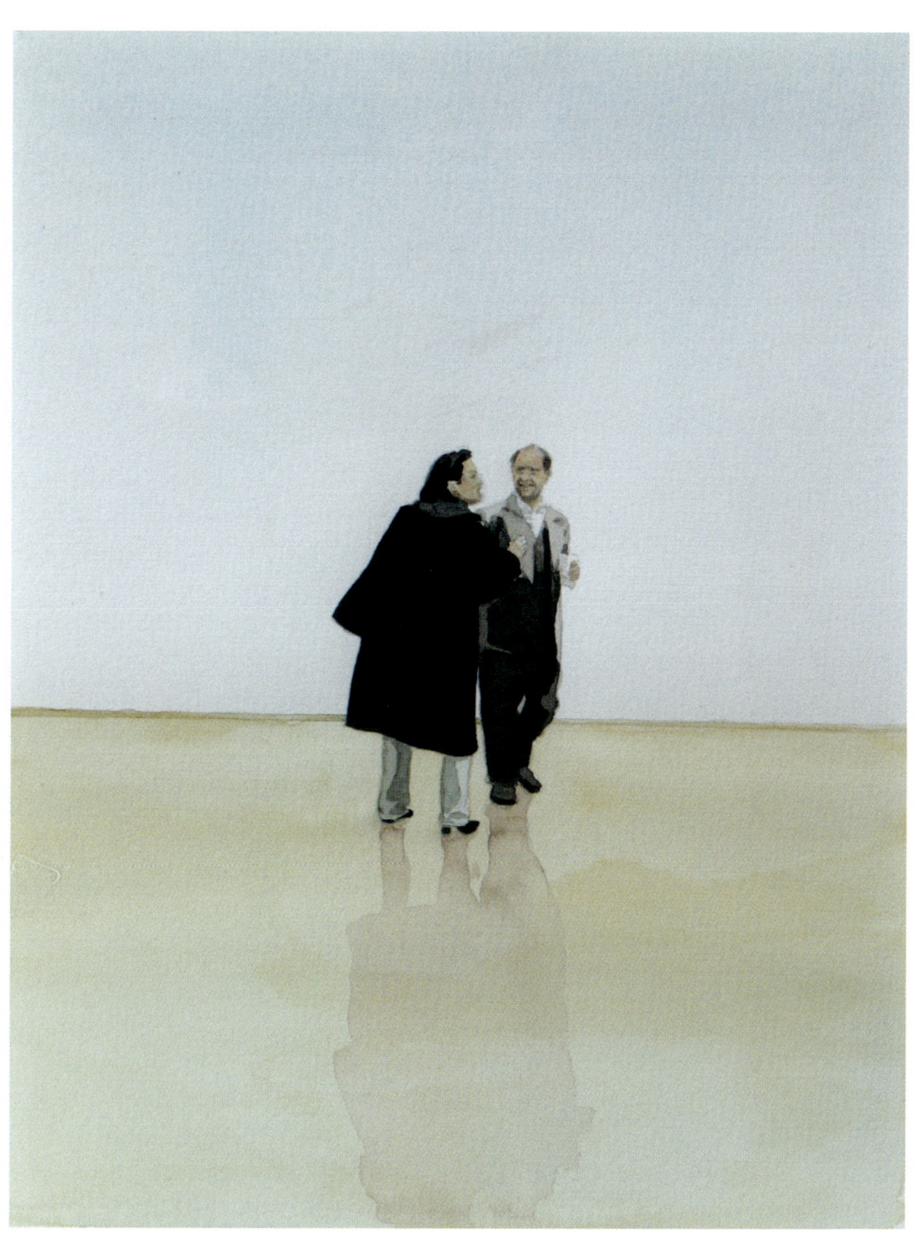

Tim Eitel
Verweis (Reference), 2003, Watercolor on paper
12 x 9 in. (30.5 x 22.8 cm)
TE1

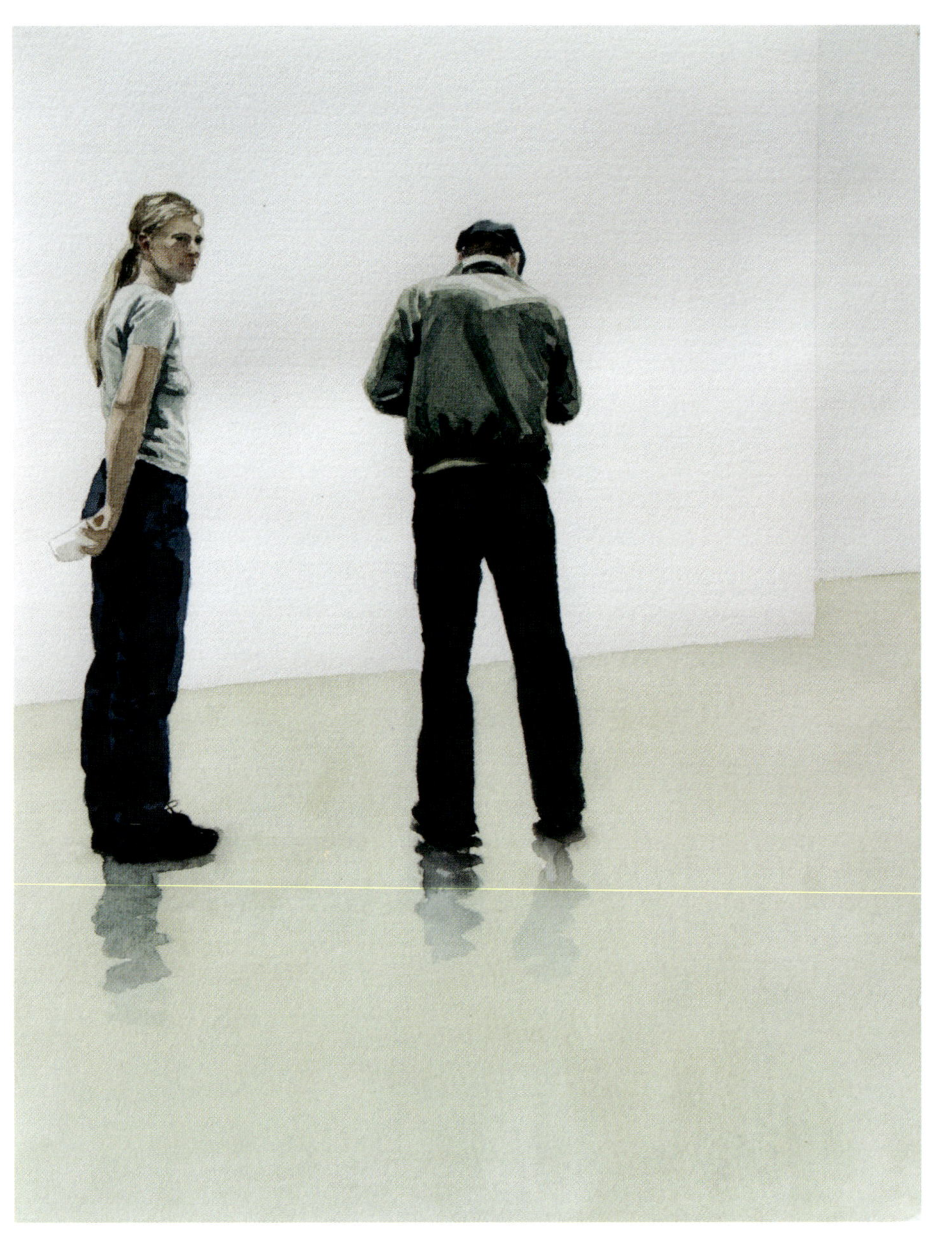

Tim Eitel
Bomberjacke (Bomber Jacket), 2003, Watercolor on paper
12 5/8 x 9 3/8 in. (32.2 x 23.7 cm)
TE2

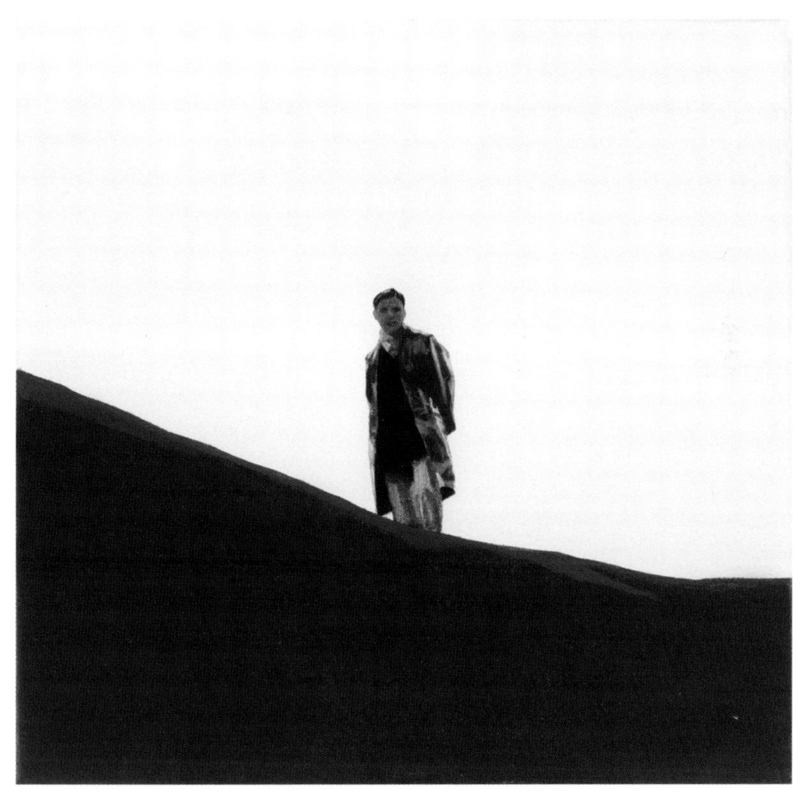

Tim Eitel
Kleine Anhöhe (Little Hill), 2003, Oil and acrylic on canvas
9 1/2 x 9 1/2 in. (24 x 24 cm)
TE3

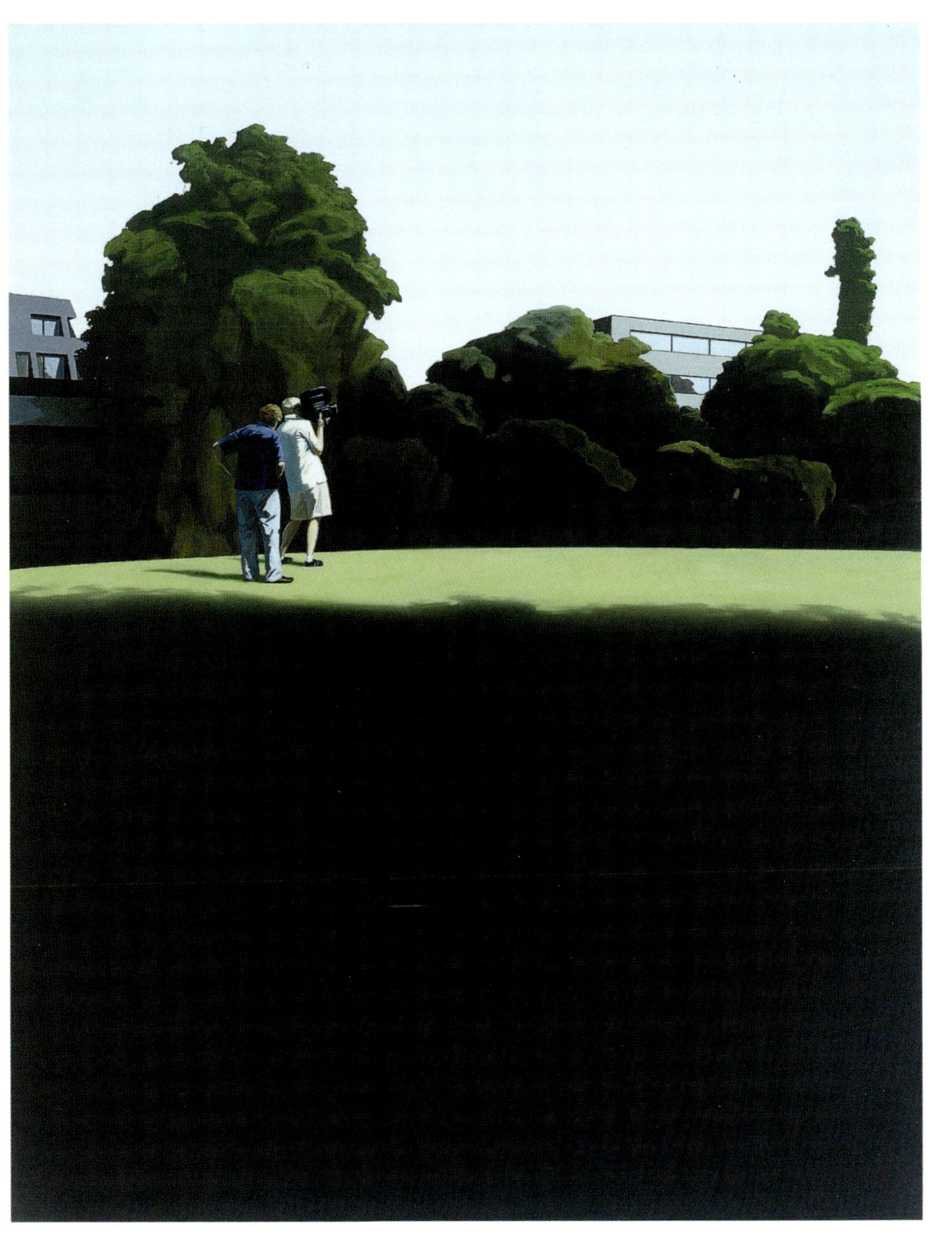

Tim Eitel
Film, 2003, Oil and acrylic on canvas
94 1/2 x 70 7/8 in. (240 x 180 cm)
TE4

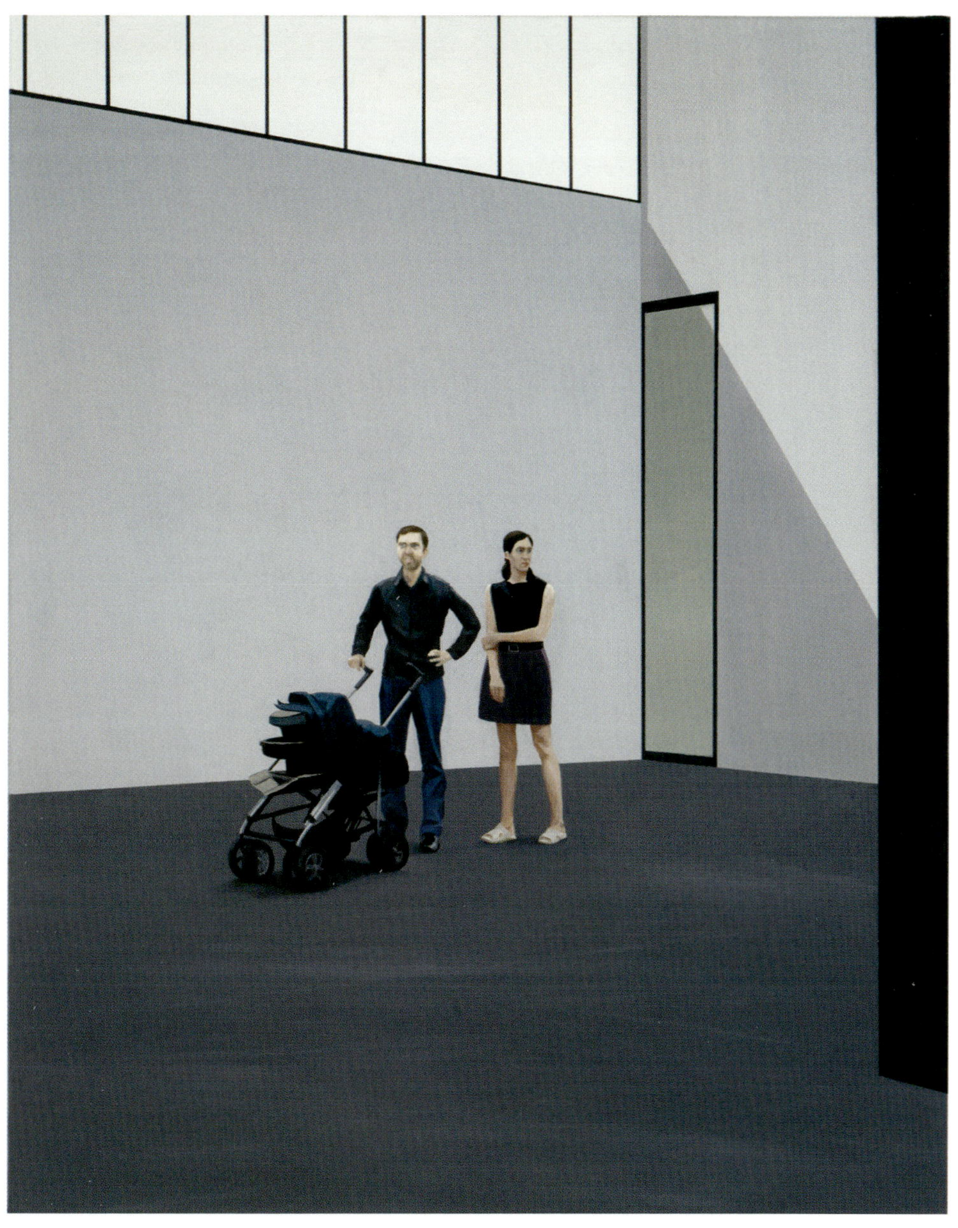

Tim Eitel
Leerer Raum (Empty Room), 2004, Oil and acrylic on canvas
35 1/2 x 27 1/2 in. (90 x 70 cm)
TE5

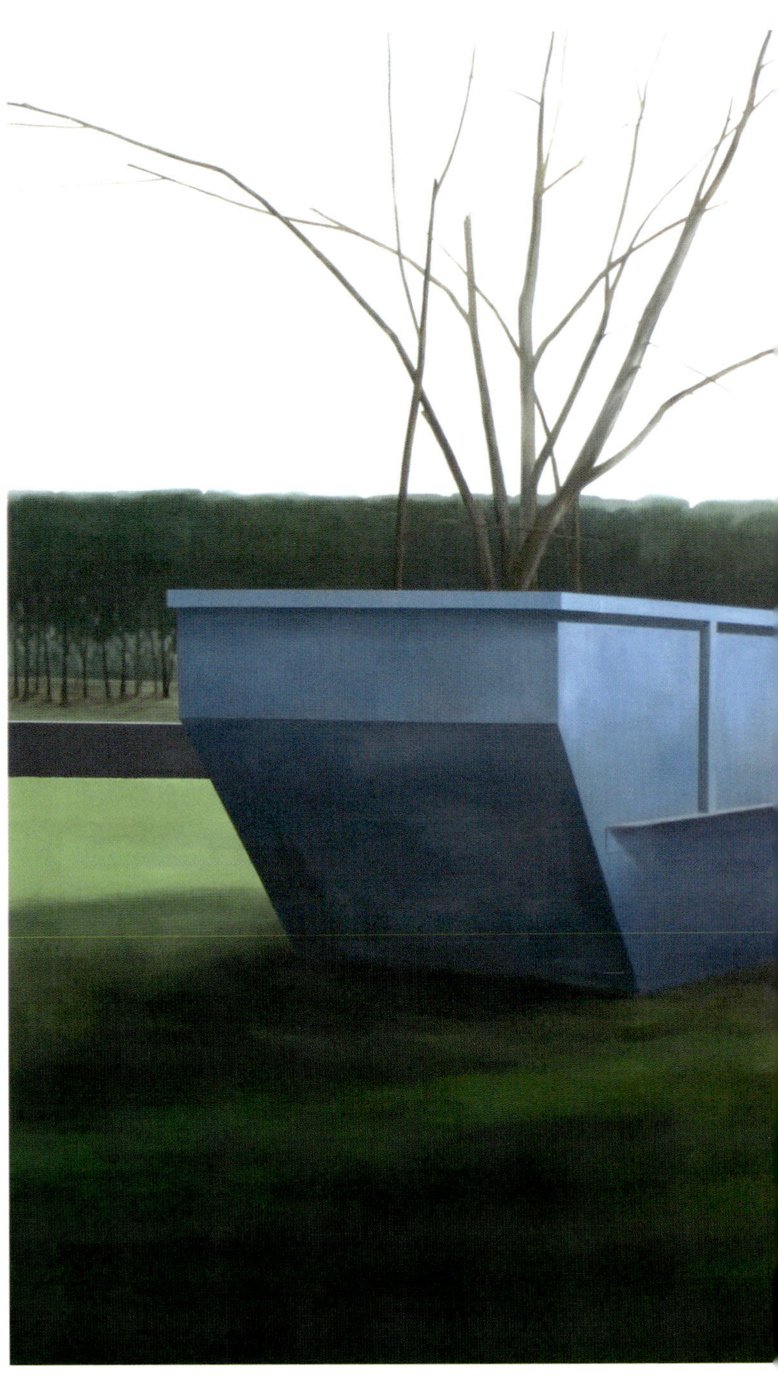

Tim Eitel
Container, 2004, Oil on canvas
82 3/4 x 118 1/8 in. (210 x 300 cm)
TE6

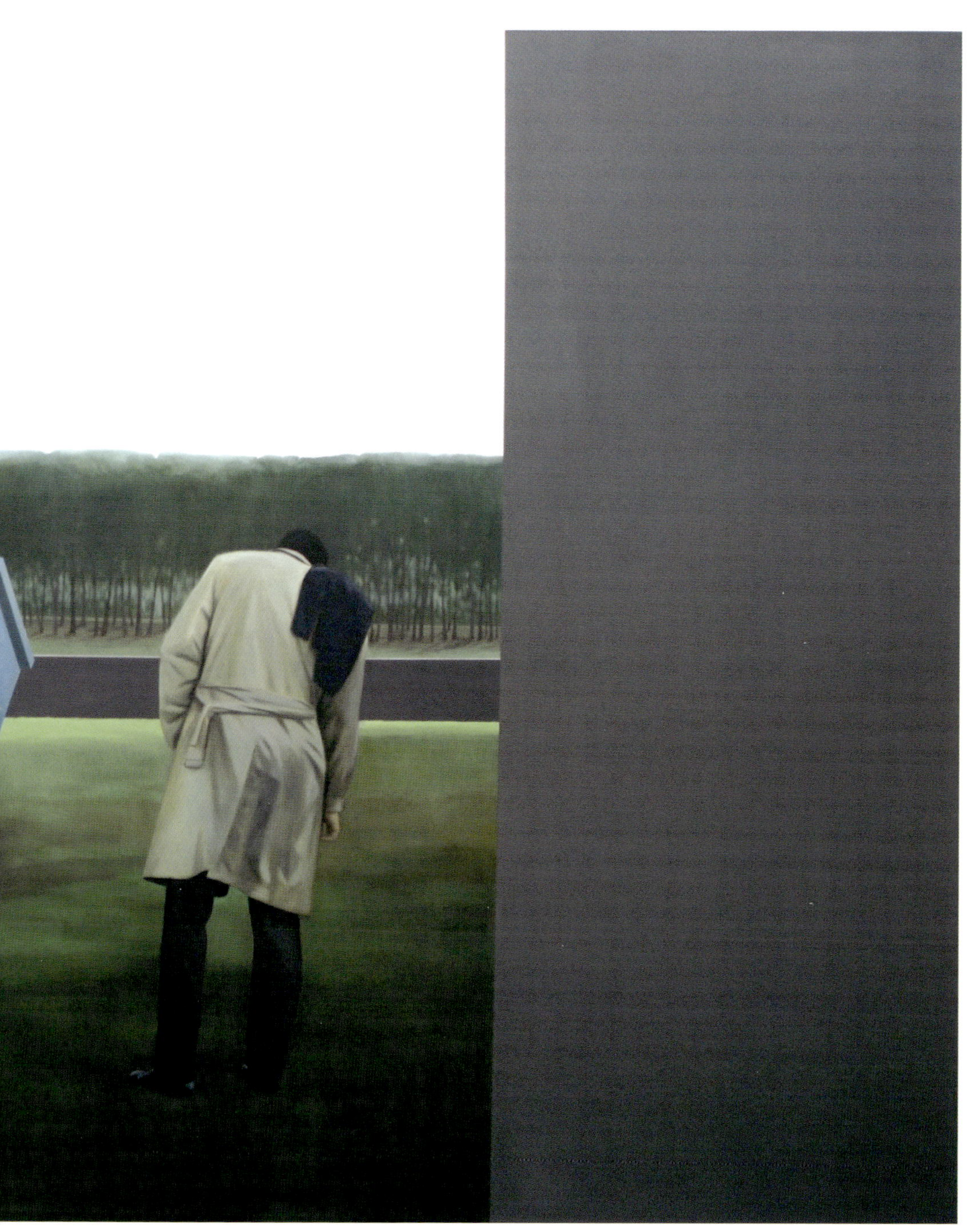

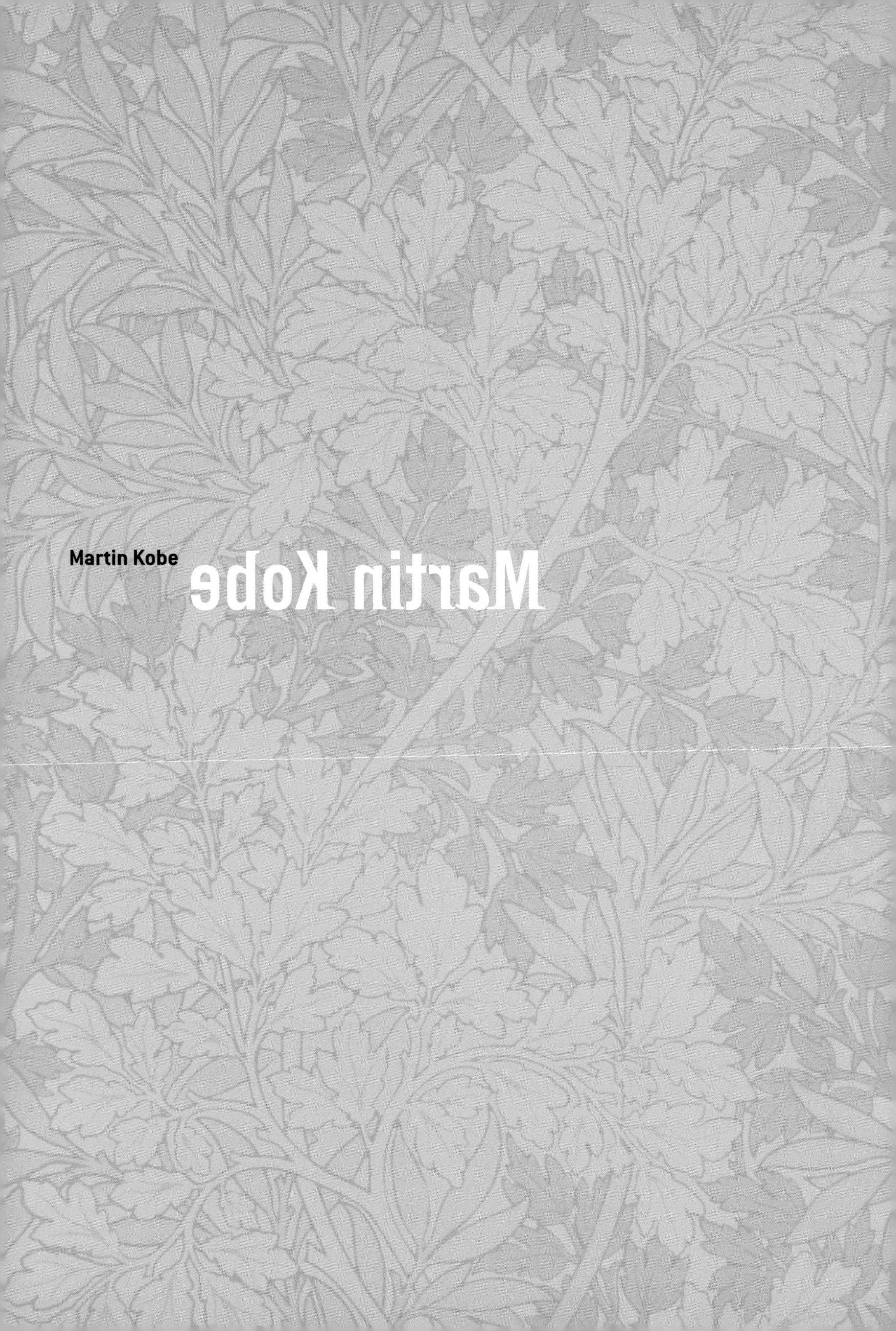
Martin Kobe

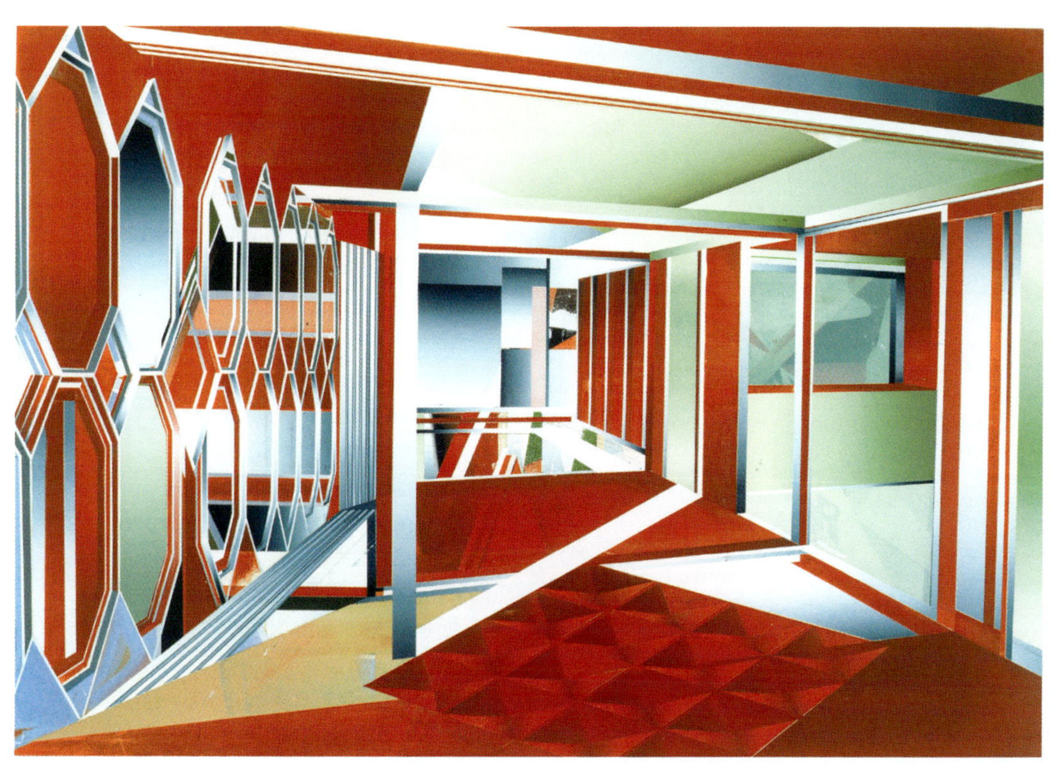

Martin Kobe
Untitled, 2003, Acrylic on canvas
64 3/4 x 90 5/8 in. (164.5 x 230 cm)
MK1

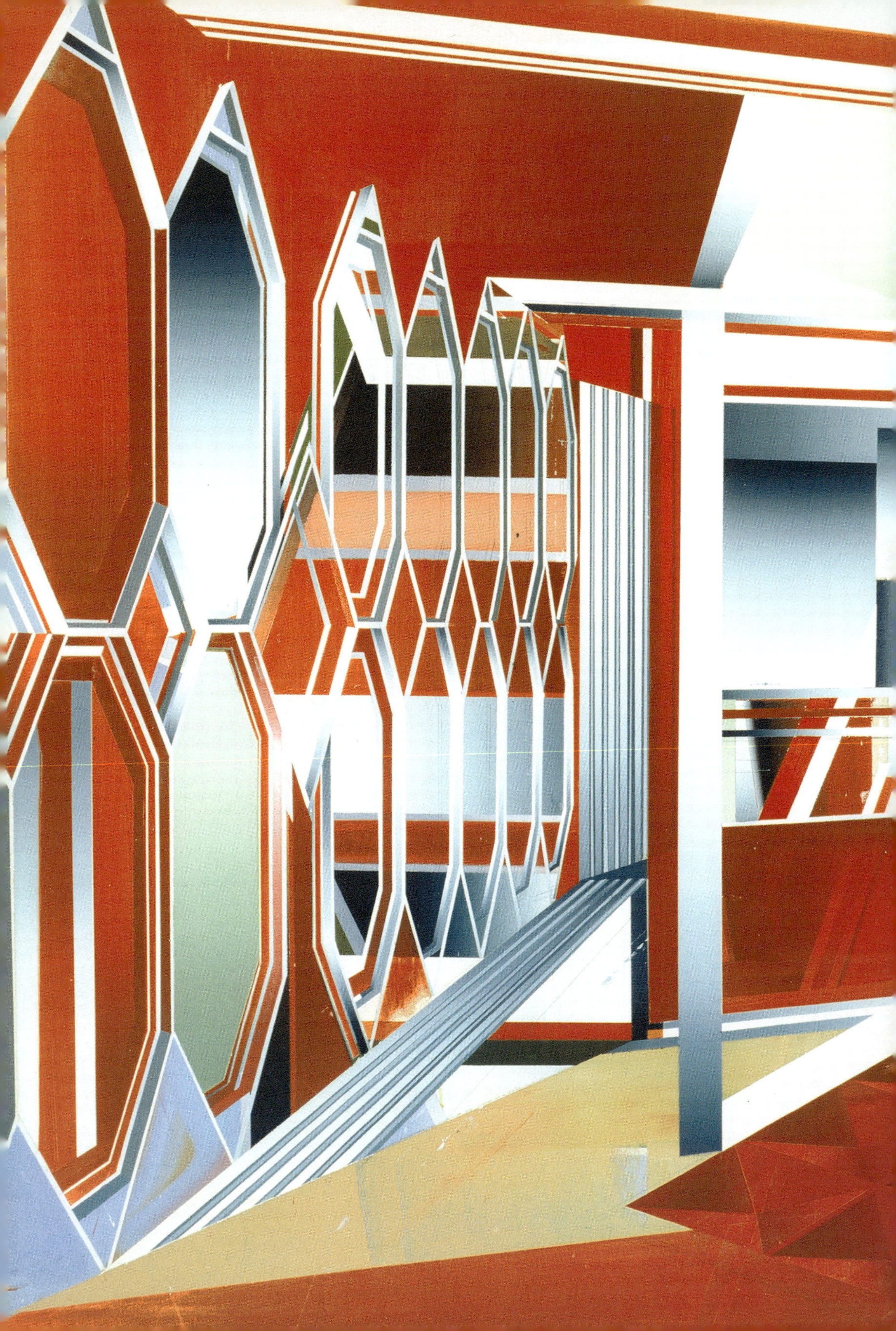

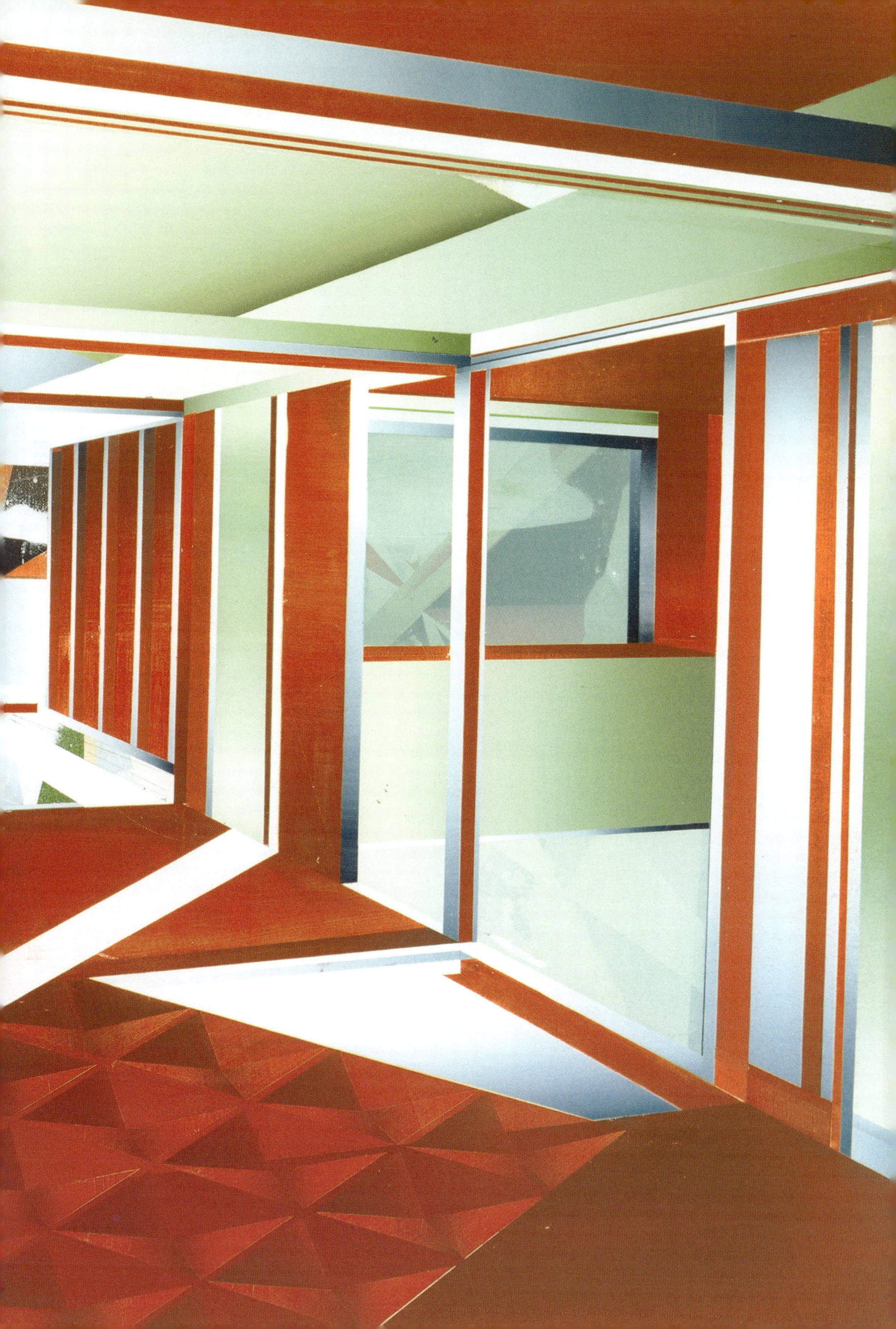

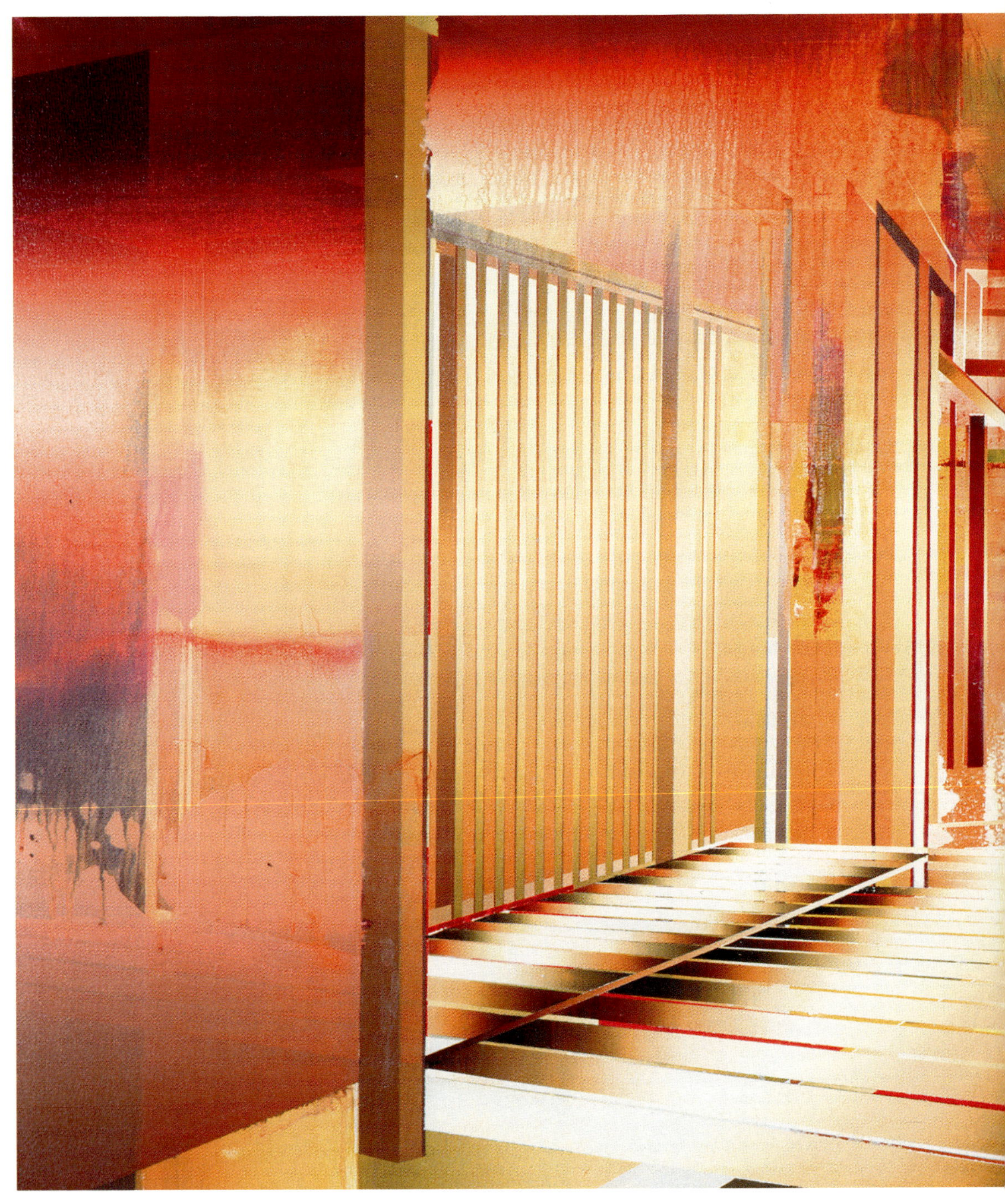

Martin Kobe
Untitled, 2005, Acrylic on canvas
34 x 58 in. (85 x 145 cm)
MK2

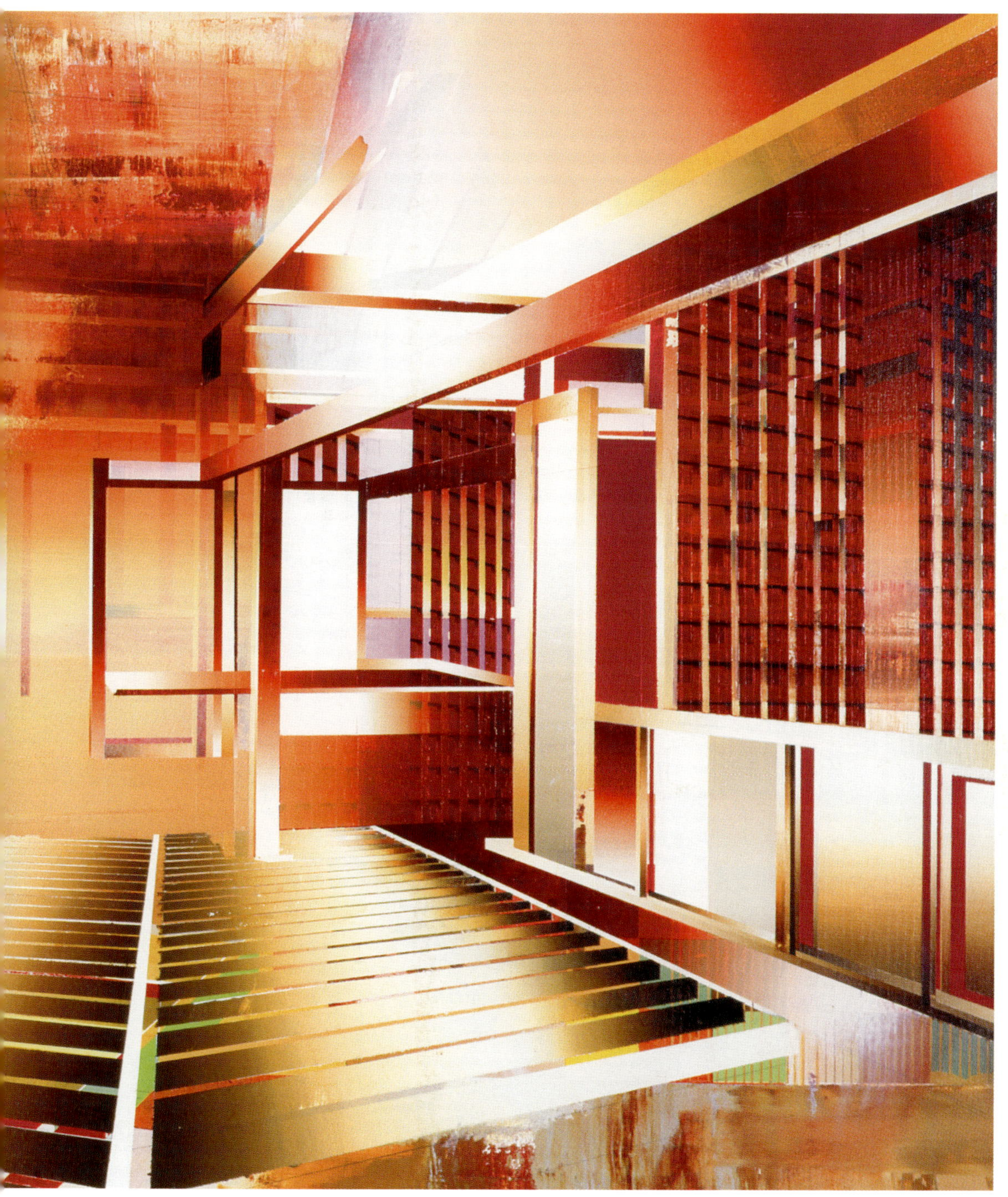

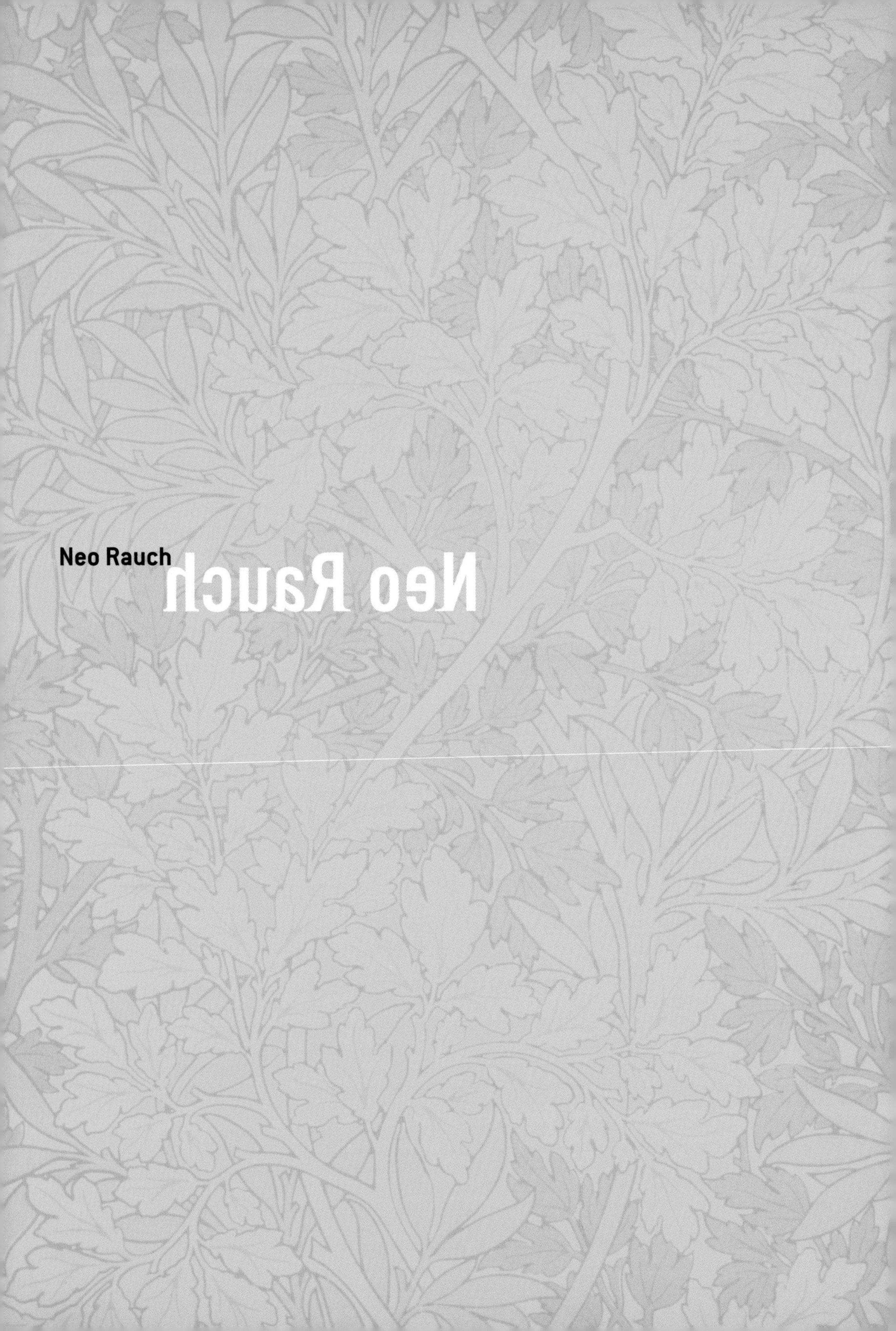

Neo Rauch

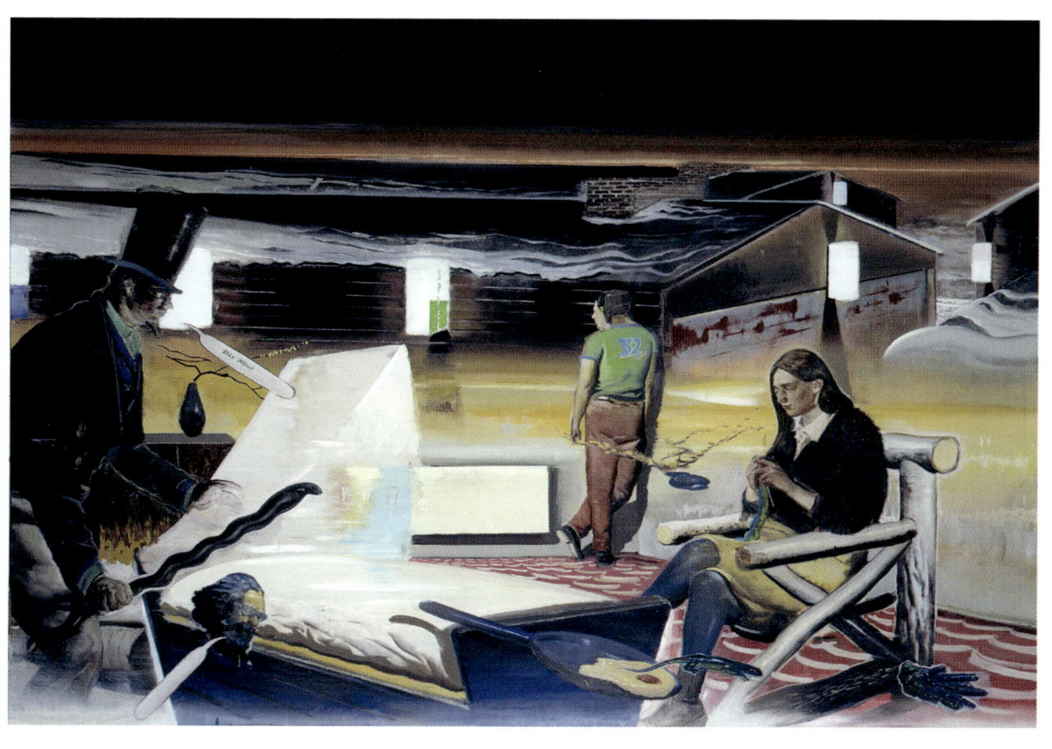

Neo Rauch
Das Neue (The New), 2003, Oil on canvas
82 1/2 x 118 1/4 in. (209.5 x 300 cm)
NR1

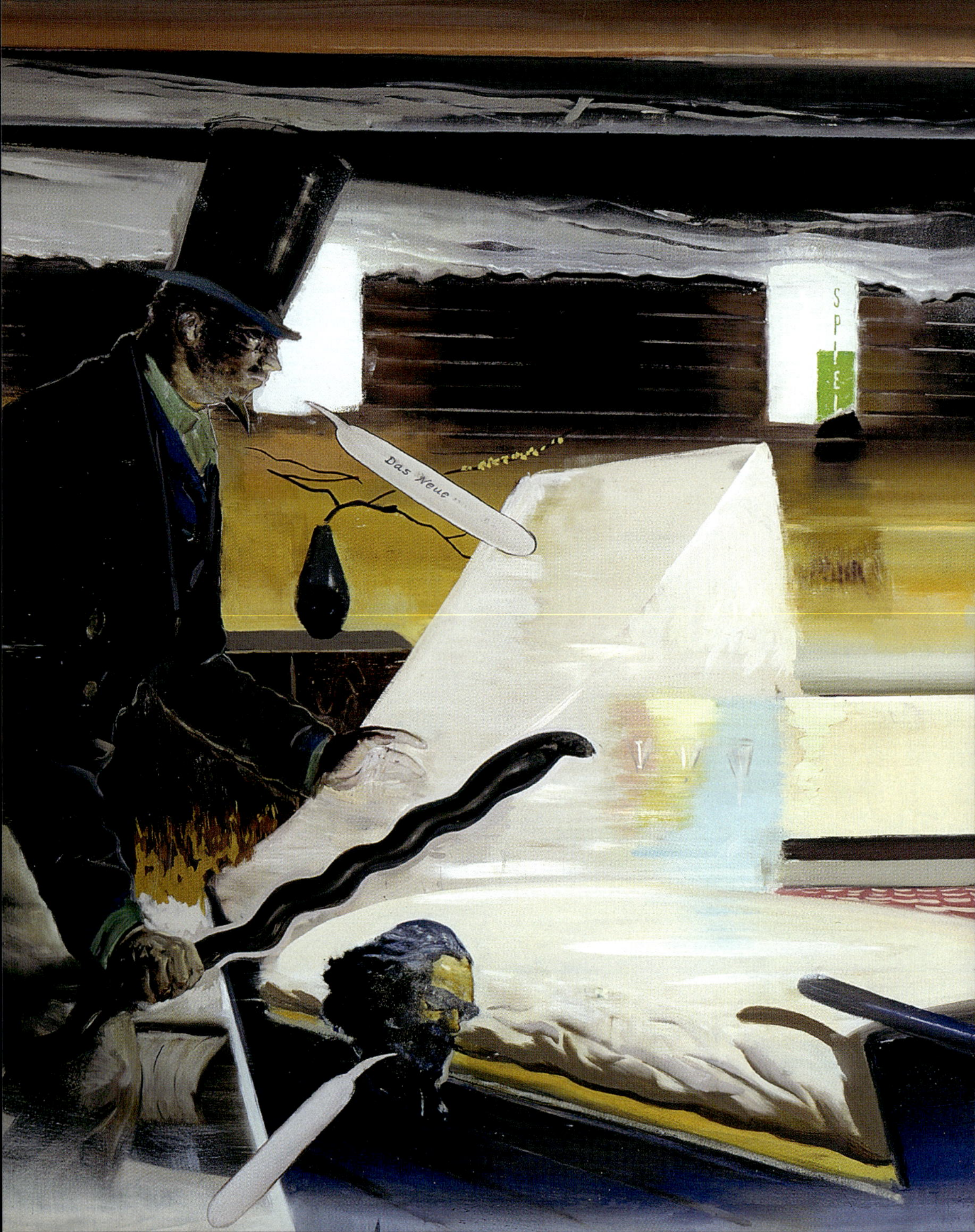
Das Neue
SPIEL

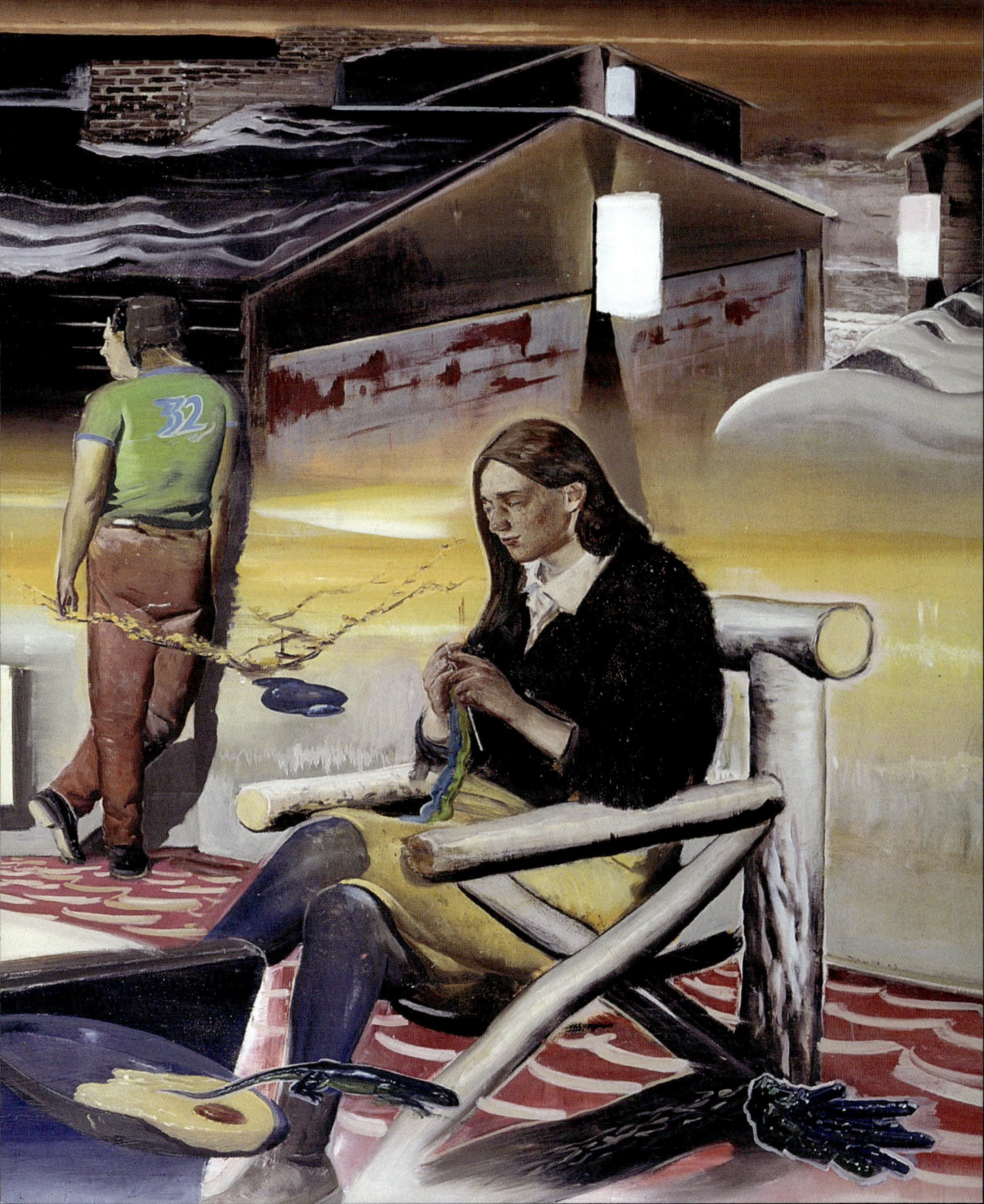
32

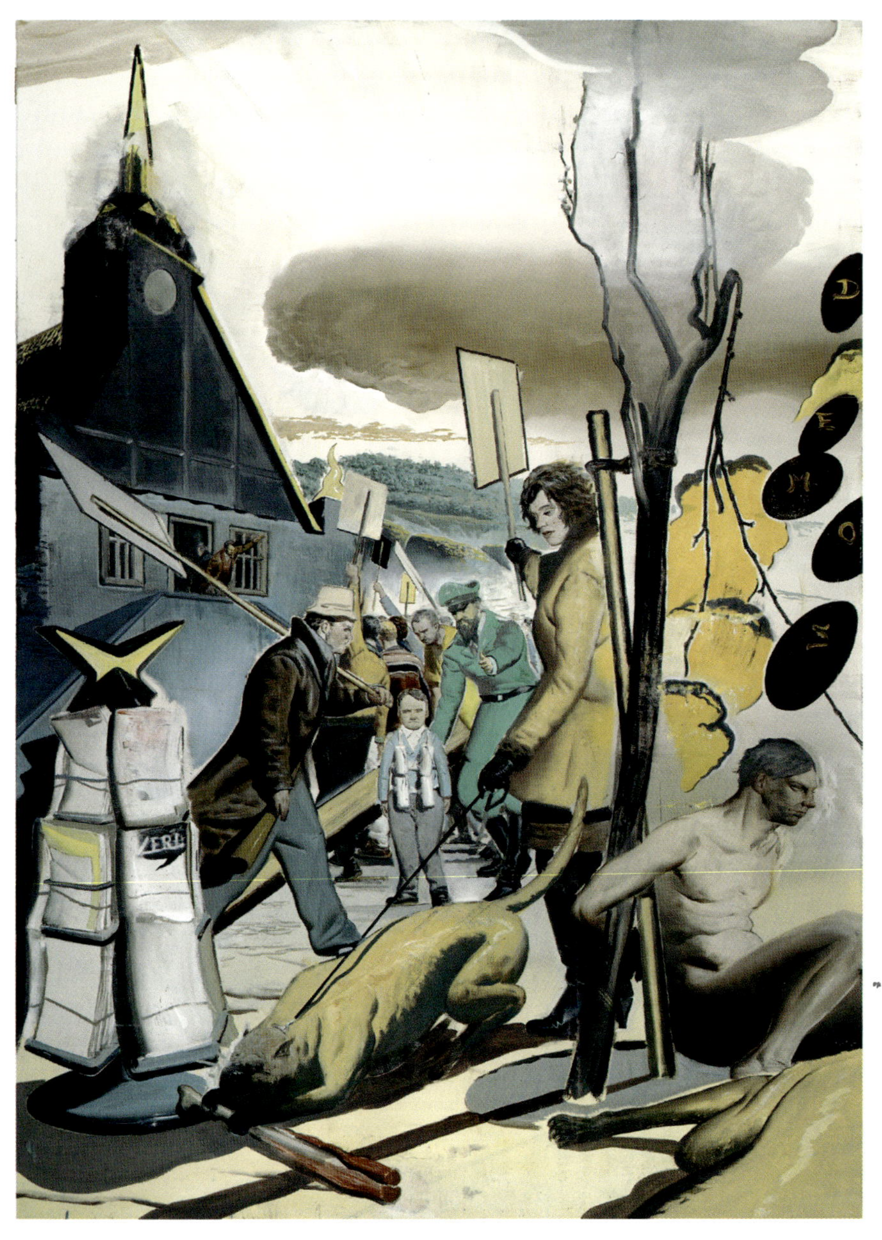

Neo Rauch
Demos (Demonstrations), 2004, Oil on canvas
118 1/8 x 82 3/4 in. (300 x 210 cm)
NR2

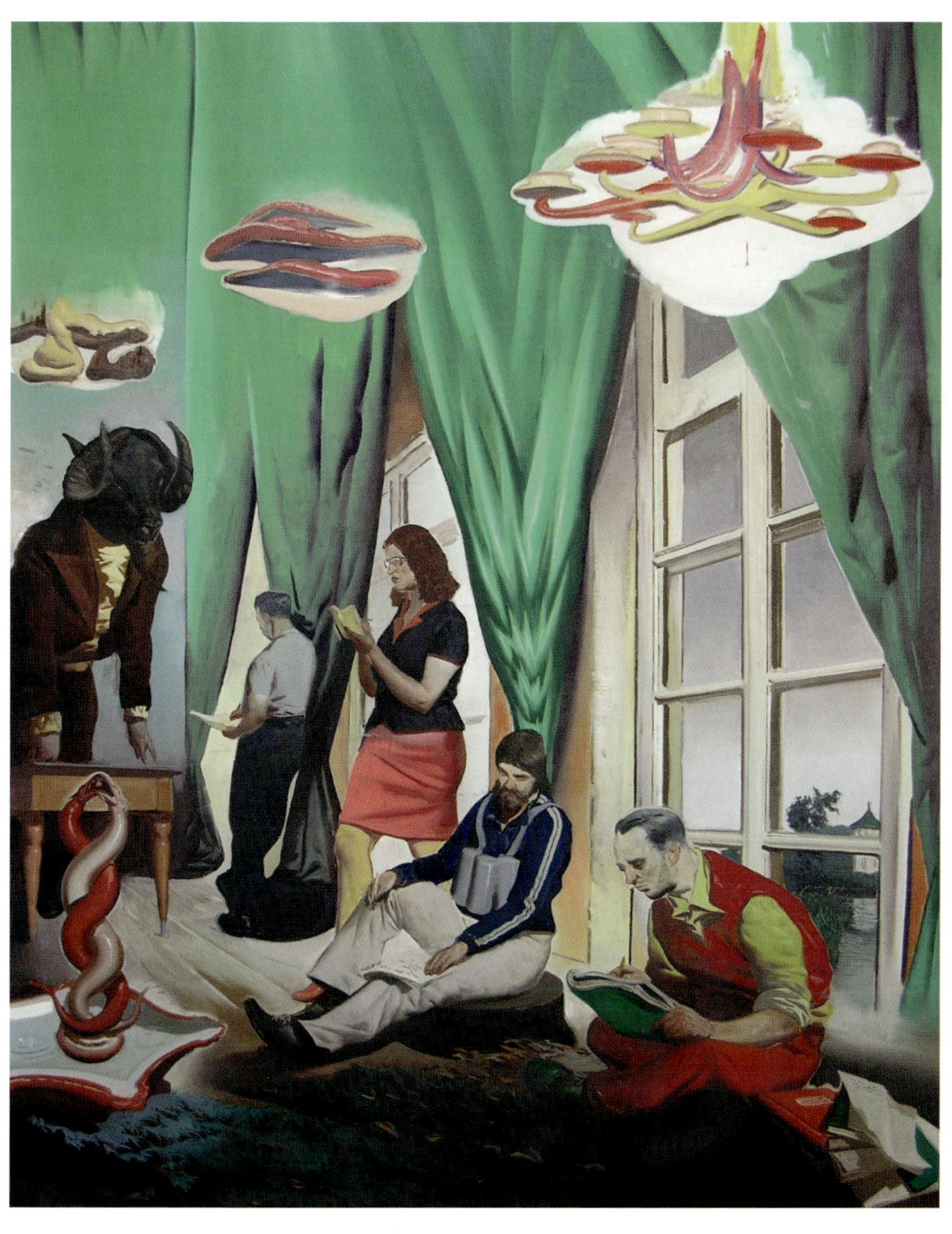

Neo Rauch
Diktat (Dictation), 2004, Oil on canvas
106 x 82 1/2 in. (269 x 209.5 cm)
NR3

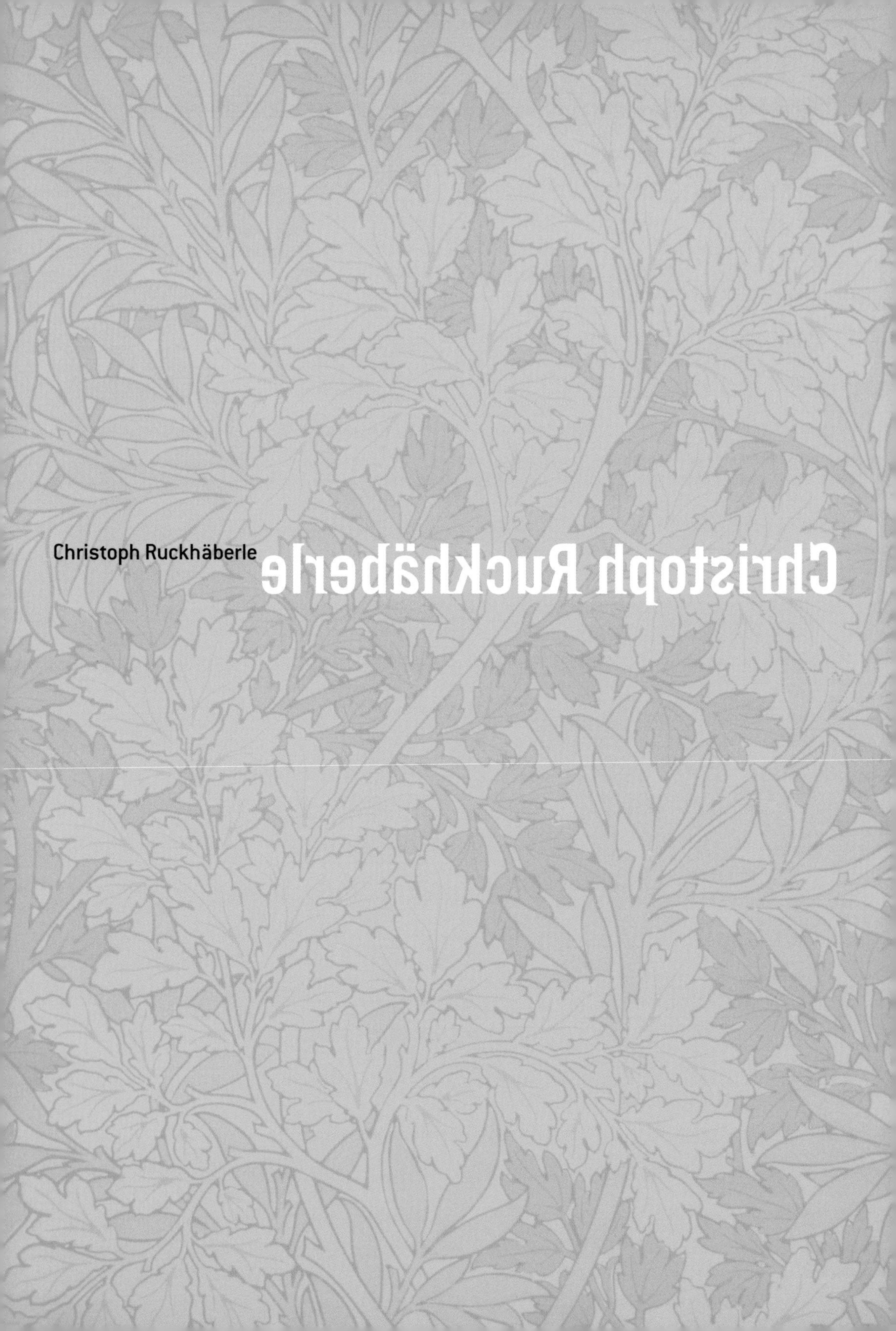
Christoph Ruckhäberle

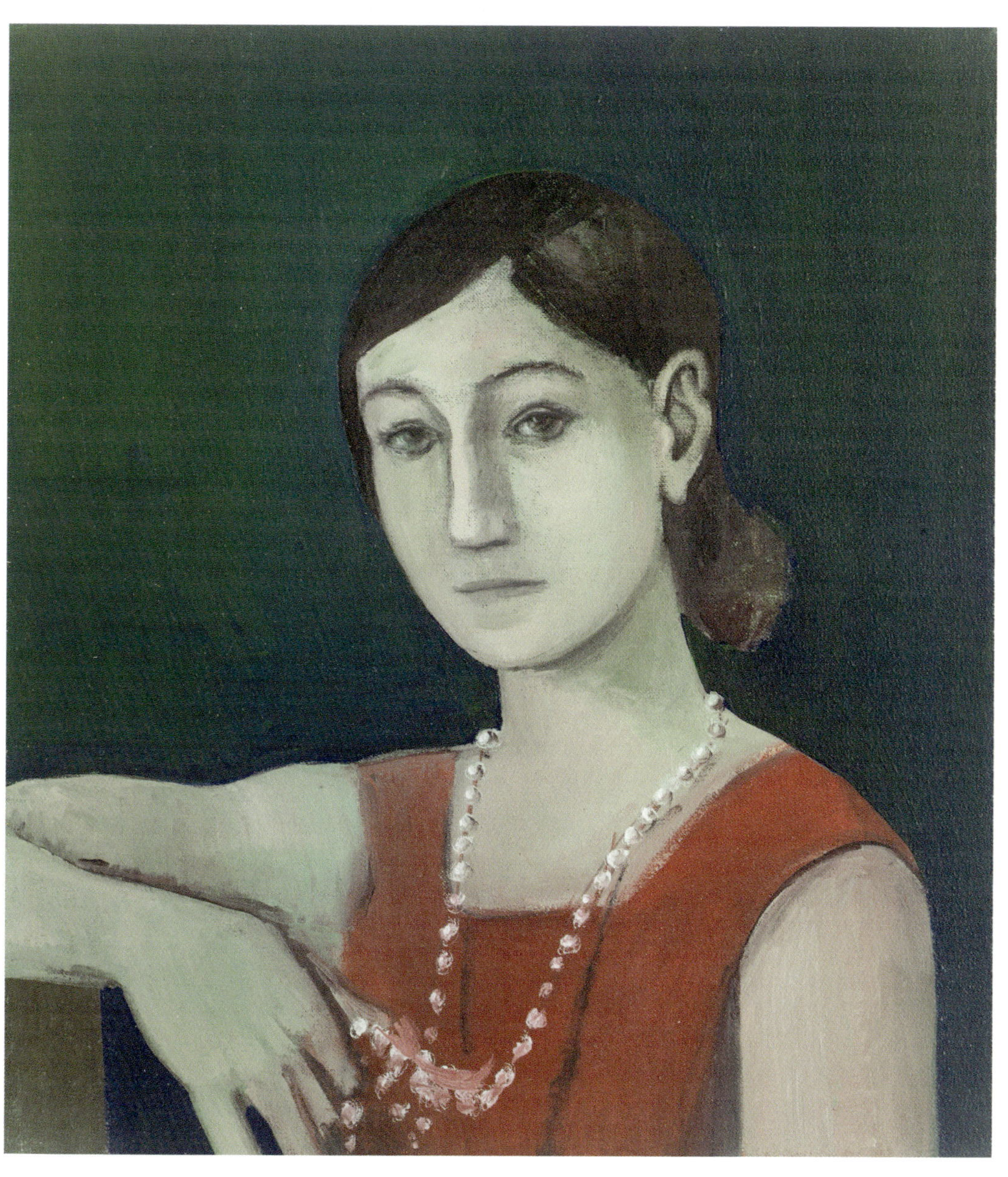

Christoph Ruckhäberle
Frau mit Perlenkette (Woman with Pearl Necklace), 2002, Oil on canvas
20 1/2 x 17 3/4 in. (52 x 45 cm)
CR1

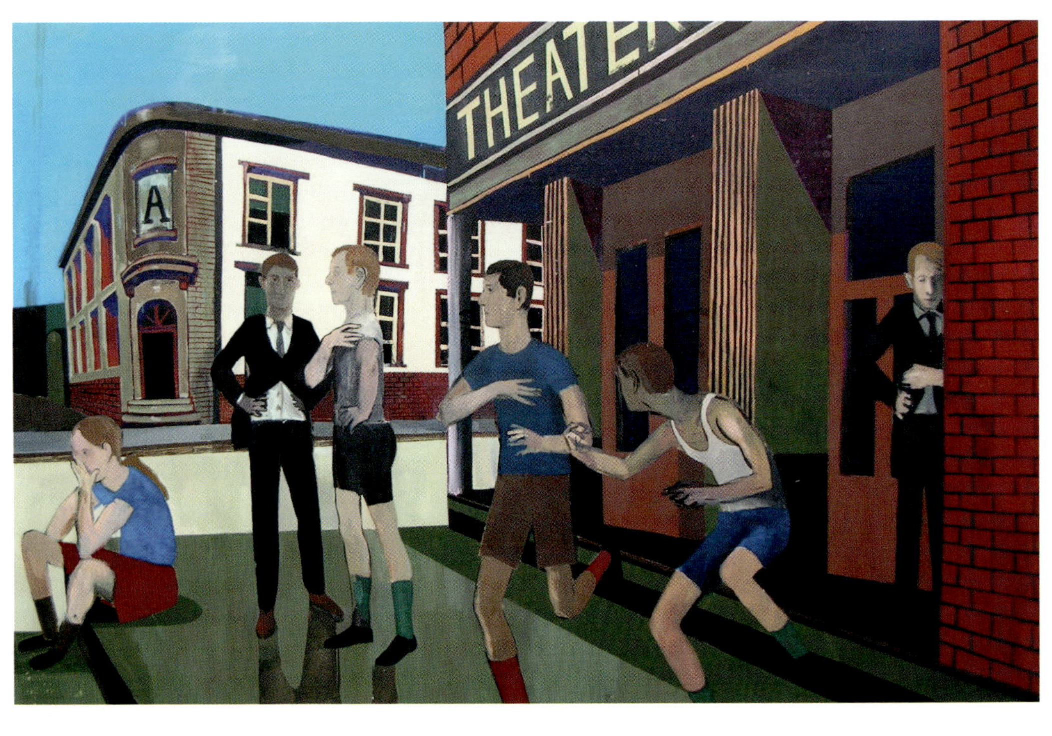

Christoph Ruckhäberle
Theater, 2003, Oil on canvas
74 3/4 x 110 1/4 in. (190 x 280 cm)
CR2

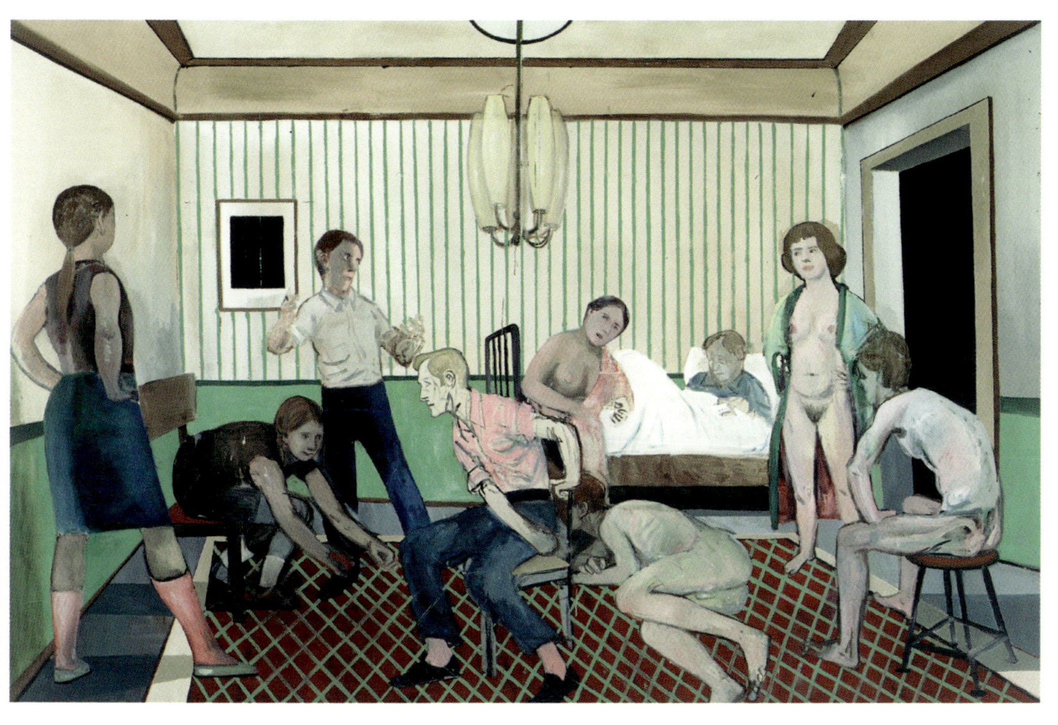

Christoph Ruckhäberle
Komödie (Comedy), 2003, Oil on canvas
75 x 110 1/4 in. (190 x 280 cm)
CR3

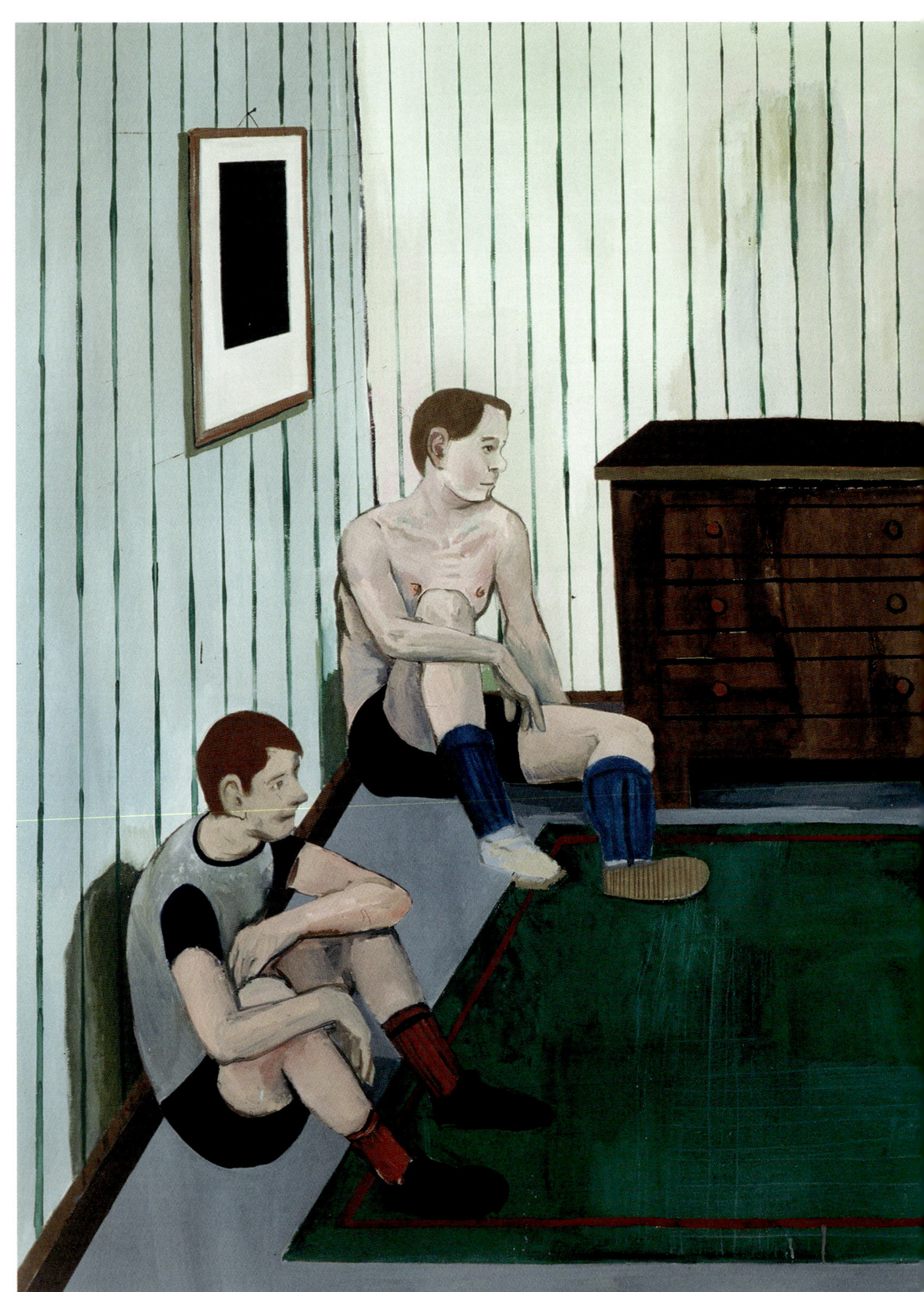

Christoph Ruckhäberle
Suite, 2003, Oil on canvas
75 x 110 1/4 in. (190.5 x 280 cm)
CR4

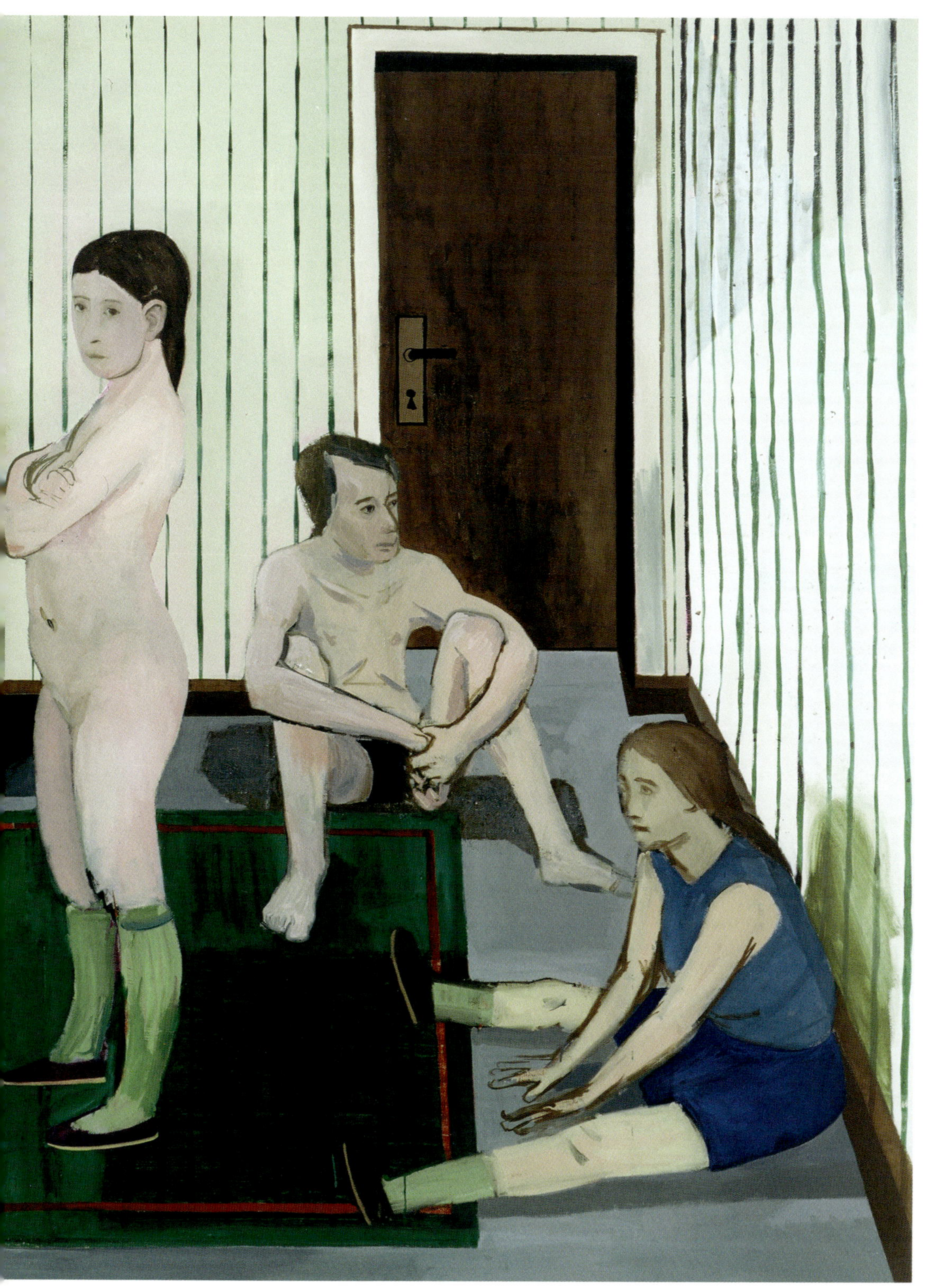

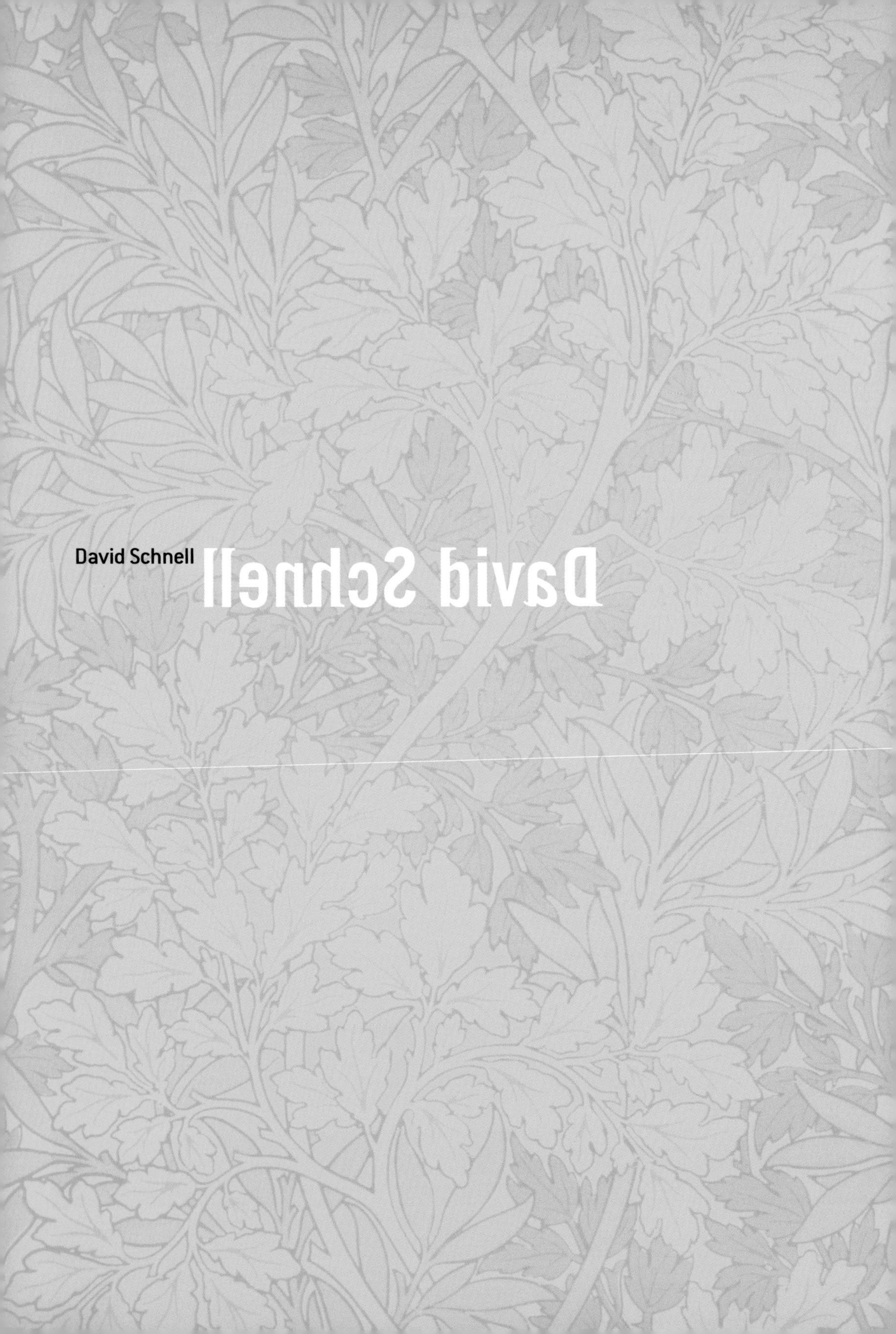

David Schnell

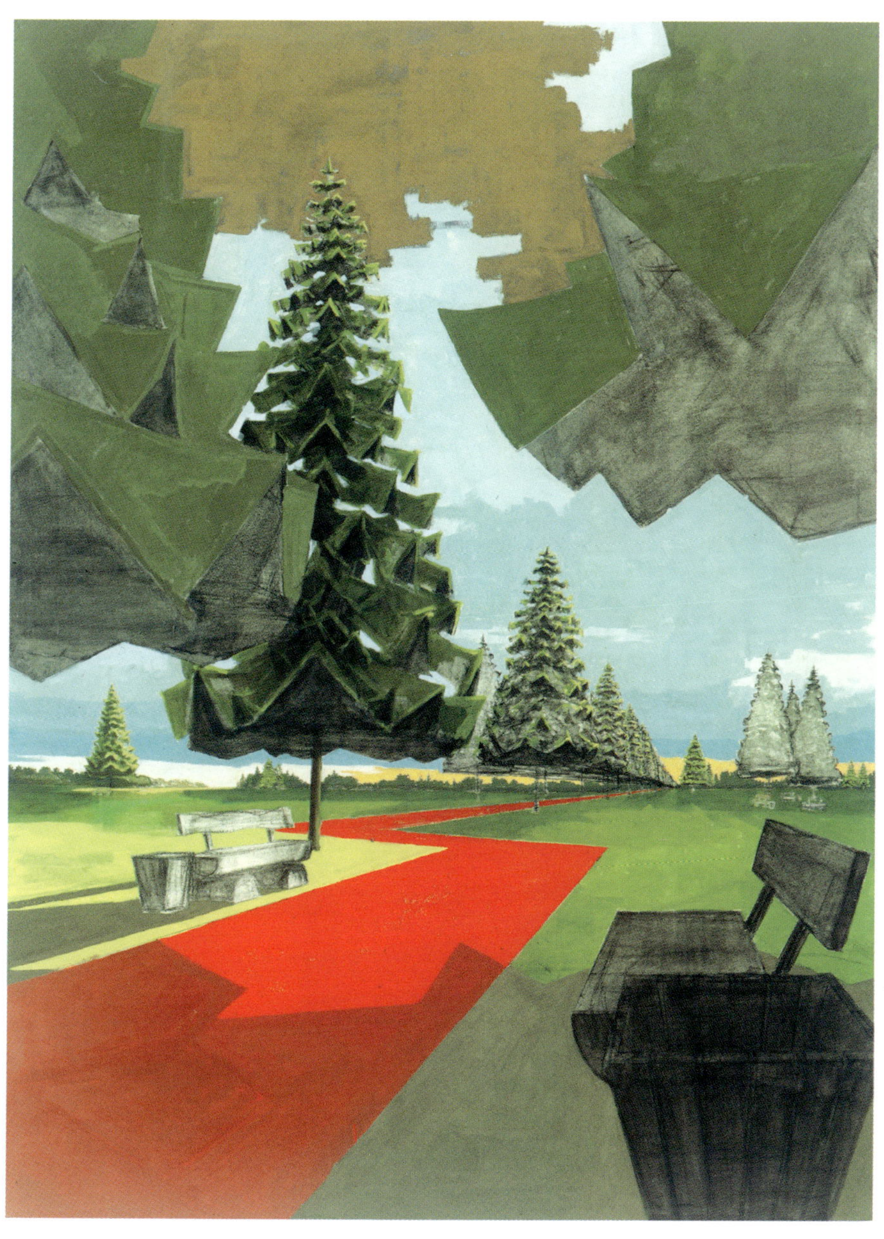

David Schnell
Park, 2000, Tempera on canvas
70 3/4 x 51 1/4 in. (179.5 x 130 cm)
DS1

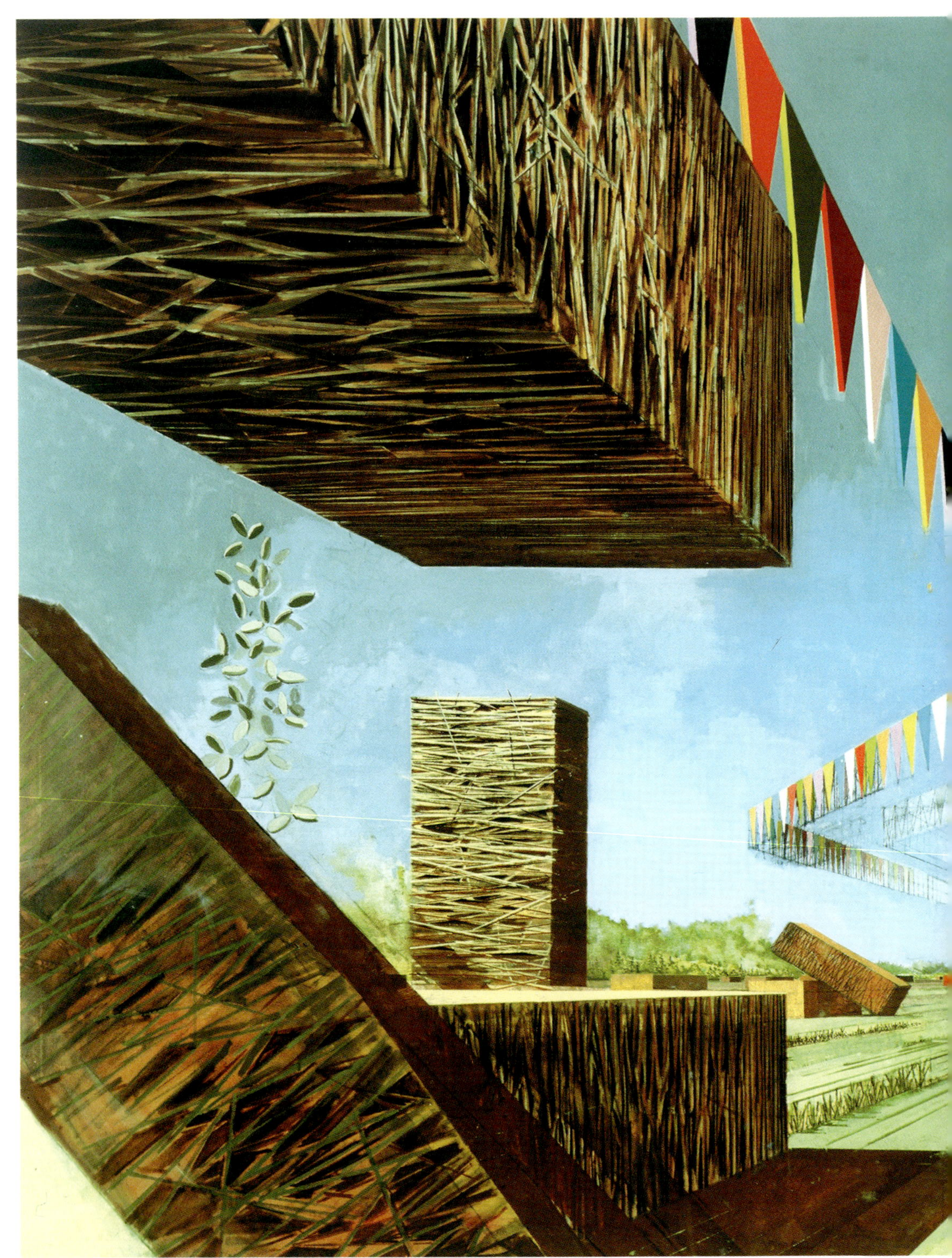

David Schnell
Ballen (Bales), 2003, Oil on canvas
71 x 110 1/4 in. (180.5 x 280 cm)
DS2

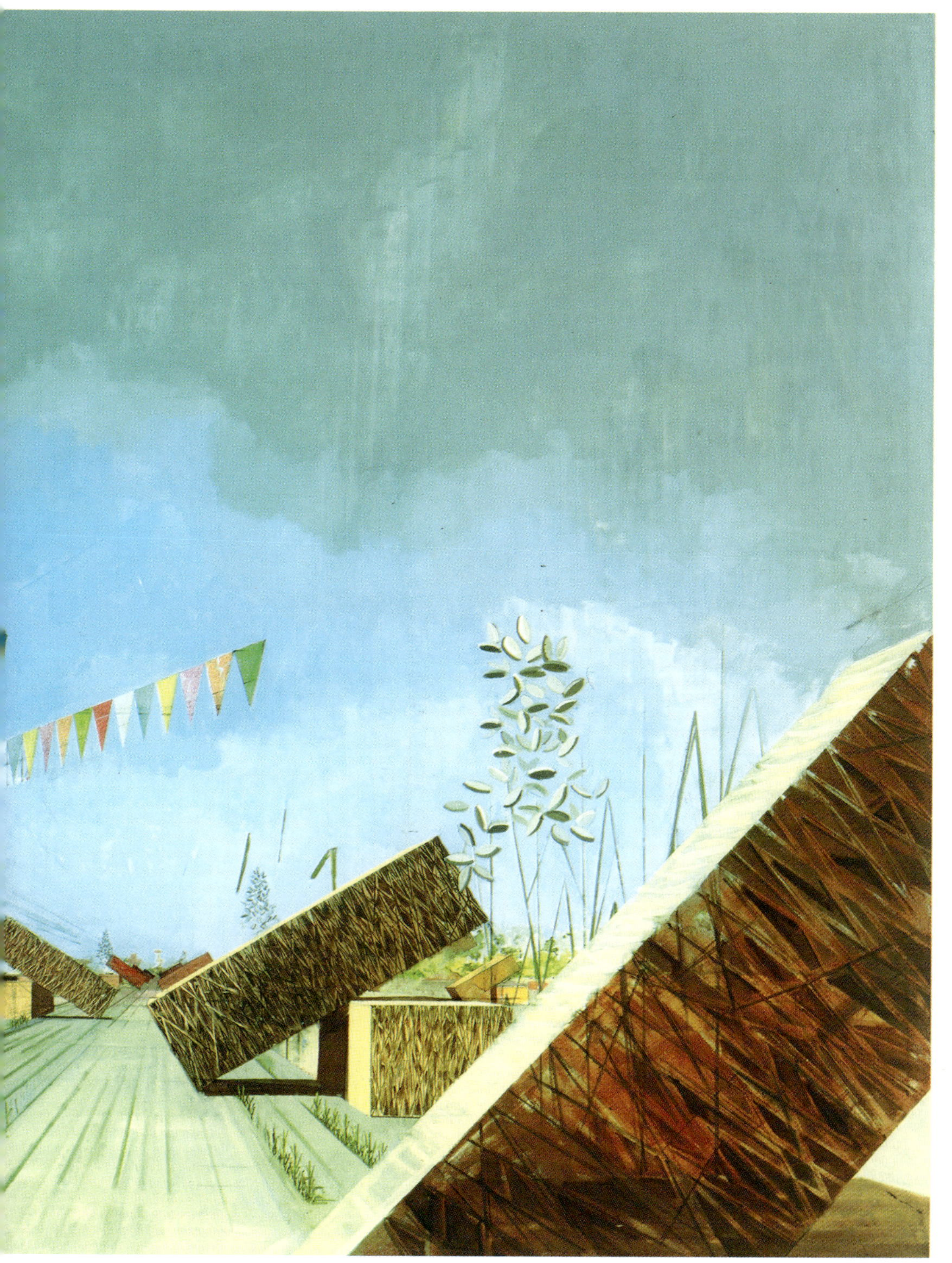

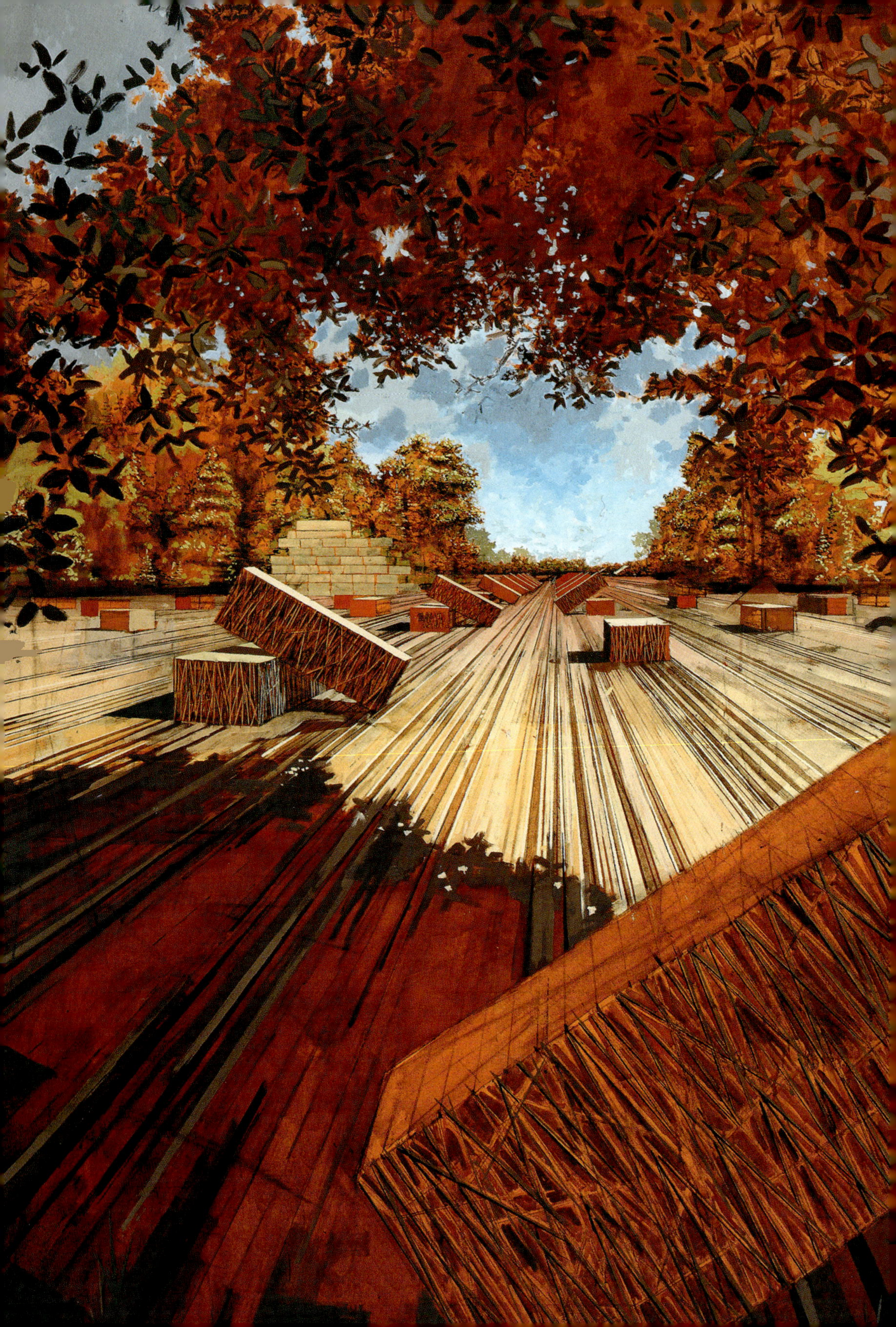

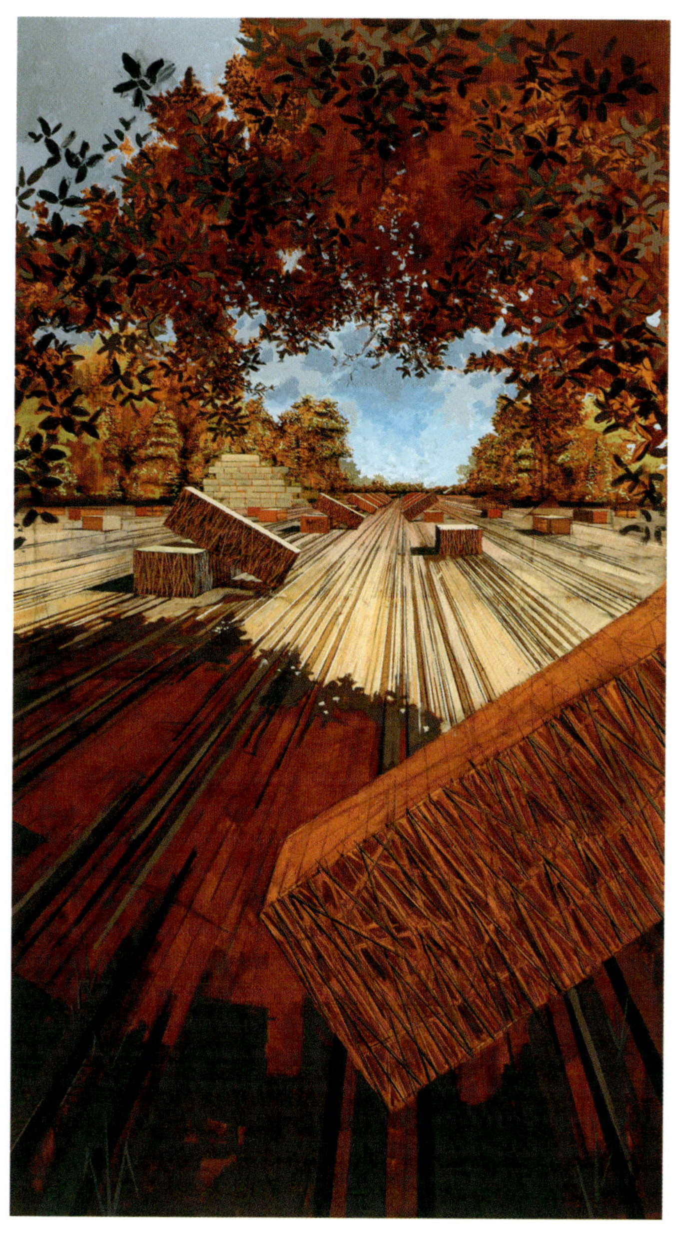

David Schnell
Durchblick (Vista), 2004, Oil on linen
90 1/2 x 49 1/8 in. (230 x 125 cm)
DS3

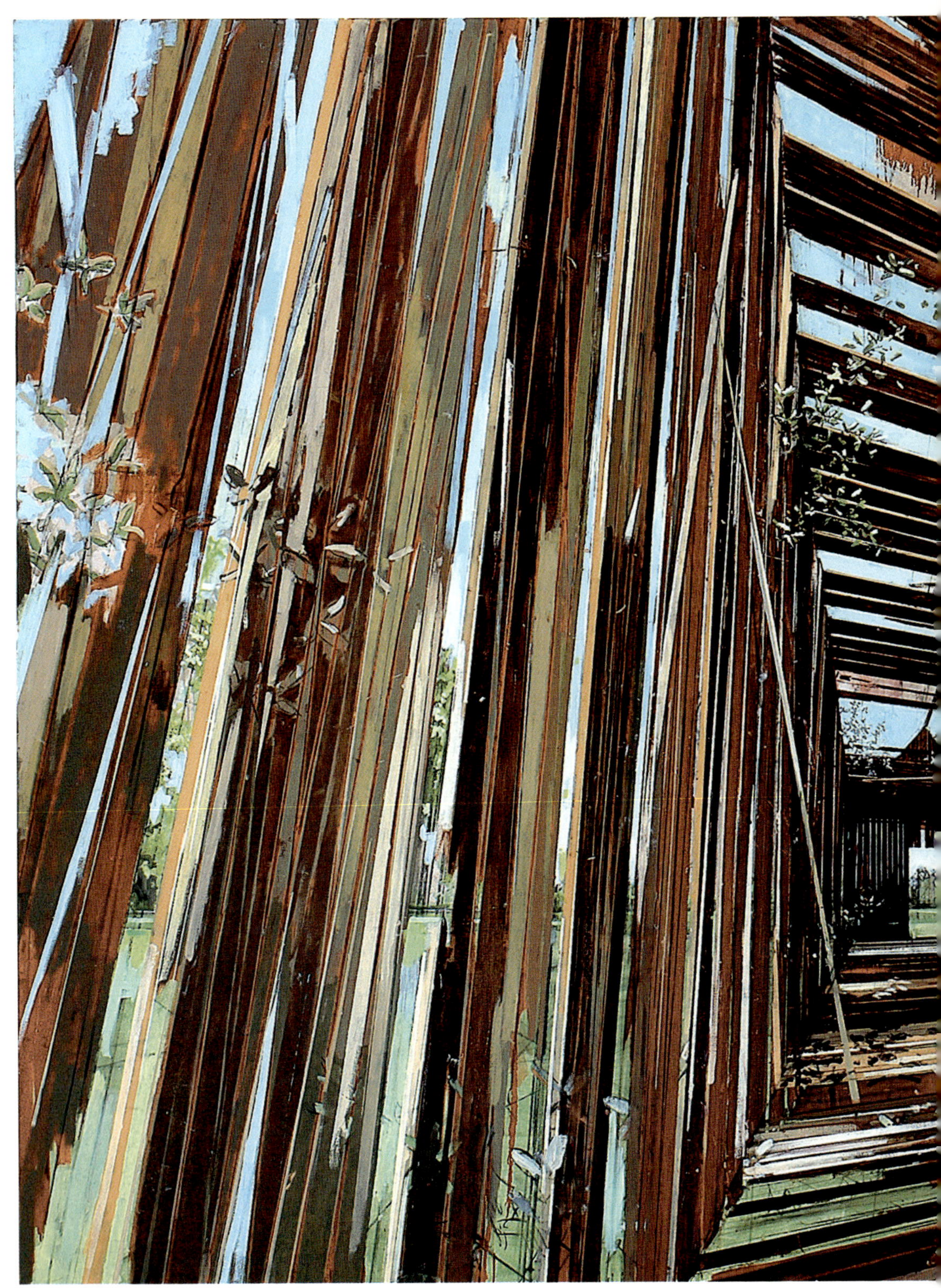

David Schnell
Bretter (Planks), 2005, Oil on canvas
78 3/4 x 118 1/8 in. (200 x 300 cm)
DS4

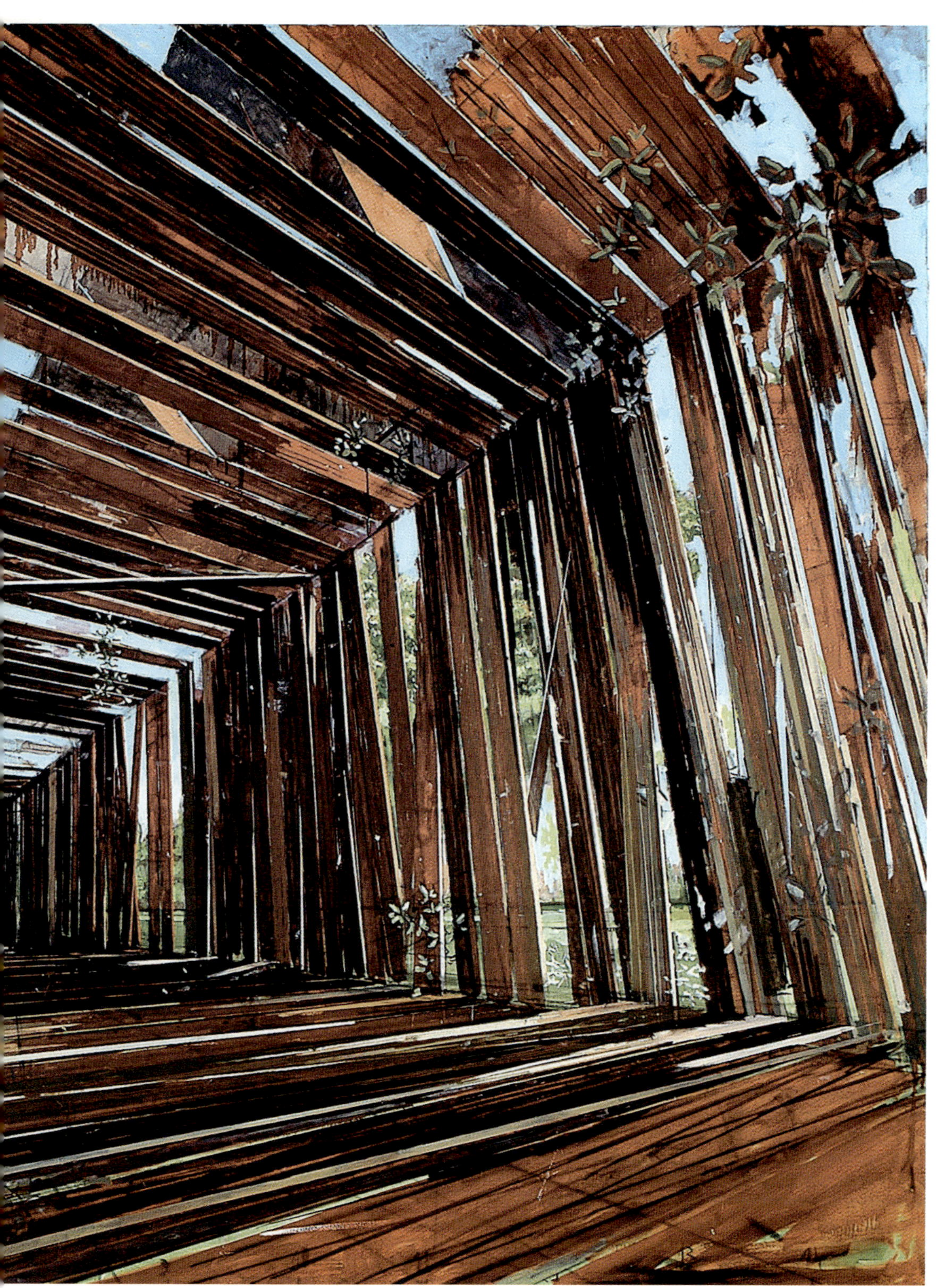

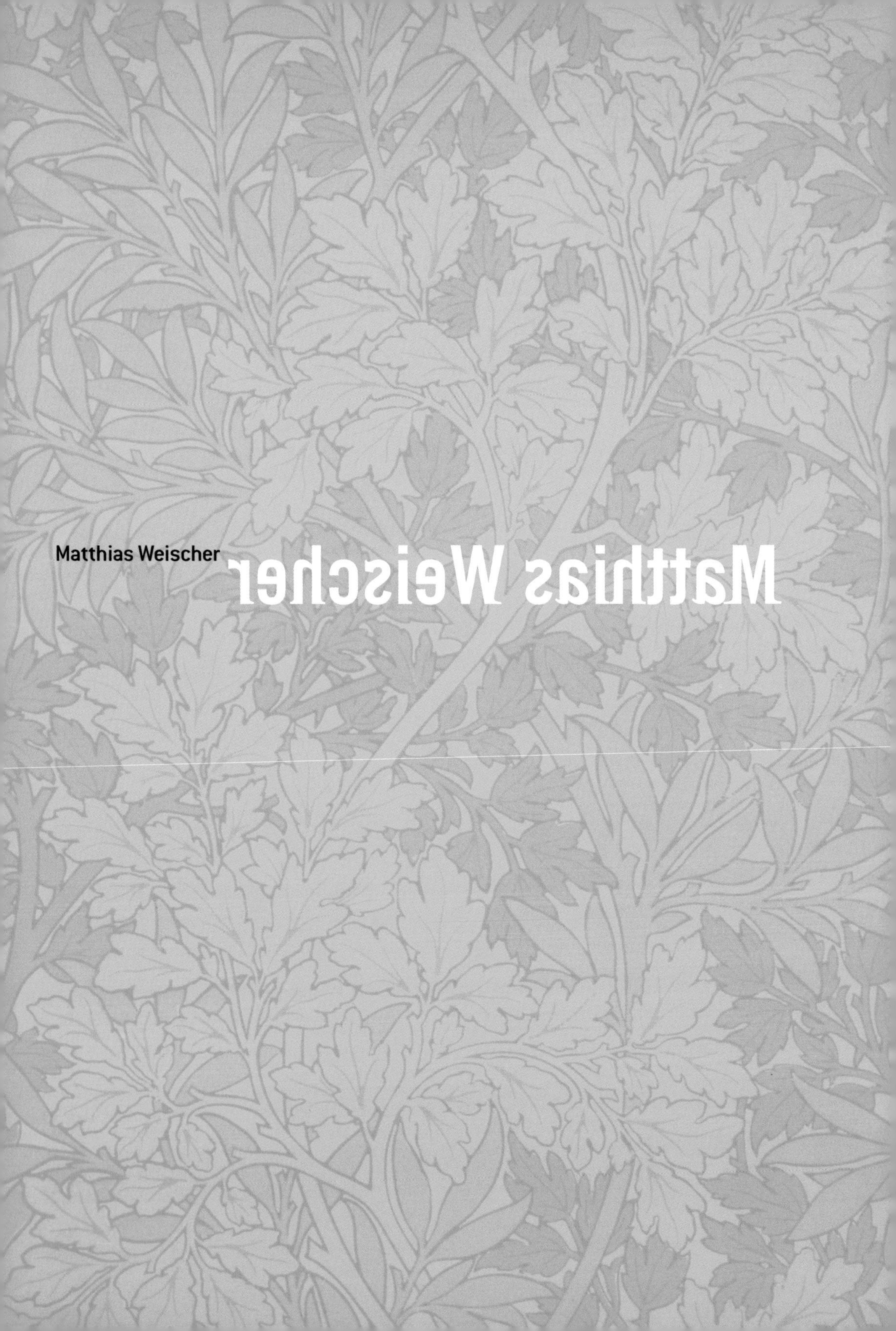

Matthias Weischer

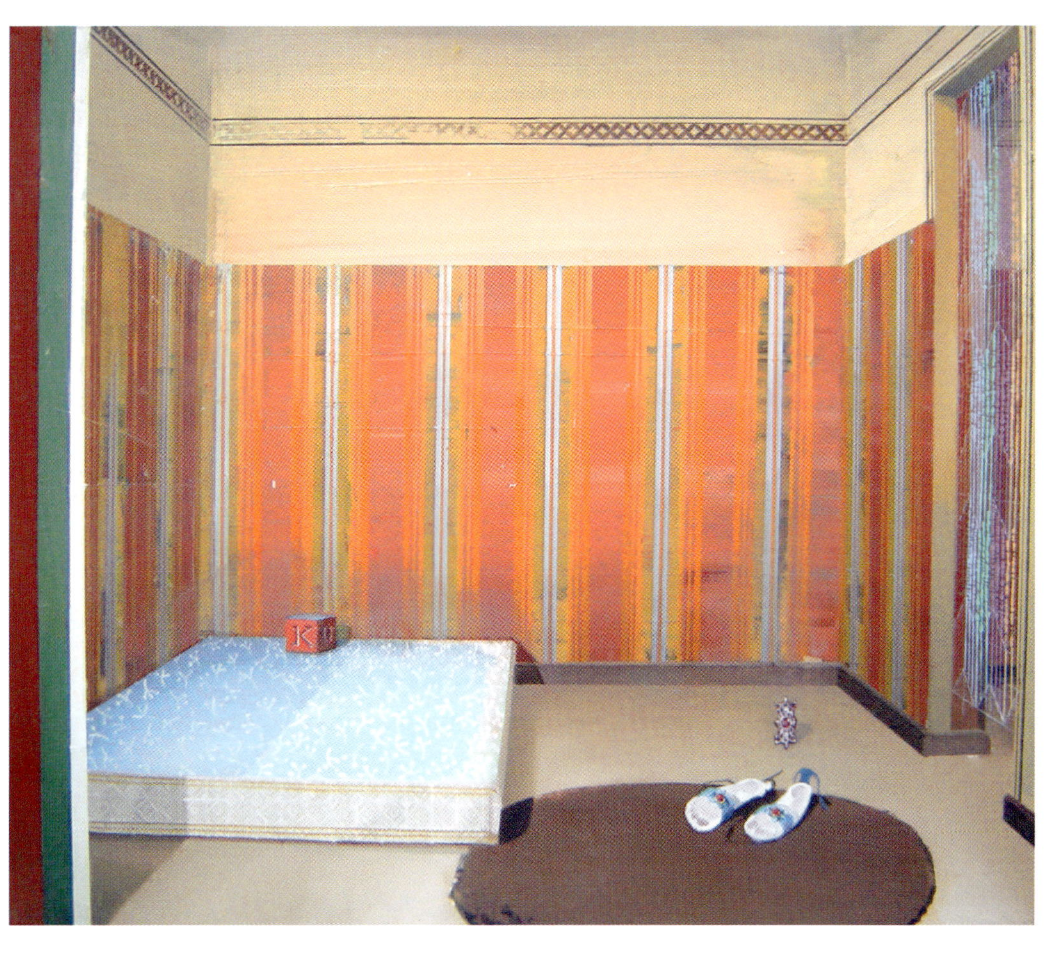

Matthias Weischer
KO, 2003, Oil on canvas
29 1/2 x 33 1/2 in. (75 x 85 cm)
MW1

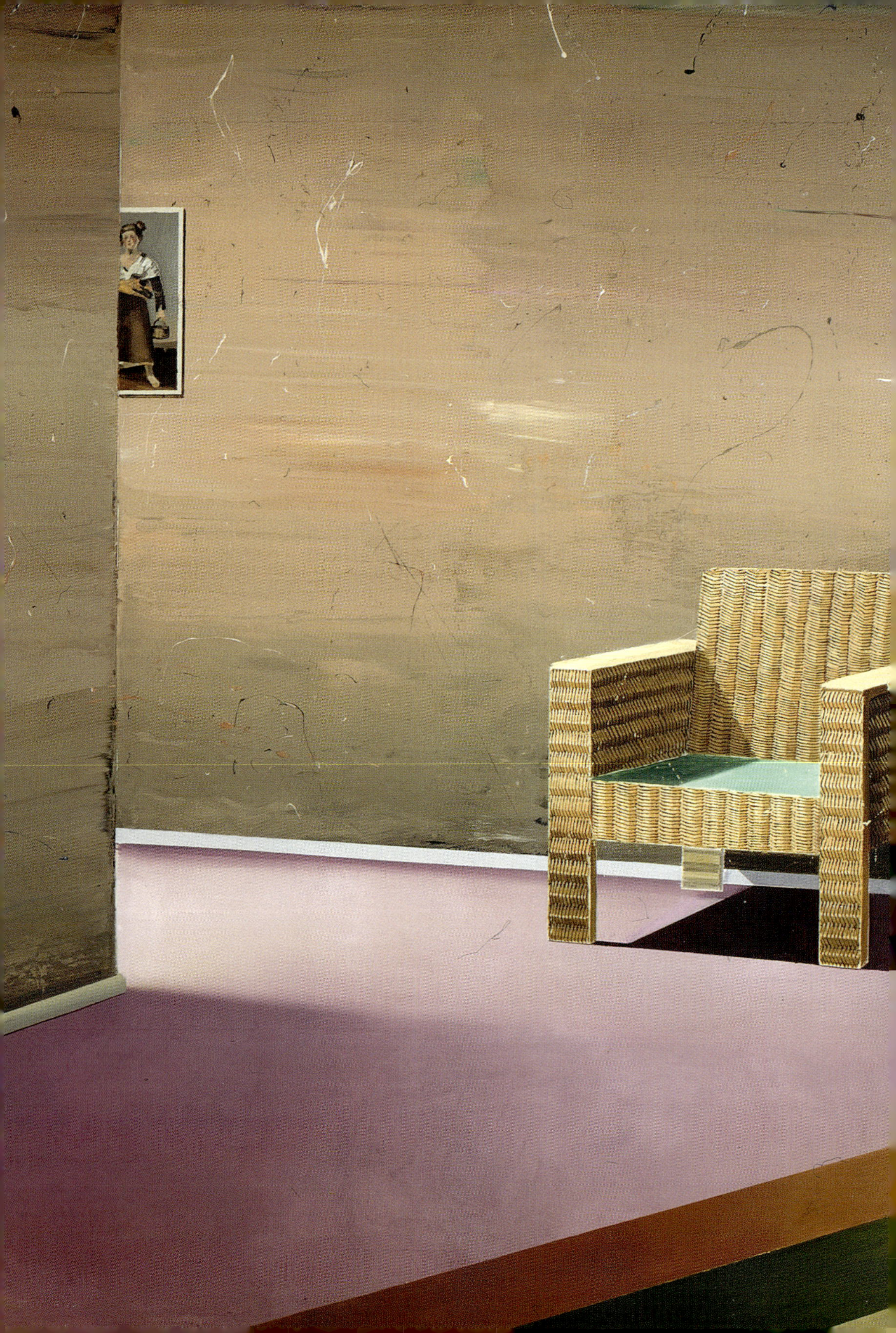

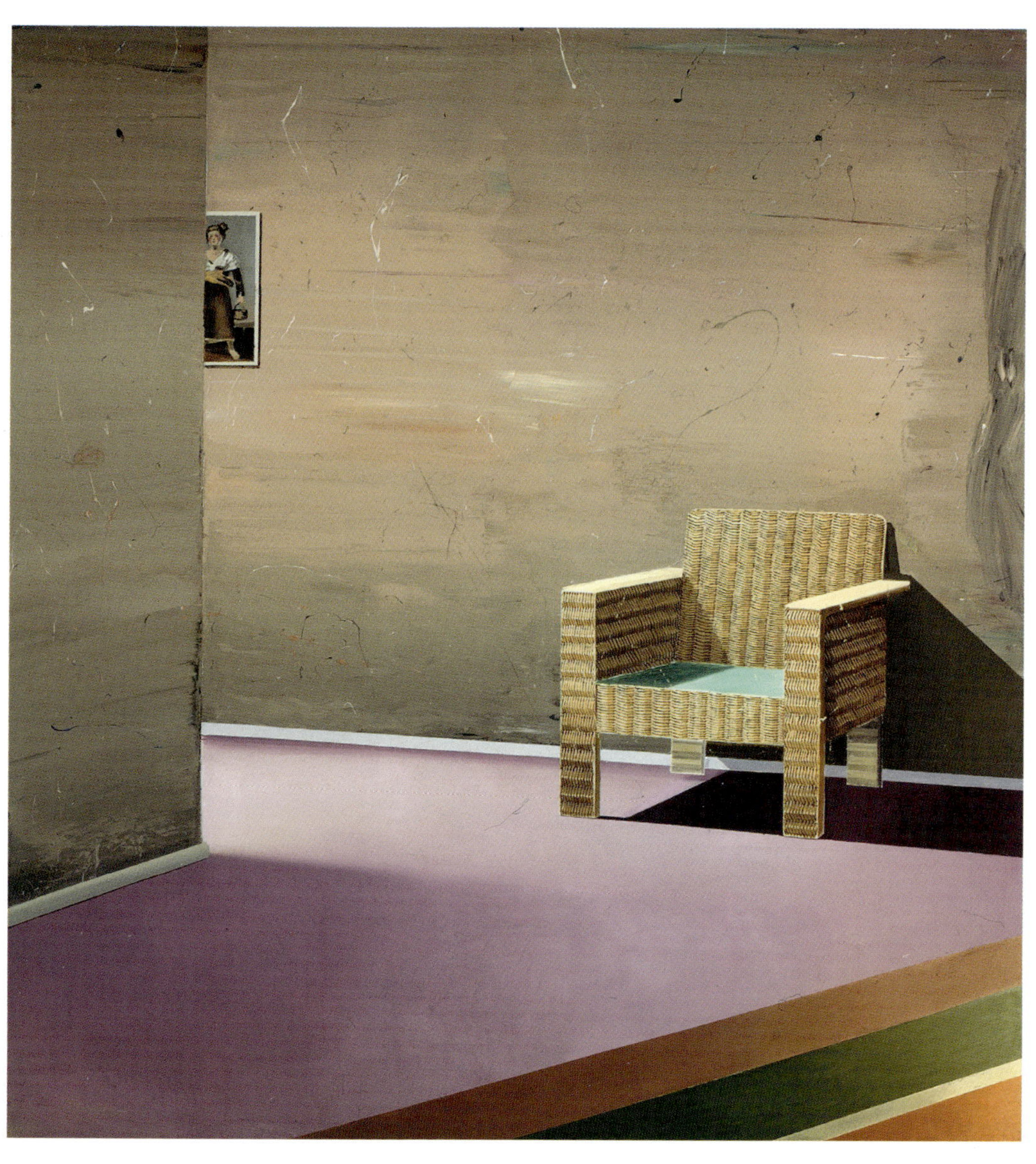

Matthias Weischer
Chair, 2003, Oil on canvas
75 x 67 in. (190.5 x 170 cm)
MW2

Matthias Weischer
Zweiteilig (Bisected), 2003, Oil on canvas
92 1/2 x 119 7/8 in. (235 x 304.5 cm)
MW3

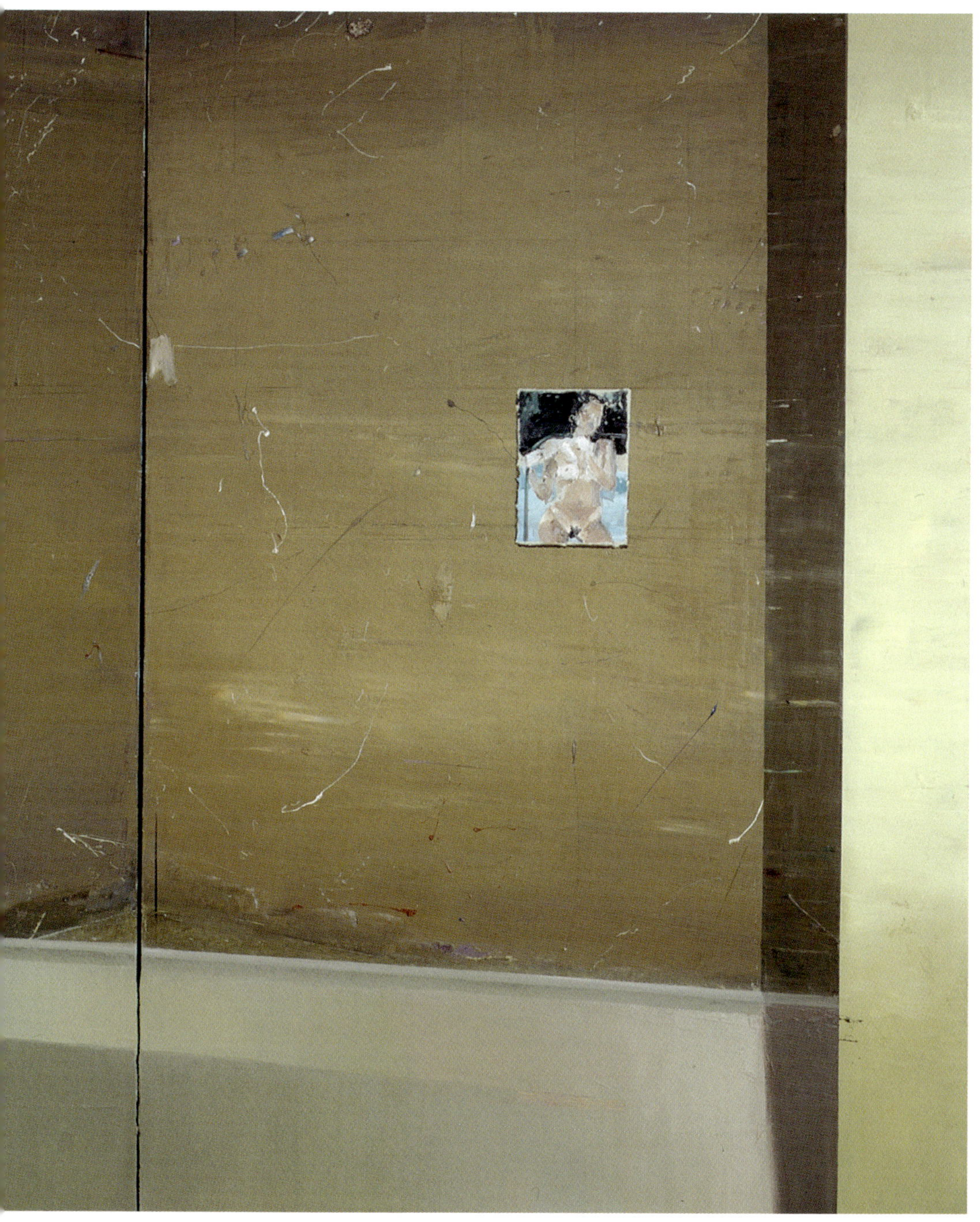

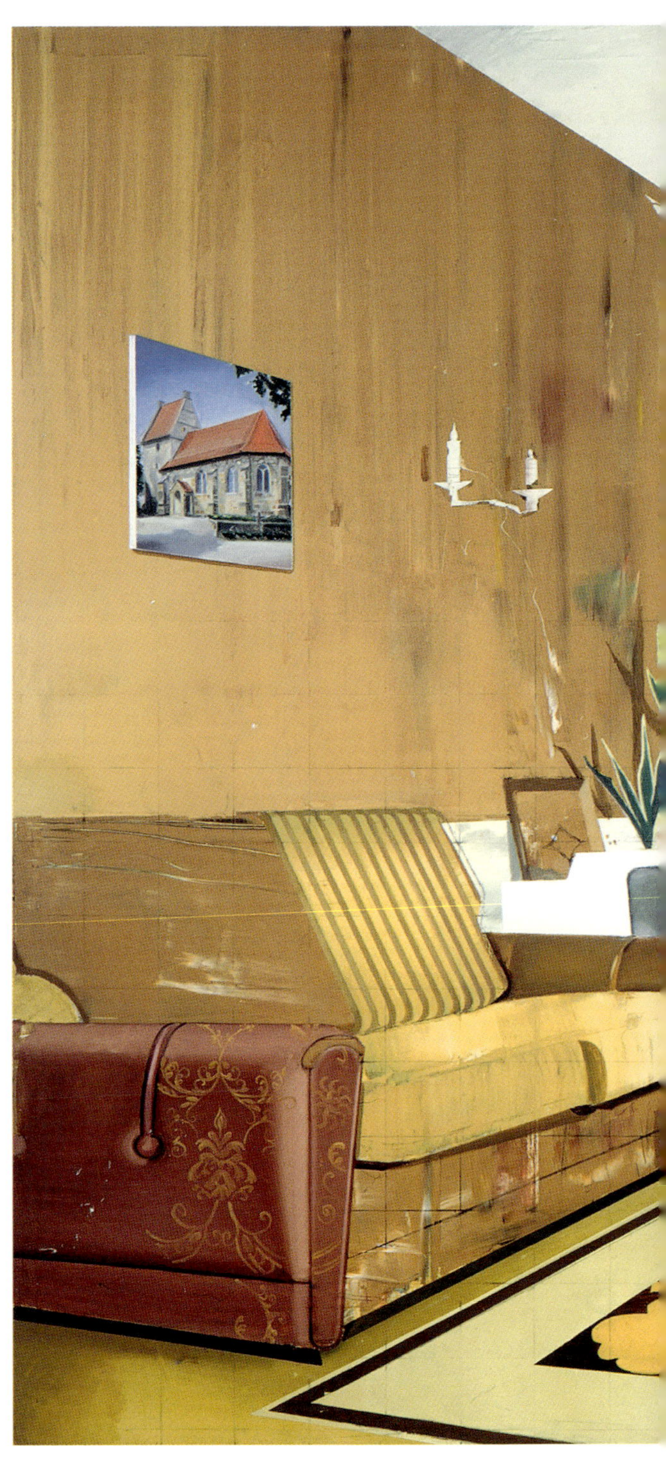

Matthias Weischer
St. Ludgerus, 2004, Oil on linen
78 3/4 x 99 in. (300 x 251.5 cm)
MW4

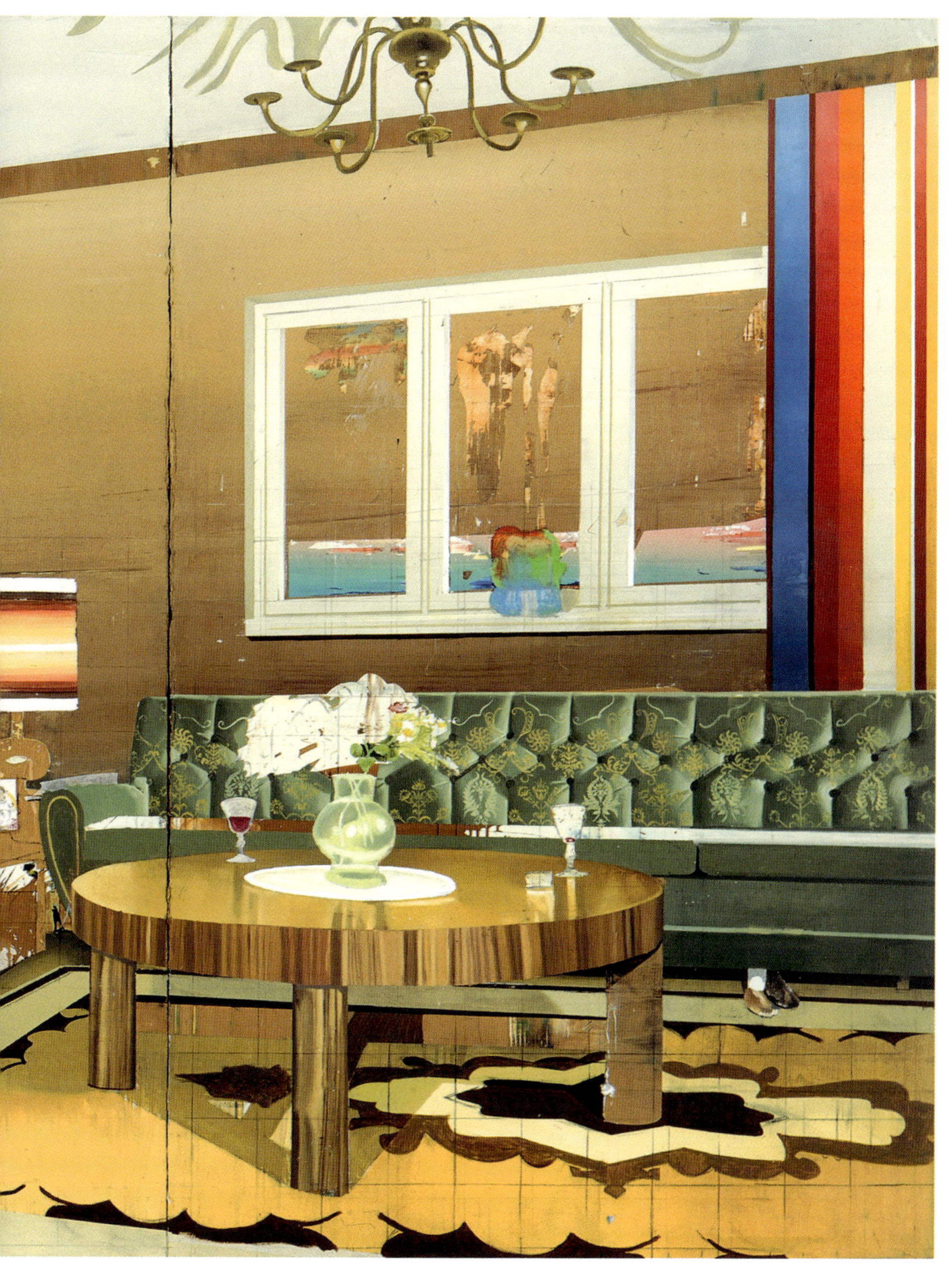

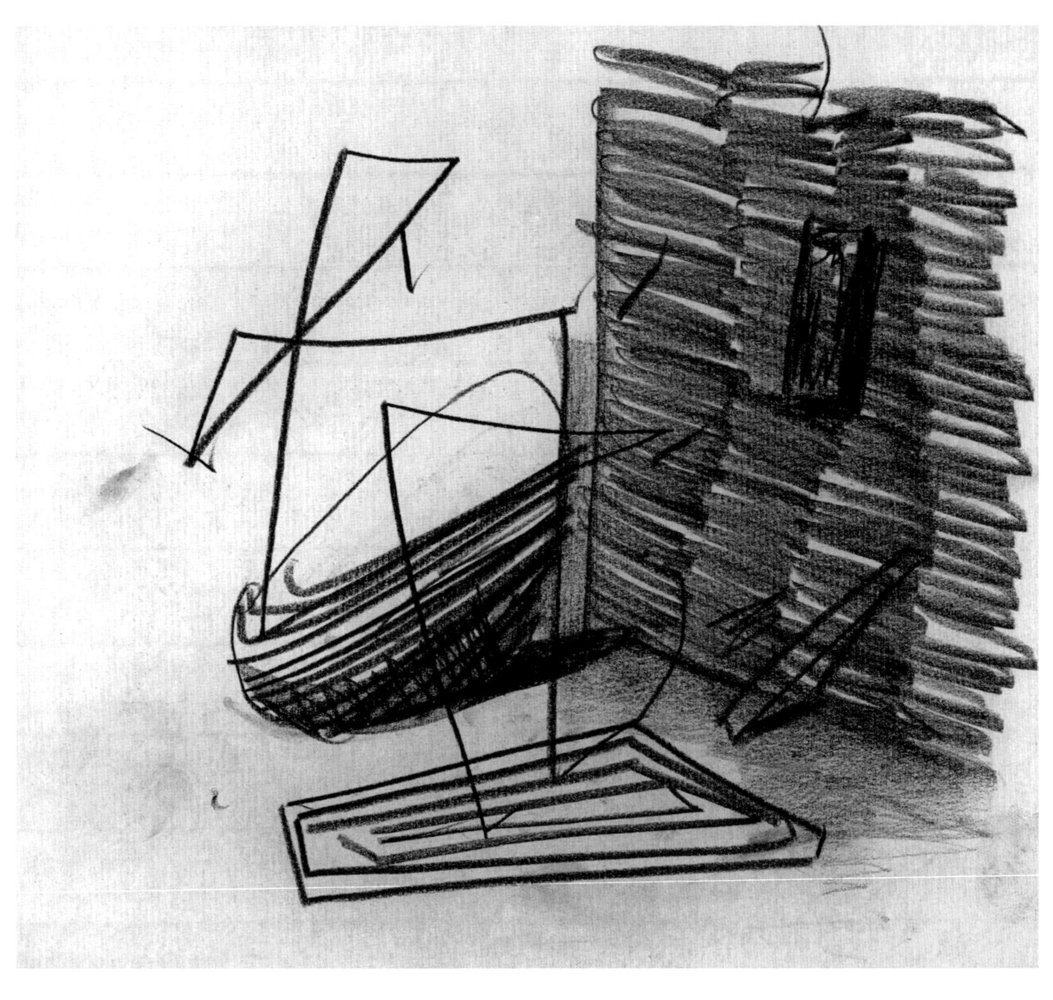

Matthias Weischer
Untitled, WV 100, 2004, Graphite on Paper
9 3/4 x 10 1/2 in. (24.8 x 26.7 cm)
MW5

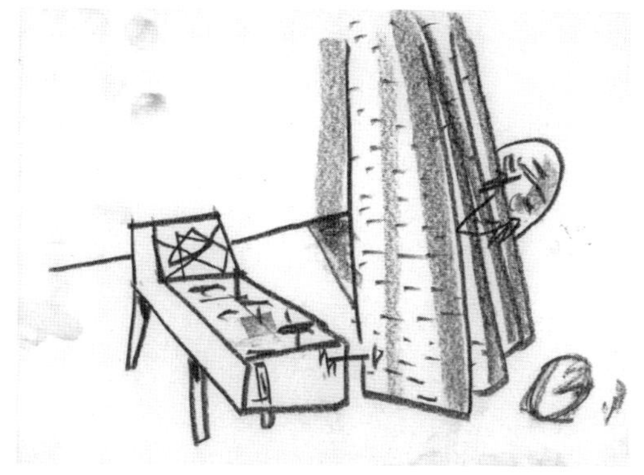

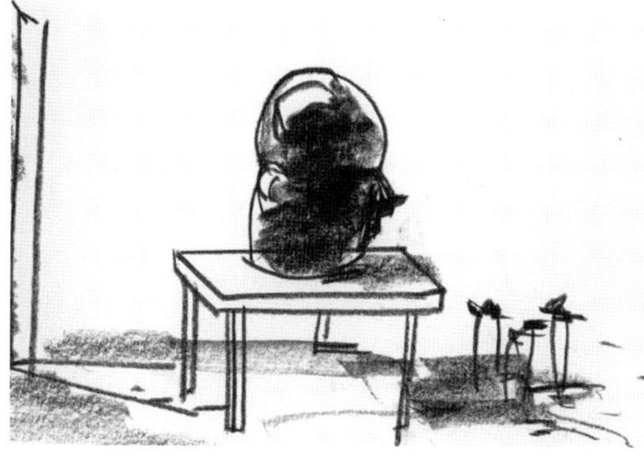

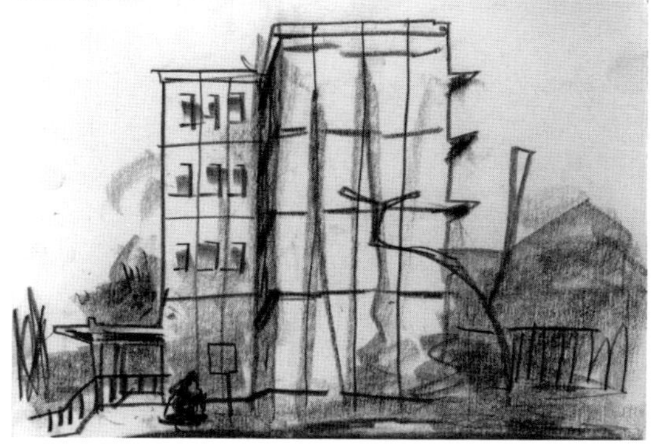

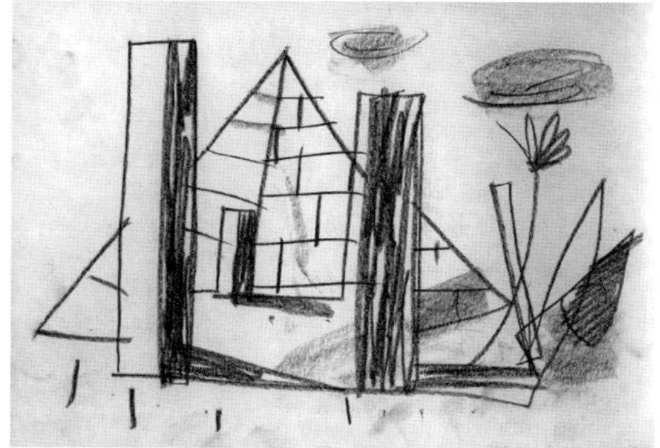

Matthias Weischer
Untitled, WV 241, 2004, Graphite on Paper
7 5/16 x 9 13/16 in. (18.5 x 25 cm)
MW6

Matthias Weischer
Untitled, WV 282, 2004, Graphite on Paper
8 1/4 x 11 13/16 in. (21 x 30 cm)
MW7

Matthias Weischer
Untitled, WV 360, 2005, Graphite on Paper
7 7/8 x 11 1/4 in. (20 x 28.5 cm)
MW8

Matthias Weischer
Untitled, WV 361, 2005, Graphite on Paper
8 1/4 x 11 5/8 in. (21 x 29.5 cm)
MW9

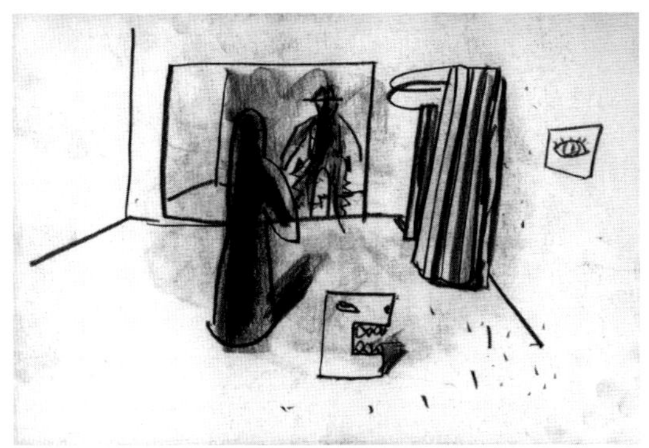

Matthias Weischer
Untitled, WV 369, (front), 2005, Graphite on Paper
7 11/16 x 11 1/2 in. (19,5 x 28.3 cm)
MW10

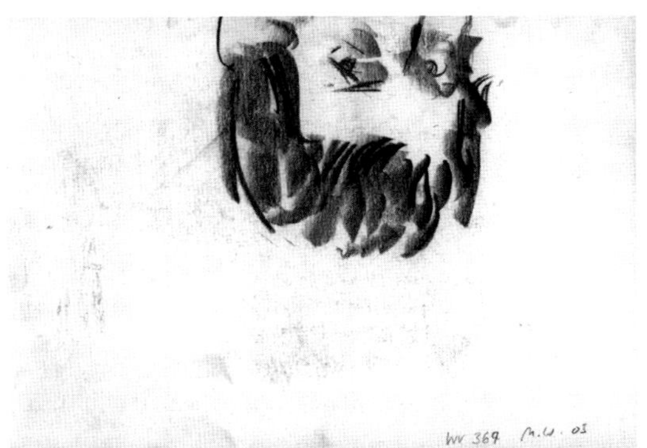

Matthias Weischer
Untitled, WV 369, (back), 2005, Graphite on Paper
7 11/16 x 11 1/2 in. (19,5 x 28.3 cm)
MW10

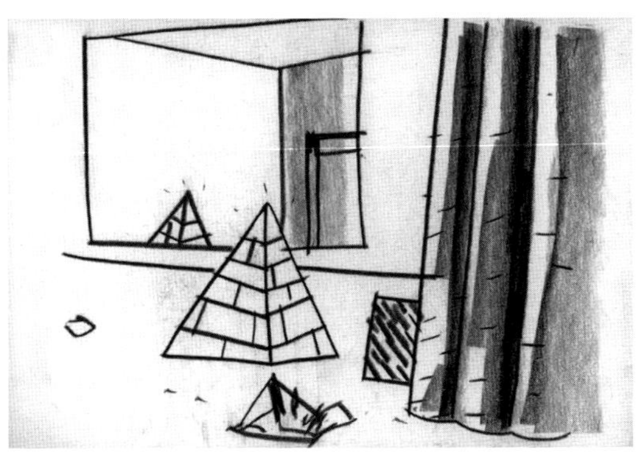

Matthias Weischer
Untitled, WV 376, 2005, Graphite on Paper
11 3/4 x 8 1/4 in. (19.6 x 28.2 cm)
MW11

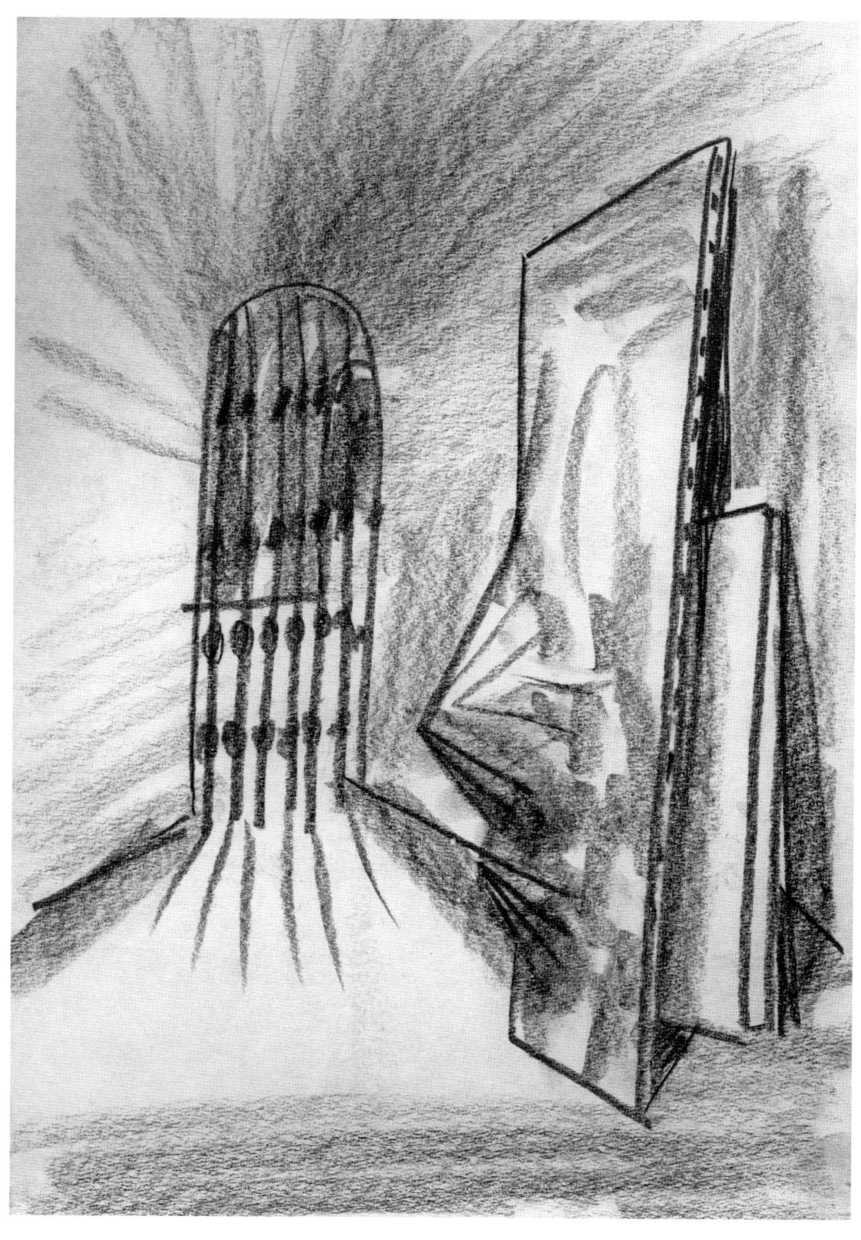

Matthias Weischer
Untitled, WV 377, 2005, Graphite on Paper
11 3/4 x 8 1/4 in. (29.8 x 21 cm)
MW12

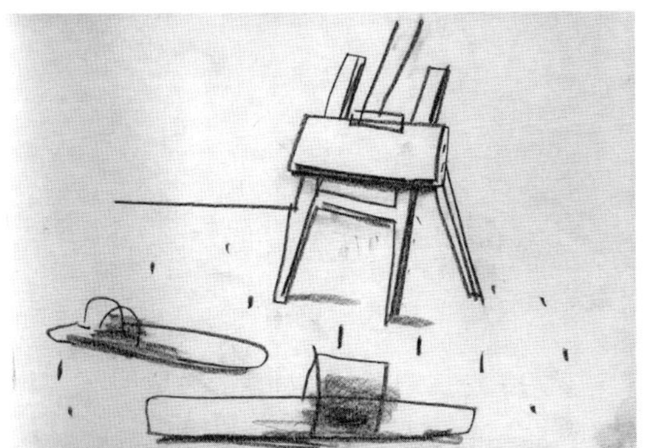

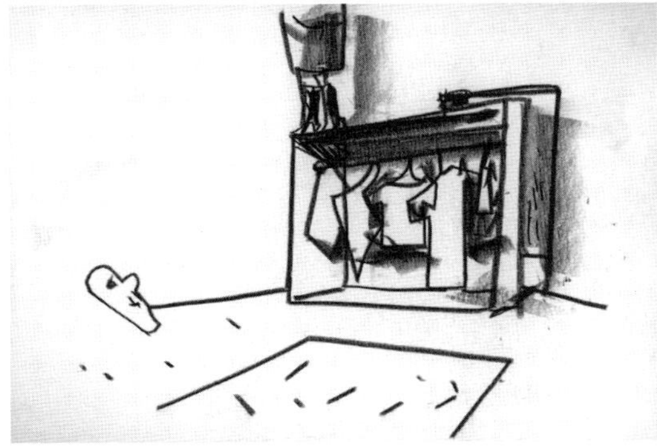

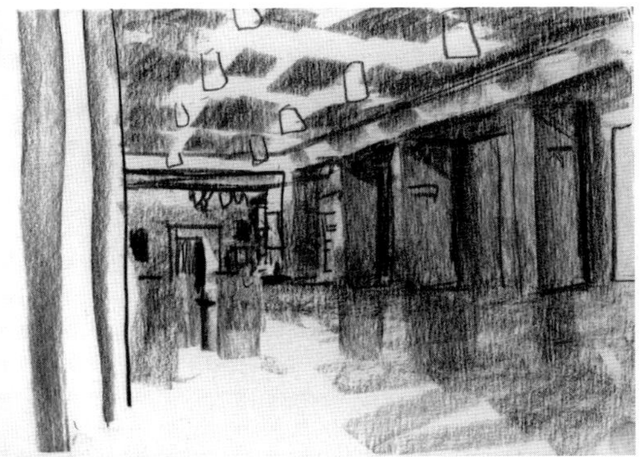

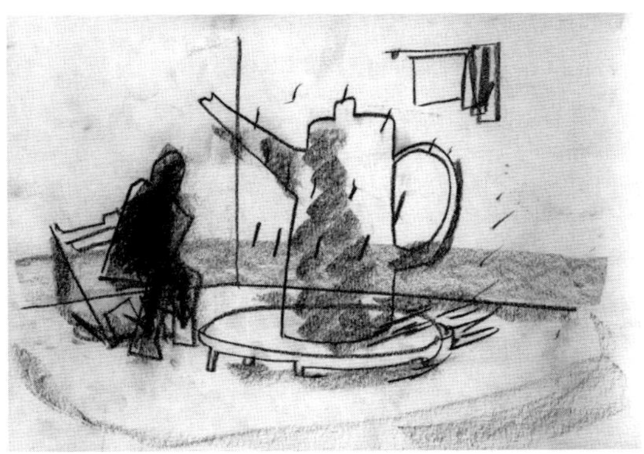

Matthias Weischer
Untitled, WV 397, 2005, Graphite on Paper
8 1/4 x 11 3/4 in. (21 x 29.8 cm)
MW13

Matthias Weischer
Untitled, WV 398, 2005, Graphite on Paper
7 11/16 x 11 1/4 in. (19.5 x 28.5 cm)
MW14

Matthias Weischer
Untitled, WV 403, 2005, Graphite on Paper
8 x 11 3/8 in. (20.3 x 29 cm)
MW15

Matthias Weischer
Untitled, WV 408, 2005, Graphite on Paper
8 5/16 x 11 3/4 in. (21.1 x 29.8 cm)
MW16

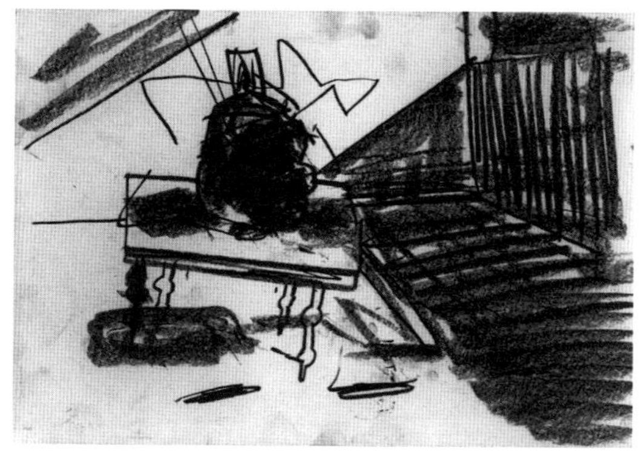

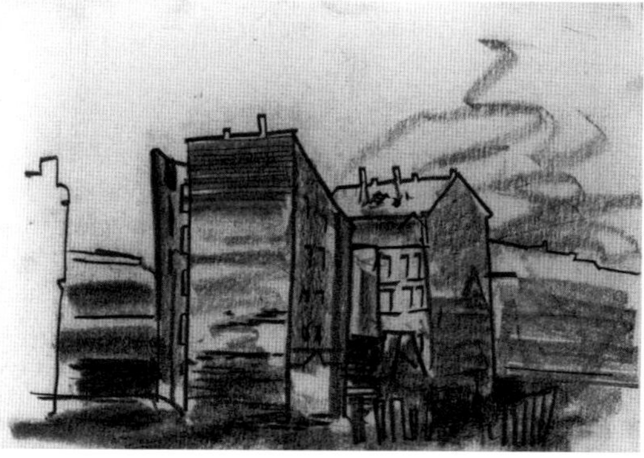

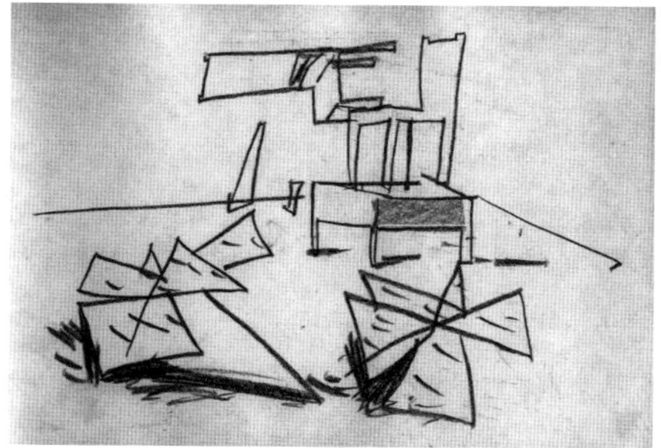

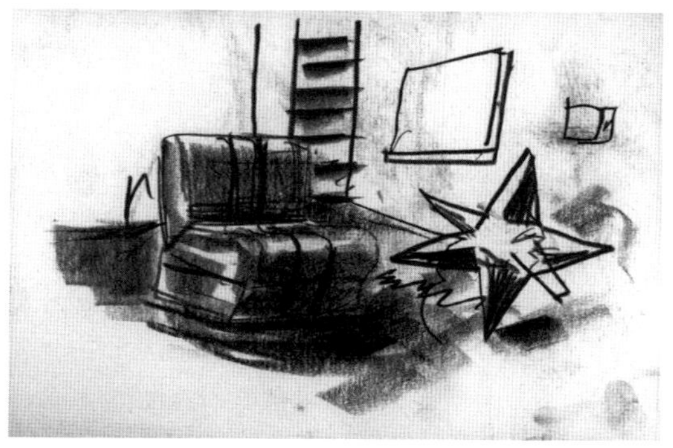

Matthias Weischer
Untitled, WV 409, 2005, Graphite on Paper
8 1/4 x 11 5/8 in. (21 x 29.5 cm)
MW17

Matthias Weischer
Untitled, WV 411, 2005, Graphite on Paper
8 x 11 3/8 in. (20.2 x 29 cm)
MW18

Matthias Weischer
Untitled, WV 416, 2005, Graphite on Paper
8 1/4 x 7 3/4 in. (21 x 29.8 cm)
MW19

Matthias Weischer
Untitled, WV 418, 2005, Graphite on Paper
7 9/16 x 11 1/8 in. (19.2 x 28.2 cm)
MW20

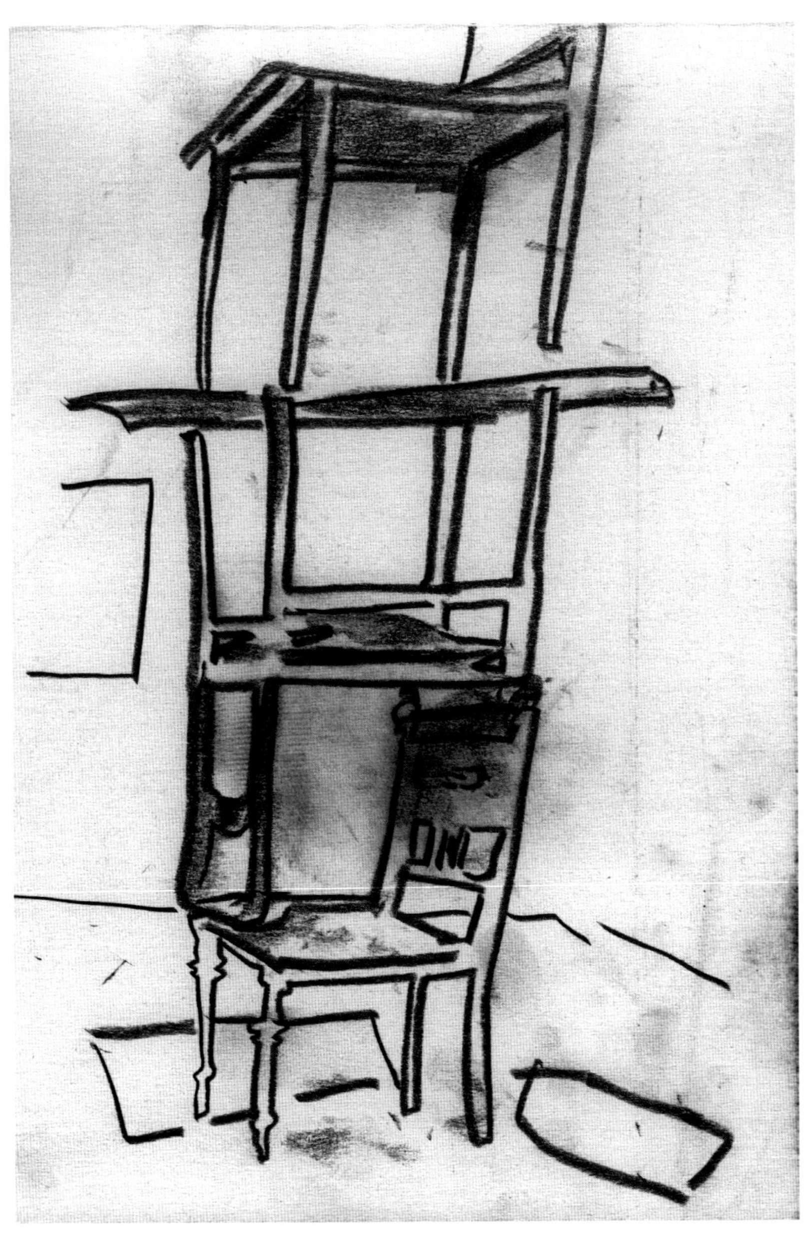

Matthias Weischer
Untitled, WV 419, 2005, Graphite on Paper
11 1/4 x 7 3/8 in. (28.5 x 18.9 cm)
MW21

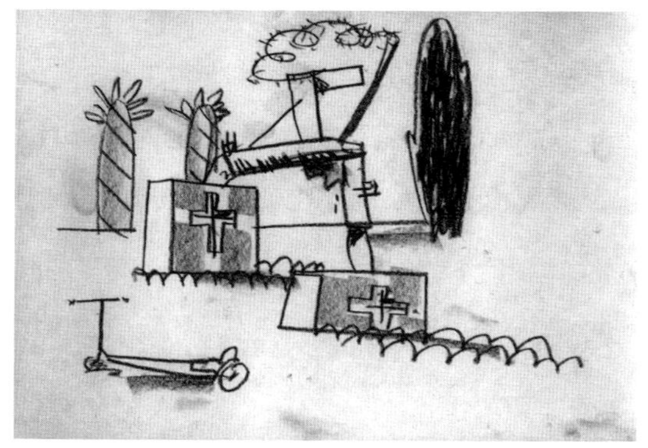

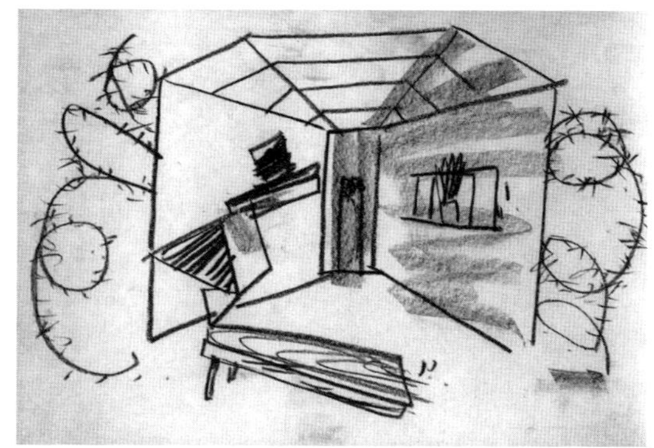

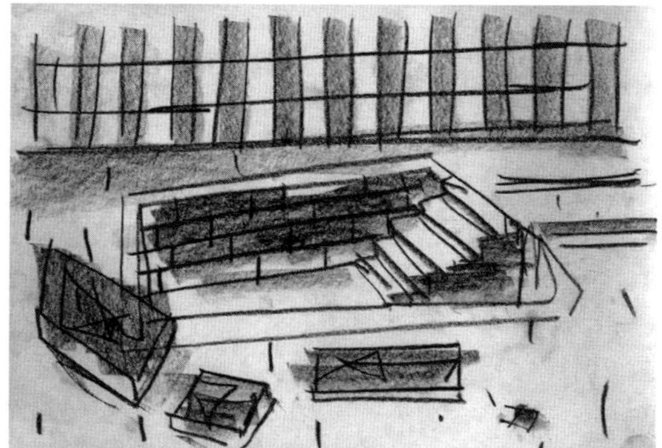

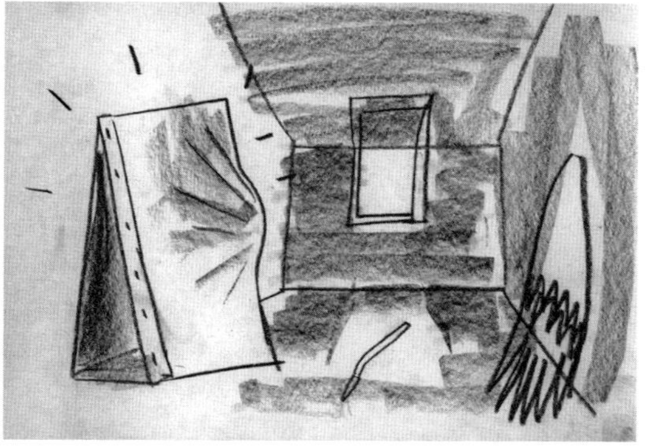

Matthias Weischer
Untitled, WV 420, 2005, Graphite on Paper
8 1/4 x 11 3/4 in. (21 x 29.8 cm)
MW22

Matthias Weischer
Untitled, WV 421, 2005, Graphite on Paper
8 1/4 x 11 3/4 in. (21 x 29.8 cm)
MW23

Matthias Weischer
Untitled, WV 422, 2005, Graphite on Paper
8 1/4 x 11 3/4 in. (21 x 29.8 cm)
MW24

Matthias Weischer
Untitled, WV 423, 2005, Graphite on Paper
8 1/4 x 11 3/4 in. (21 x 29.8 cm)
MW25

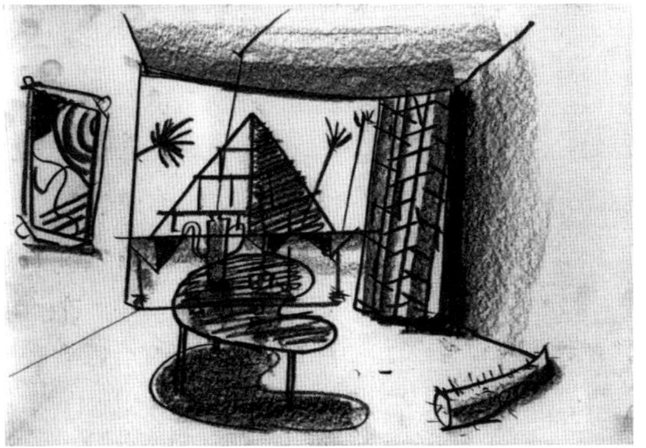

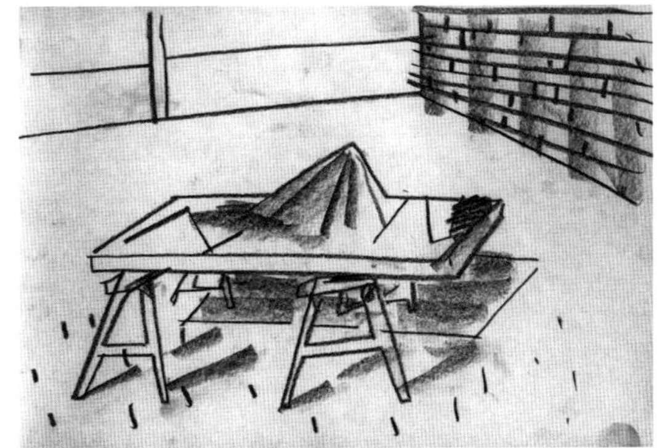

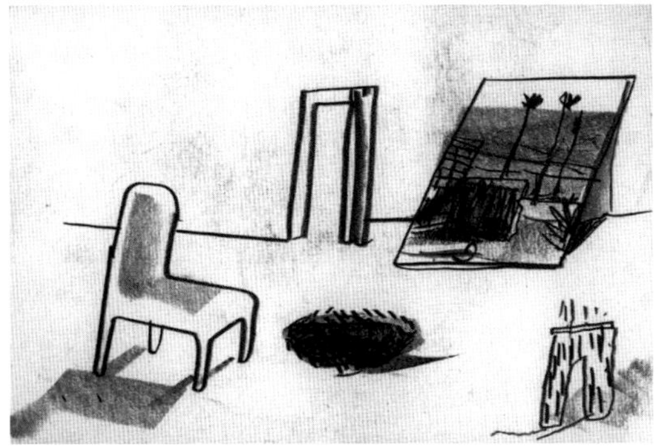

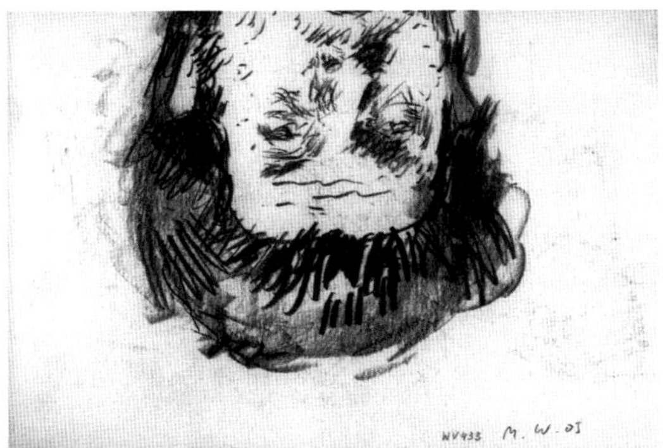

Matthias Weischer
Untitled, WV 424, 2005, Graphite on Paper
8 1/4 x 11 5/8 in. (21 x 29.5cm)
MW26

Matthias Weischer
Untitled, WV 432, 2005, Graphite on Paper
8 1/4 x 11 3/4 in. (21 x 29.8 cm)
MW27

Matthias Weischer
Untitled, WV 433, (front), 2005, Graphite on Paper
7 11/16 x 11 7/16 in. (19.5 x 29.4 cm)
MW28

Matthias Weischer
Untitled, WV 433, (back), 2005, Graphite on Paper
7 11/16 x 11 7/16 in. (19.5 x 29.4 cm)
MW28

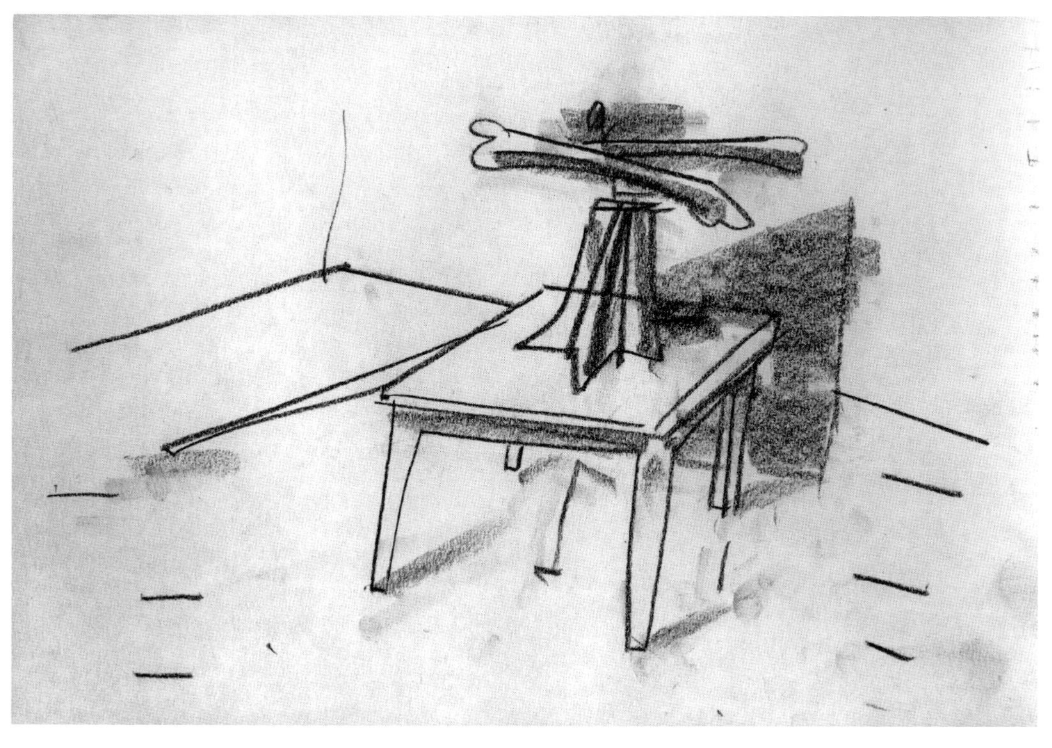

Matthias Weischer
Untitled, WV 436, 2005, Graphite on Paper
8 1/4 x 11 3/4 in. (21 x 29.8 cm)
MW29

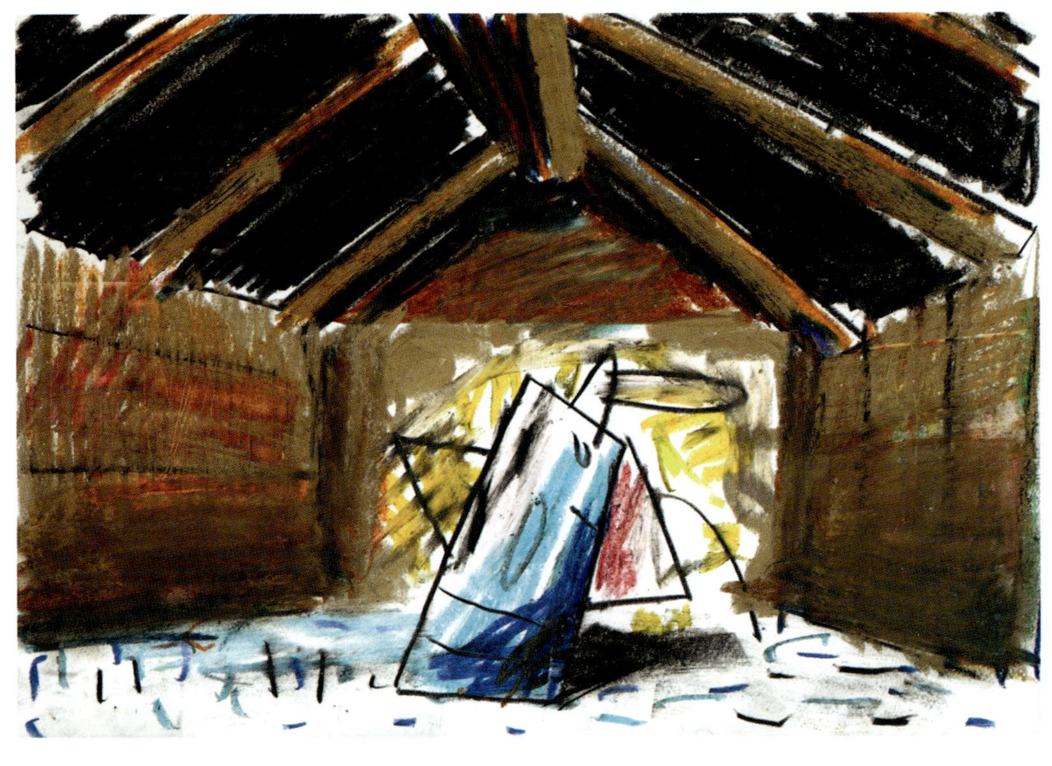

Matthias Weischer

Untitled, WV 510, 2005, Oil pastel and graphite on paper

8 1/4 x 11 5/8 in. (21 x 29.5 cm)

MW30

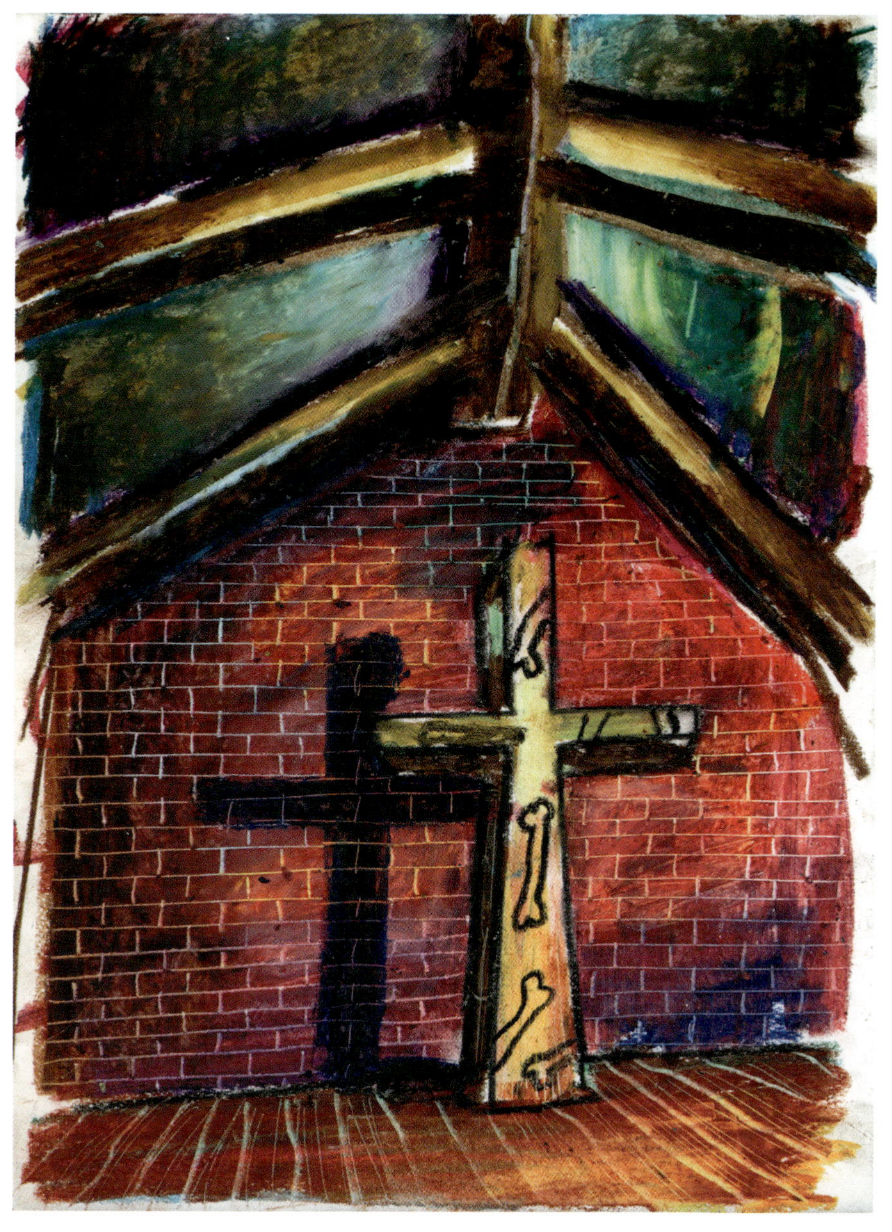

Matthias Weischer
Untitled, WV 512, 2005, Oil pastel and graphite on paper
11 5/8 x 8 1/4 in. (29.5 x 21 cm)
MW31

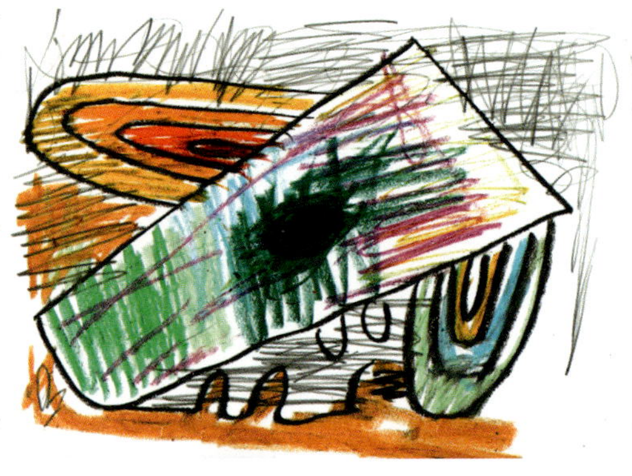

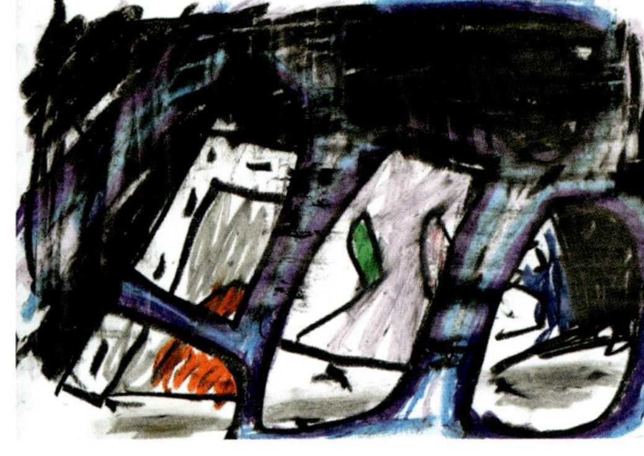

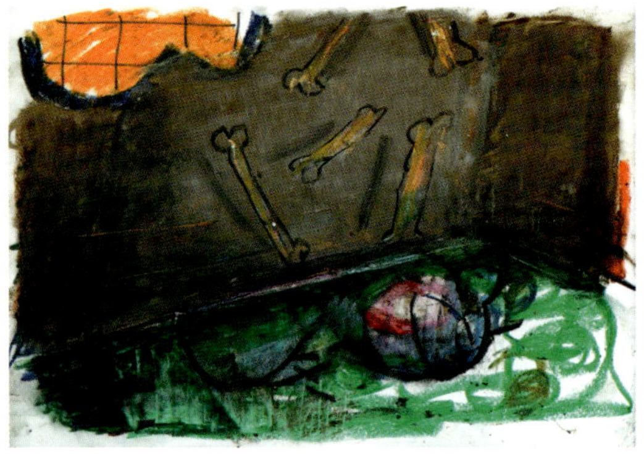

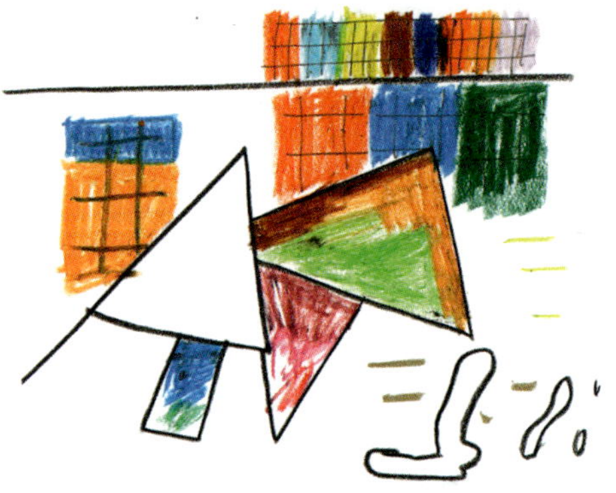

Matthias Weischer
Untitled, WV 514, 2005, Oil pastel and graphite on paper
8 1/4 x 11 5/8 in. (21 x 29.5 cm)
MW32

Matthias Weischer
Untitled, WV 518, 2005, Oil pastel and graphite on paper
8 1/4 x 11 5/8 in. (21 x 29.5 cm)
MW33

Matthias Weischer
Untitled, WV 520, 2005, Oil pastel and graphite on paper
8 1/4 x 11 5/8 in. (21 x 29.5 cm)
MW34

Matthias Weischer
Untitled, WV 521, 2005, Oil pastel and graphite on paper
8 1/4 x 11 5/8 in. (21 x 29.5 cm)
MW35

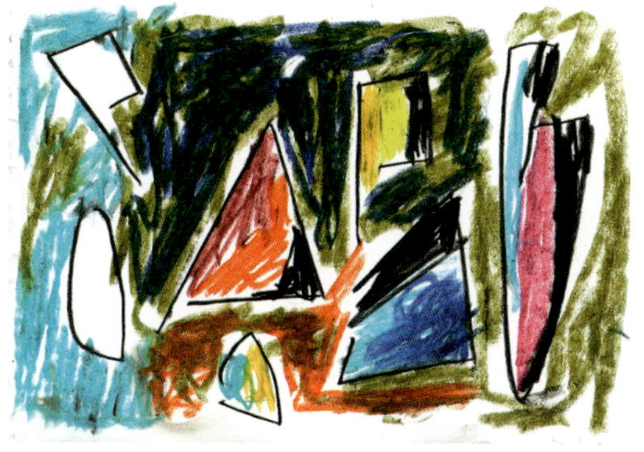

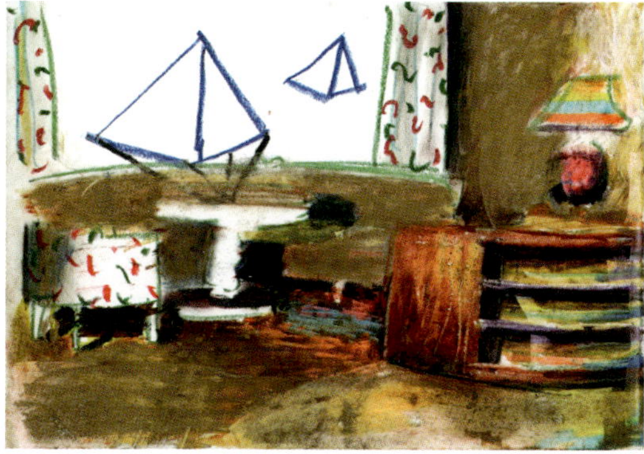

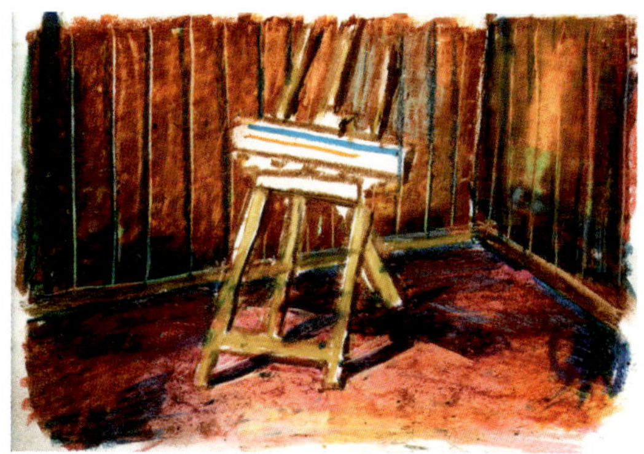

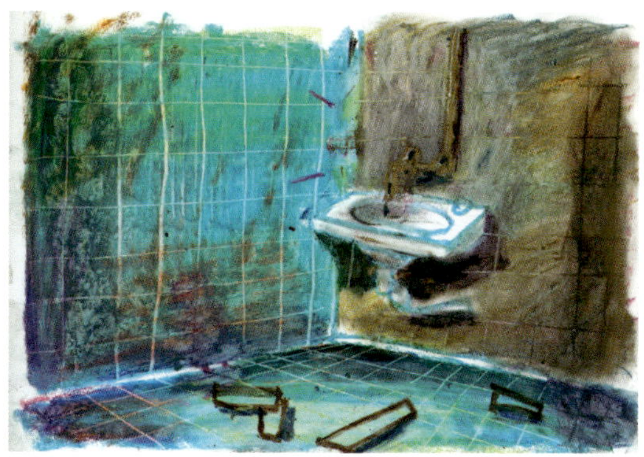

Matthias Weischer
Untitled, WV 523, 2005, Oil pastel and graphite on paper
8 1/4 x 11 5/8 in. (21 x 29.5 cm)
MW36

Matthias Weischer
Untitled, WV 524, 2005, Oil pastel and graphite on paper
8 1/4 x 11 5/8 in. (21 x 29.5 cm)
MW37

Matthias Weischer
Untitled, WV 525, 2005, Oil pastel and graphite on paper
8 1/4 x 11 5/8 in. (21 x 29.5 cm)
MW38

Matthias Weischer
Untitled, WV 526, 2005, Oil pastel and graphite on paper
8 1/4 x 11 5/8 in. (21 x 29.5 cm)
MW39

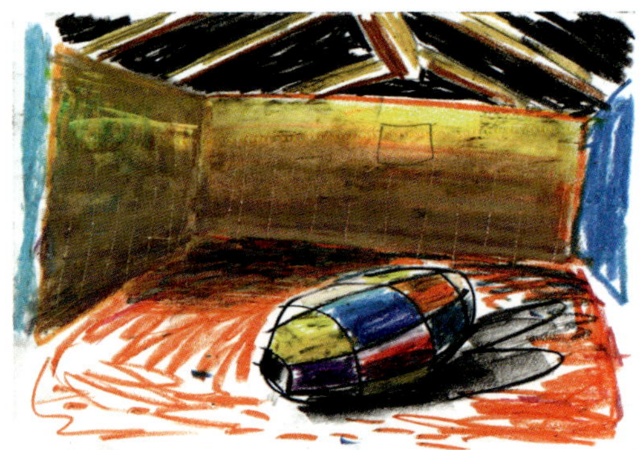

Matthias Weischer
Untitled, WV 530, 2005, Oil pastel and graphite on paper
8 1/4 x 11 5/8 in. (21 x 29.5 cm)
MW40

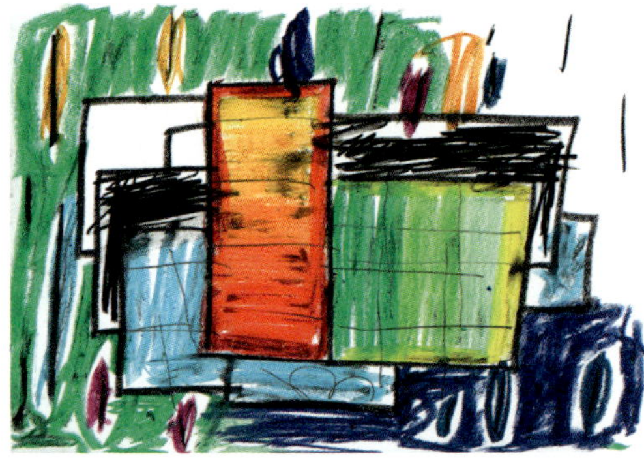

Matthias Weischer
Untitled, WV 531, 2005, Oil pastel and graphite on paper
8 1/4 x 11 5/8 in. (21 x 29.5 cm)
MW41

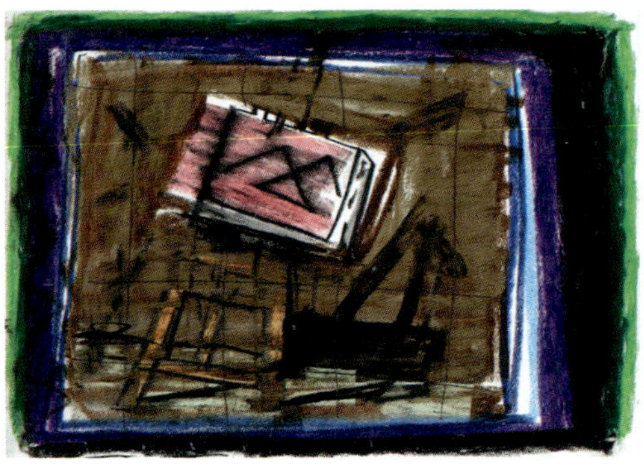

Matthias Weischer
Untitled, WV 534, 2005, Oil pastel and graphite on paper
8 1/4 x 11 5/8 in. (21 x 29.5 cm)
MW42

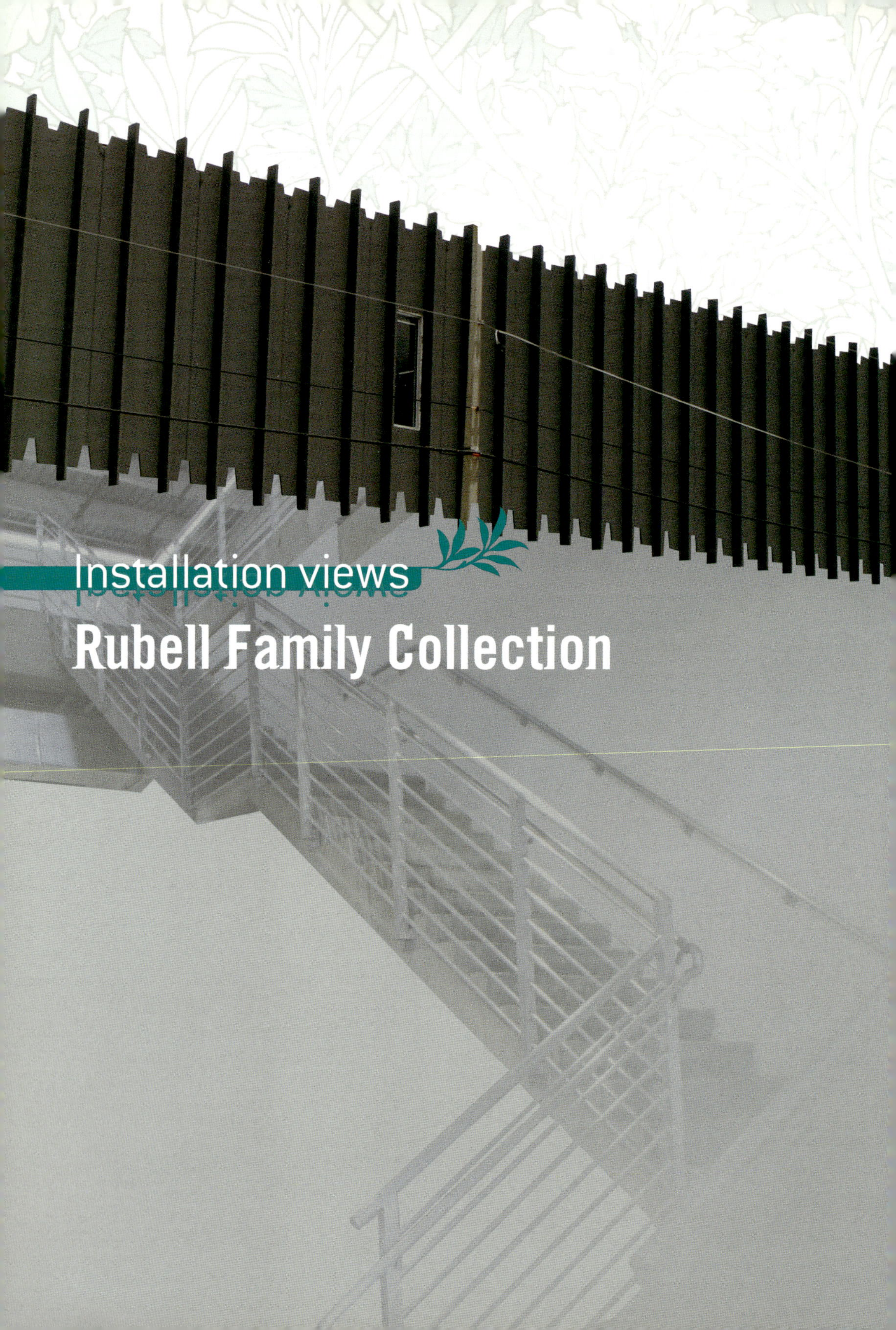

Installation views

Rubell Family Collection

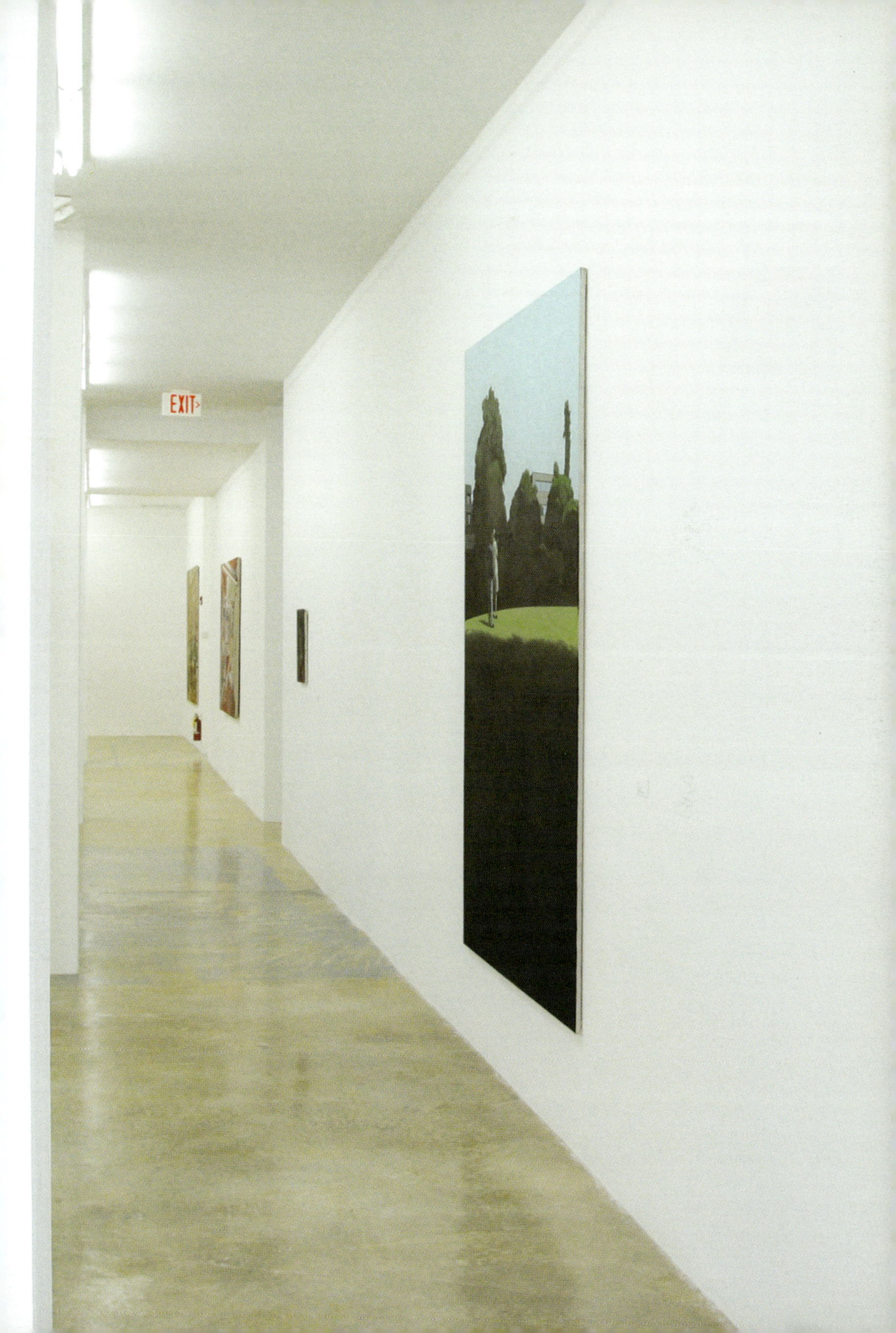
EXIT

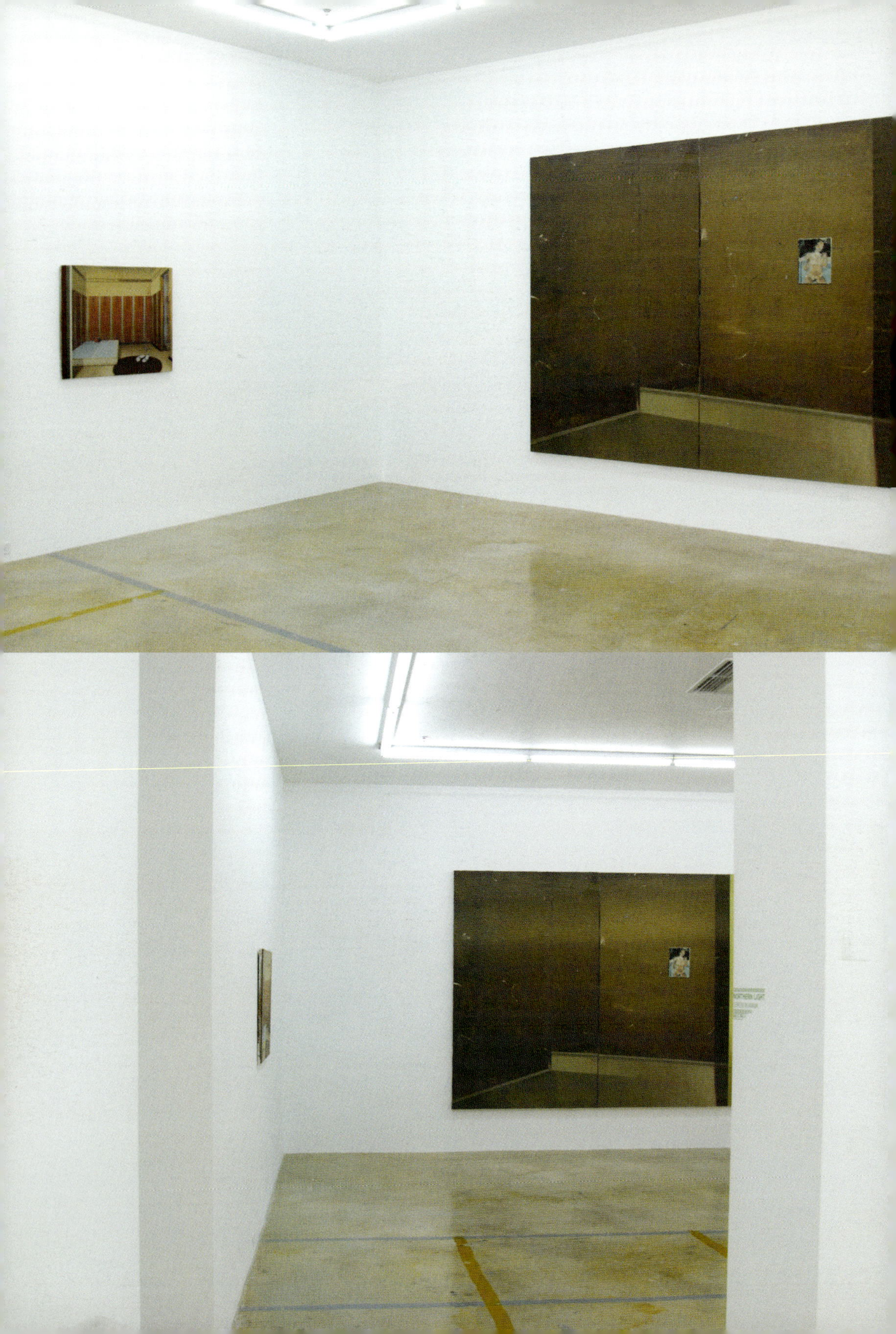

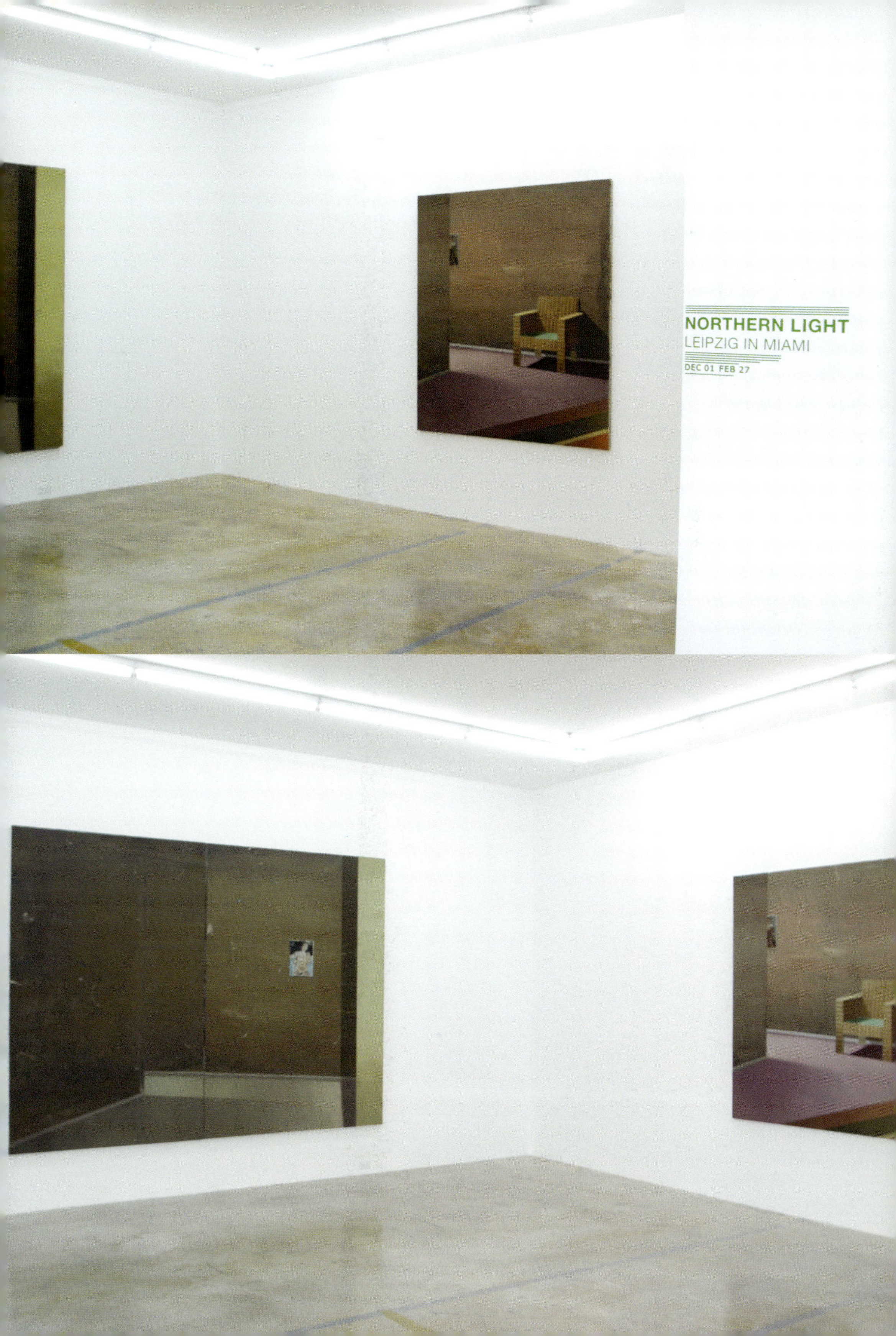
NORTHERN LIGHT
LEIPZIG IN MIAMI
DEC 01 FEB 27

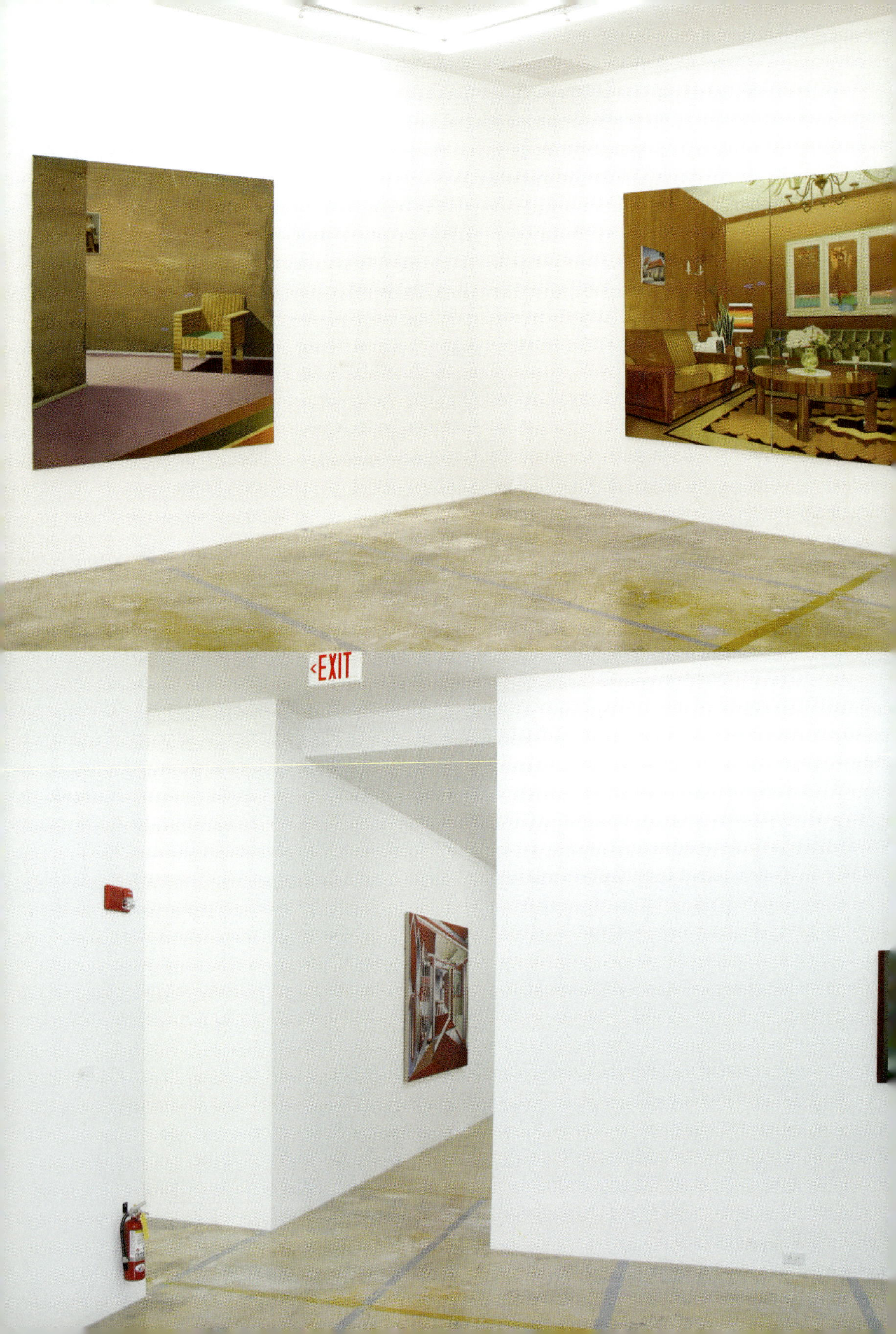
EXIT

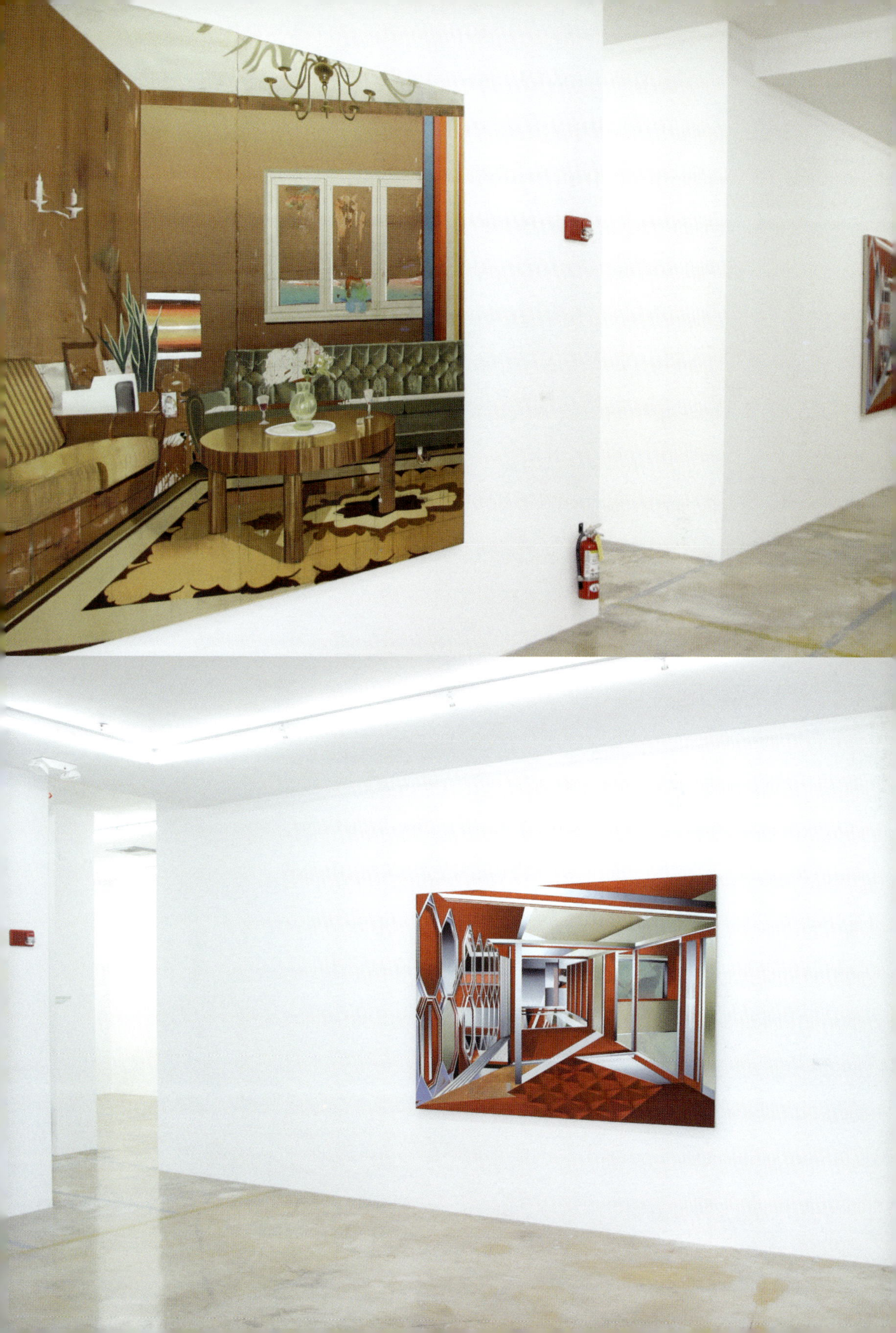

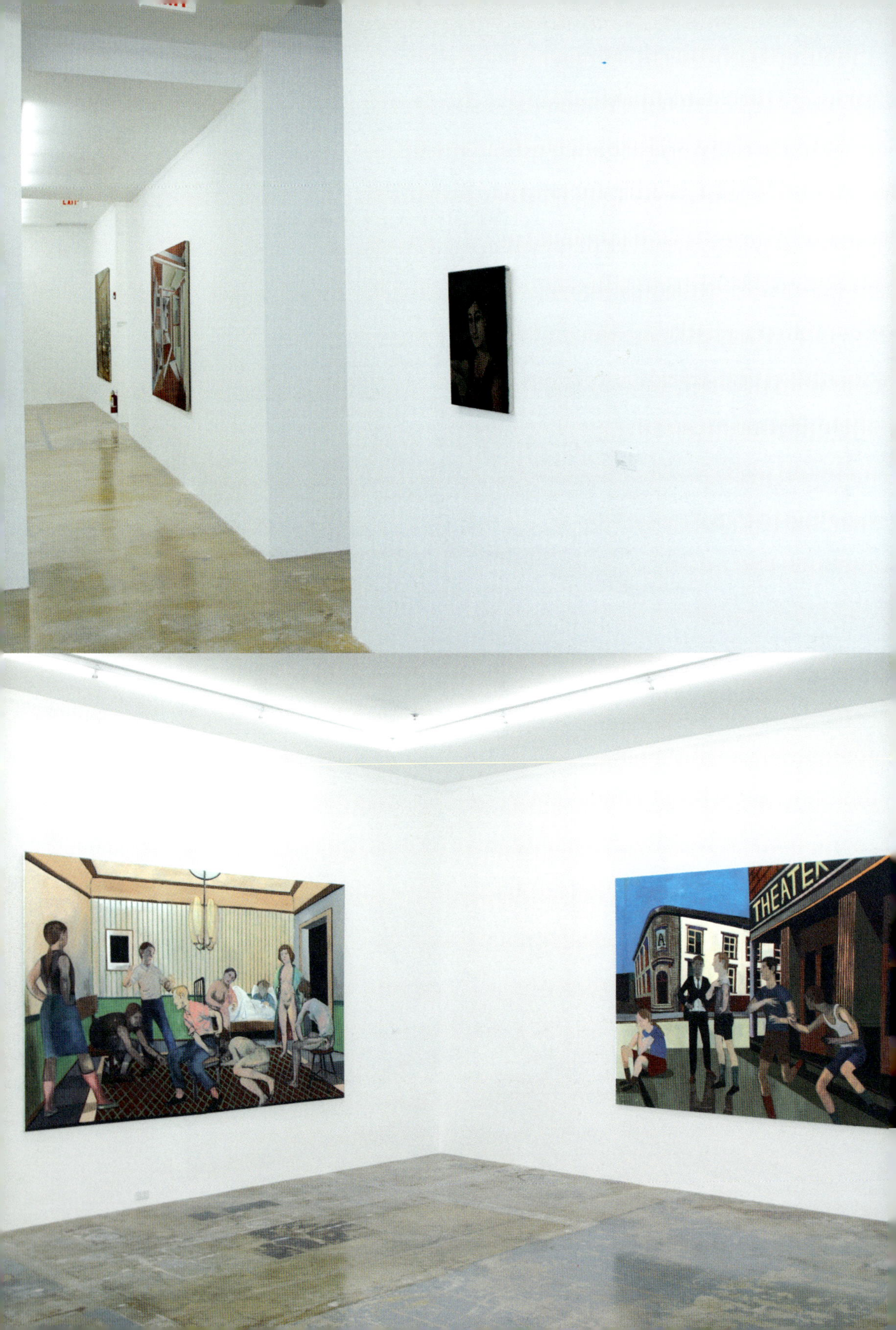
THEATER

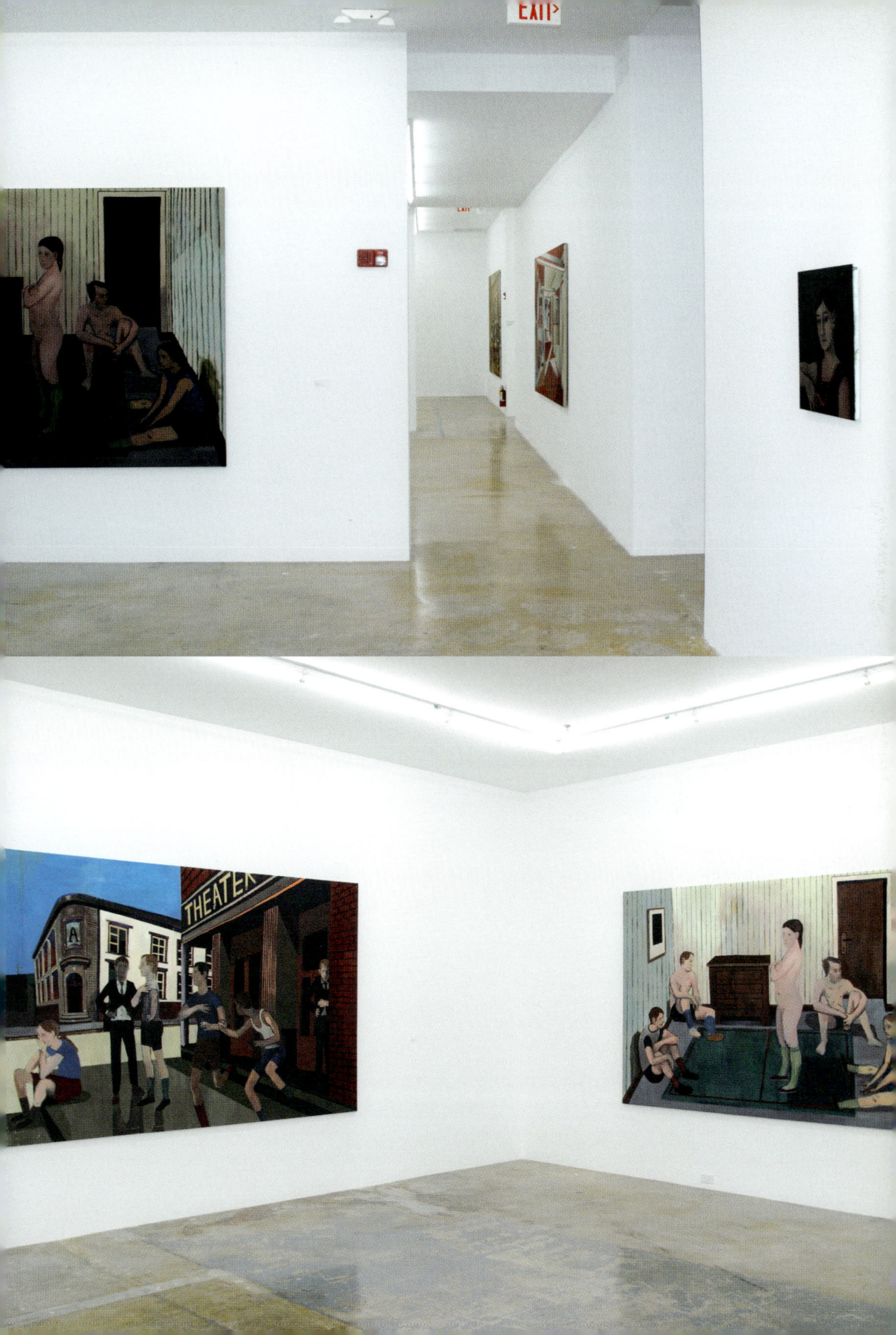
EXIT
THEATER
A

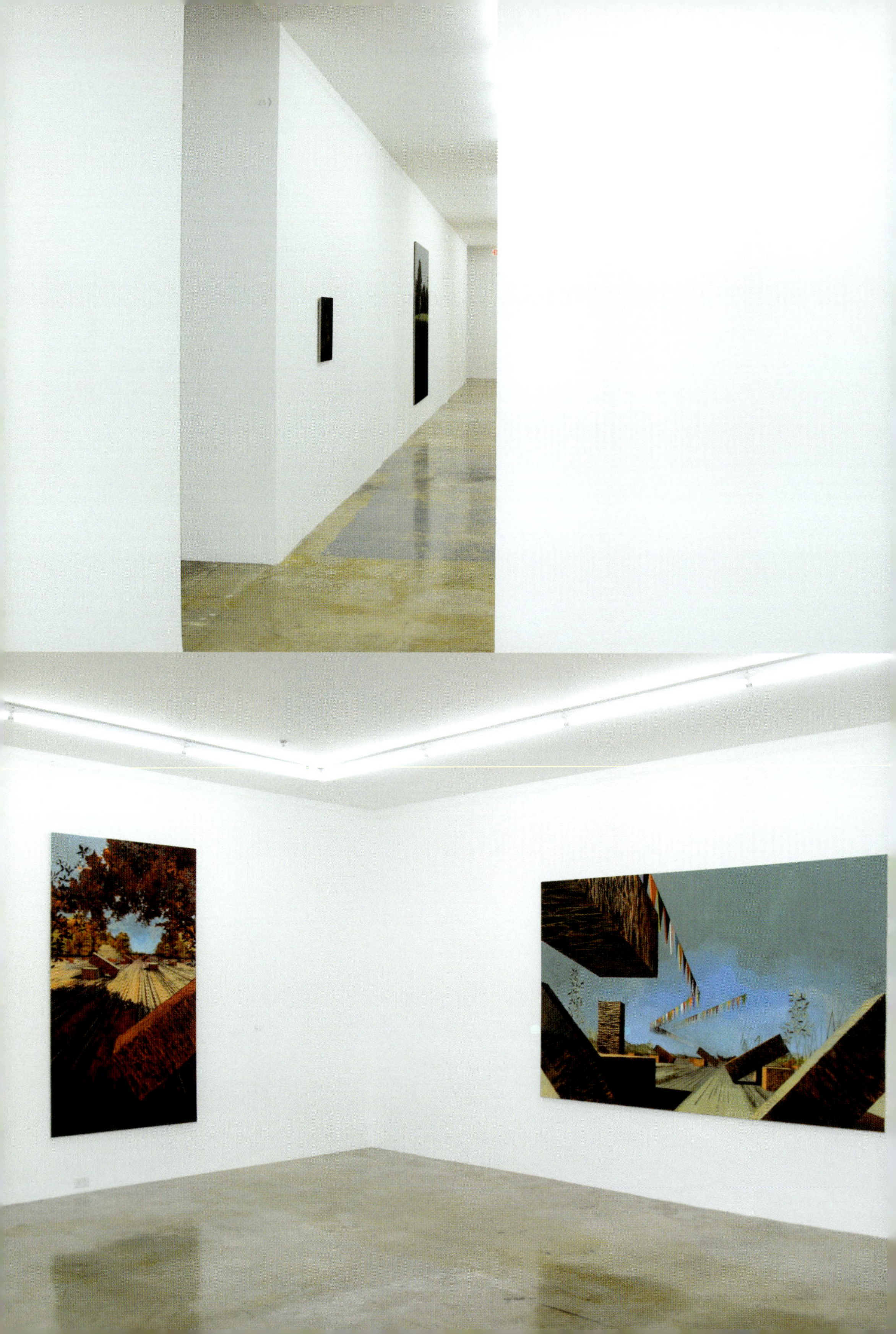

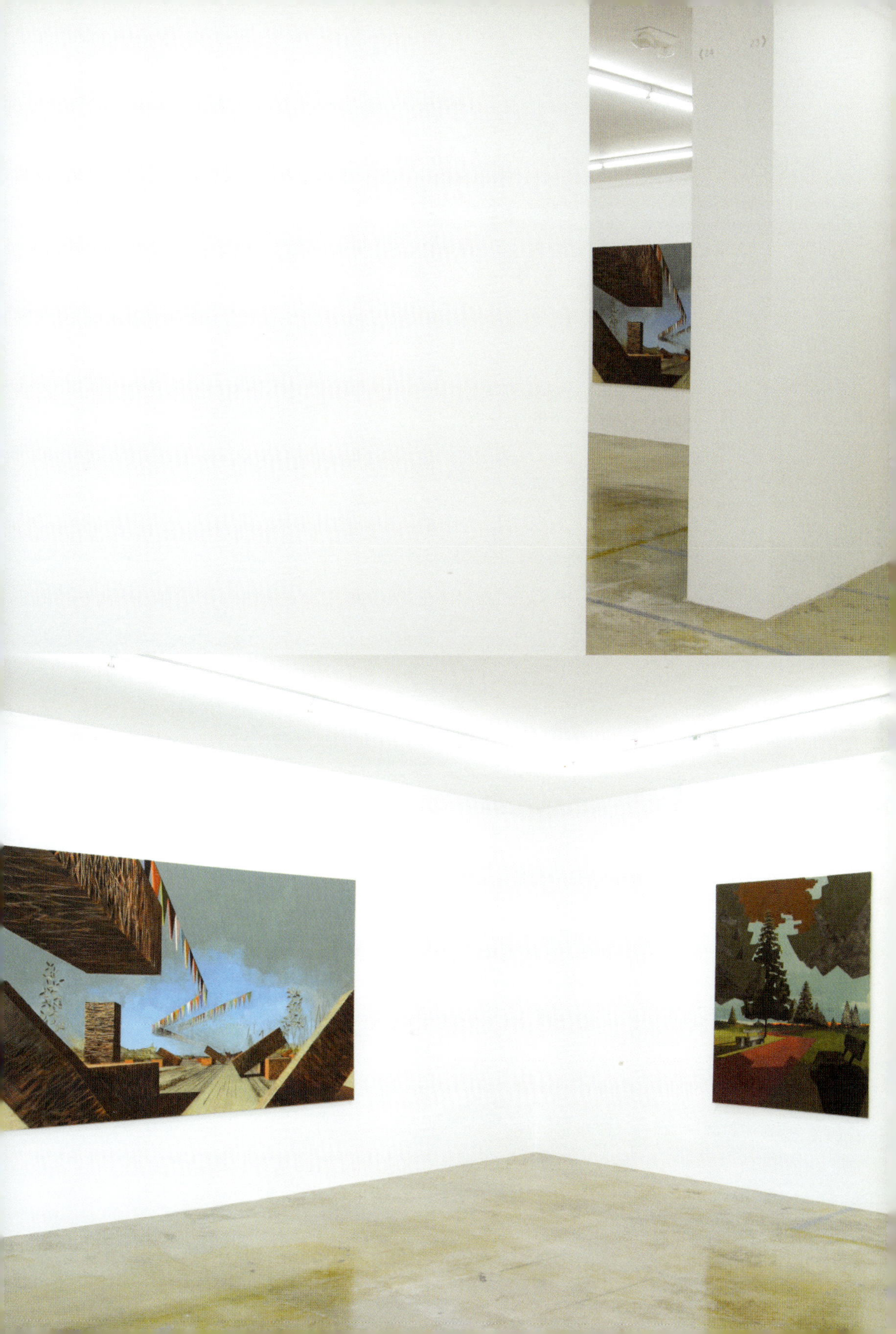

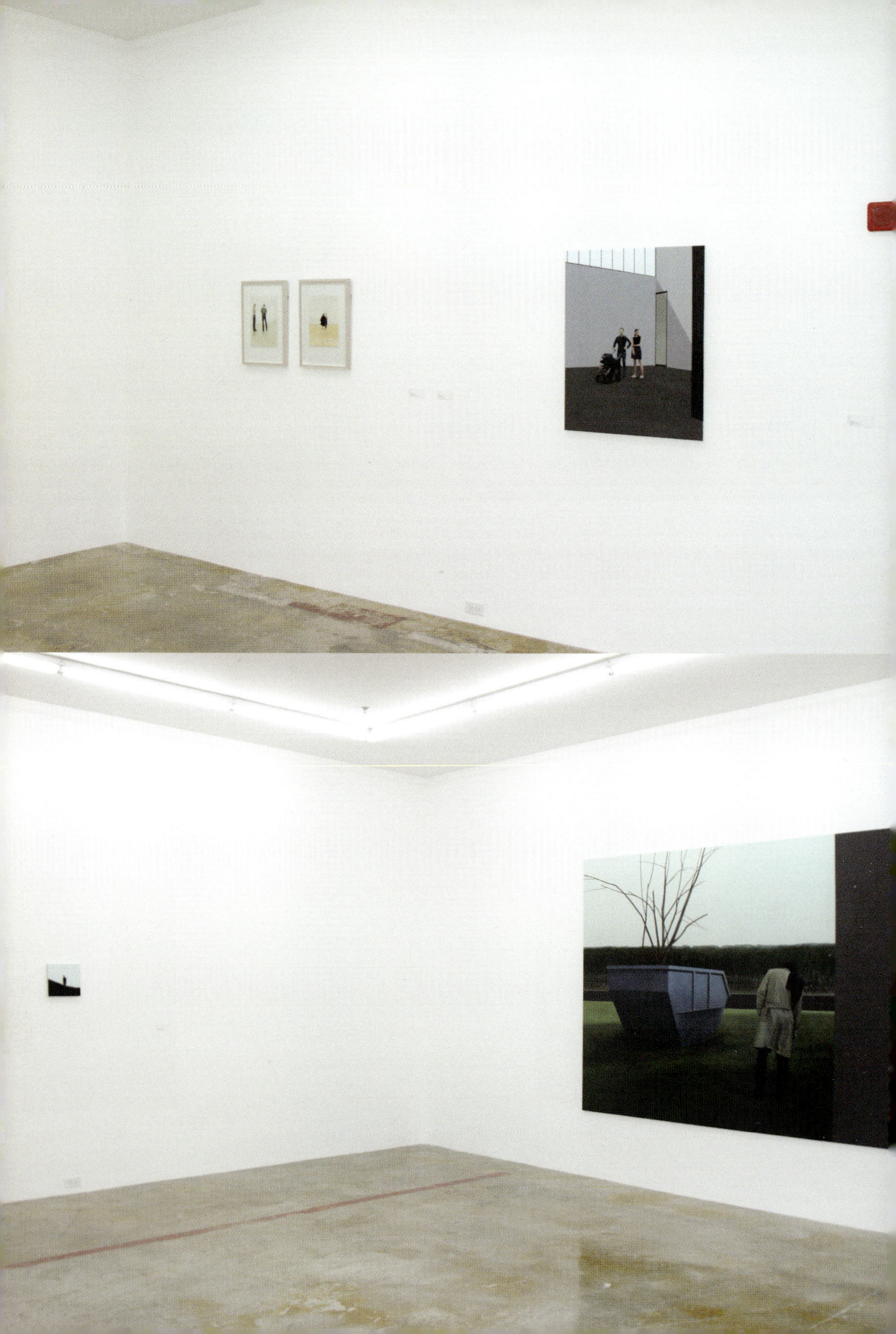

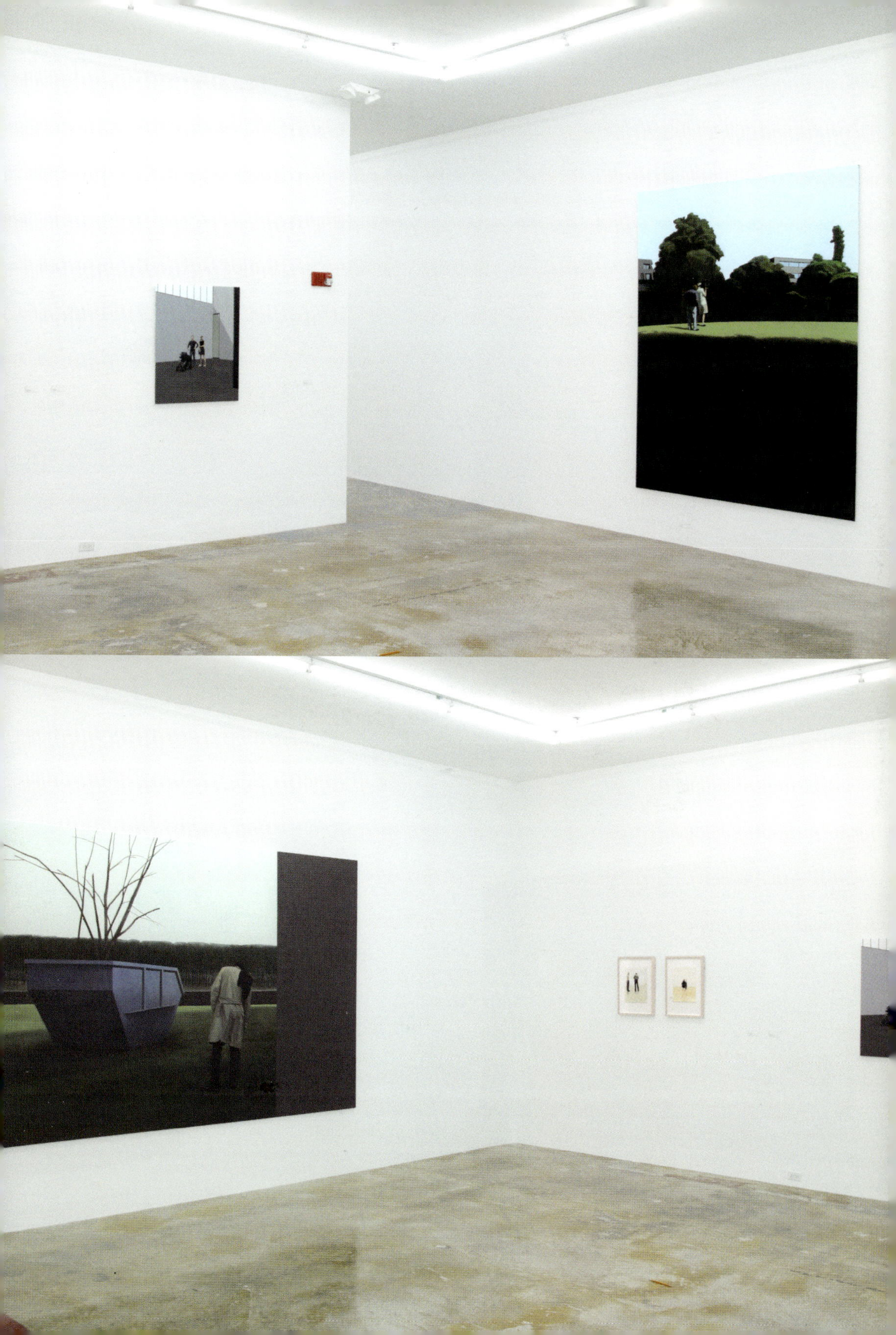

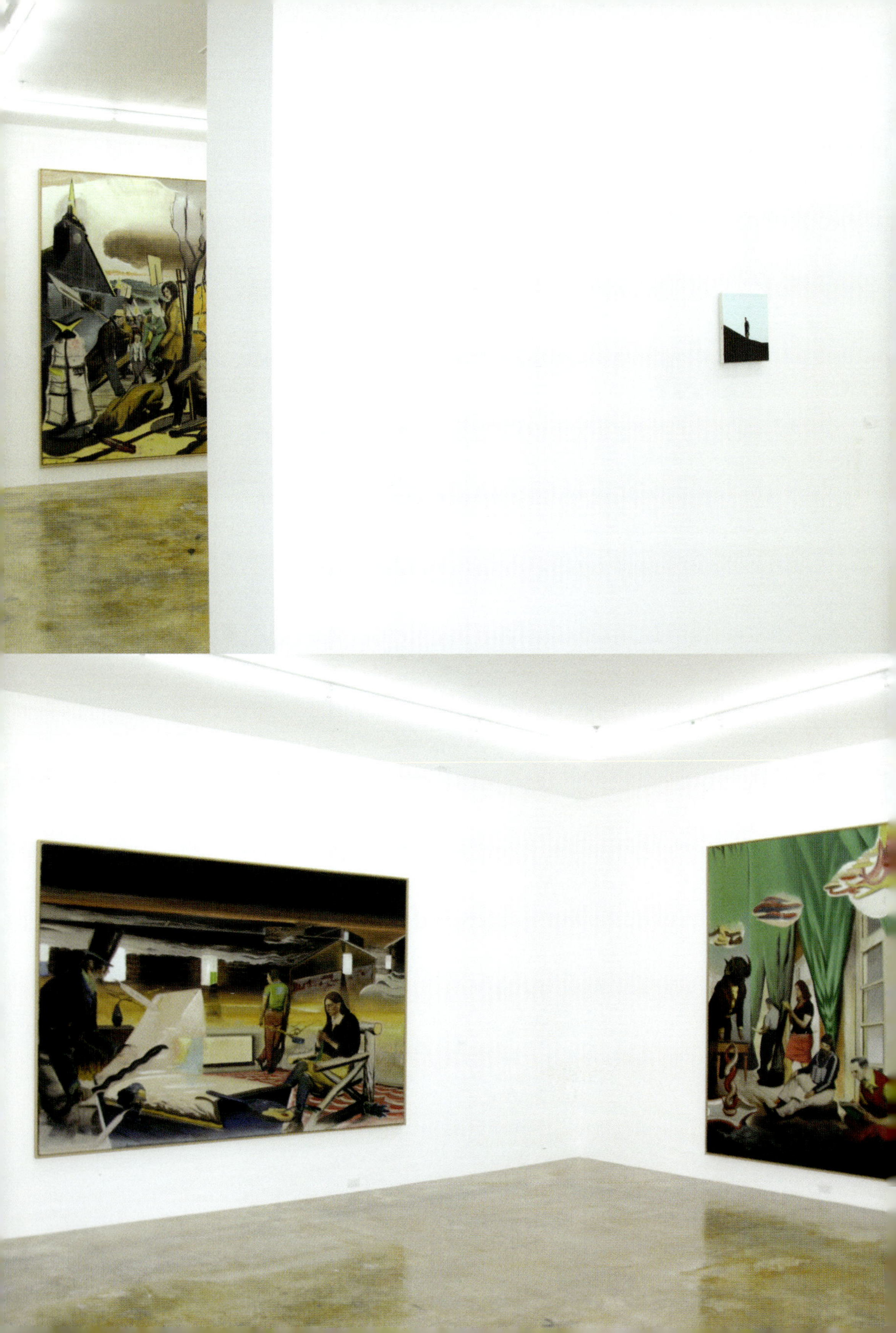

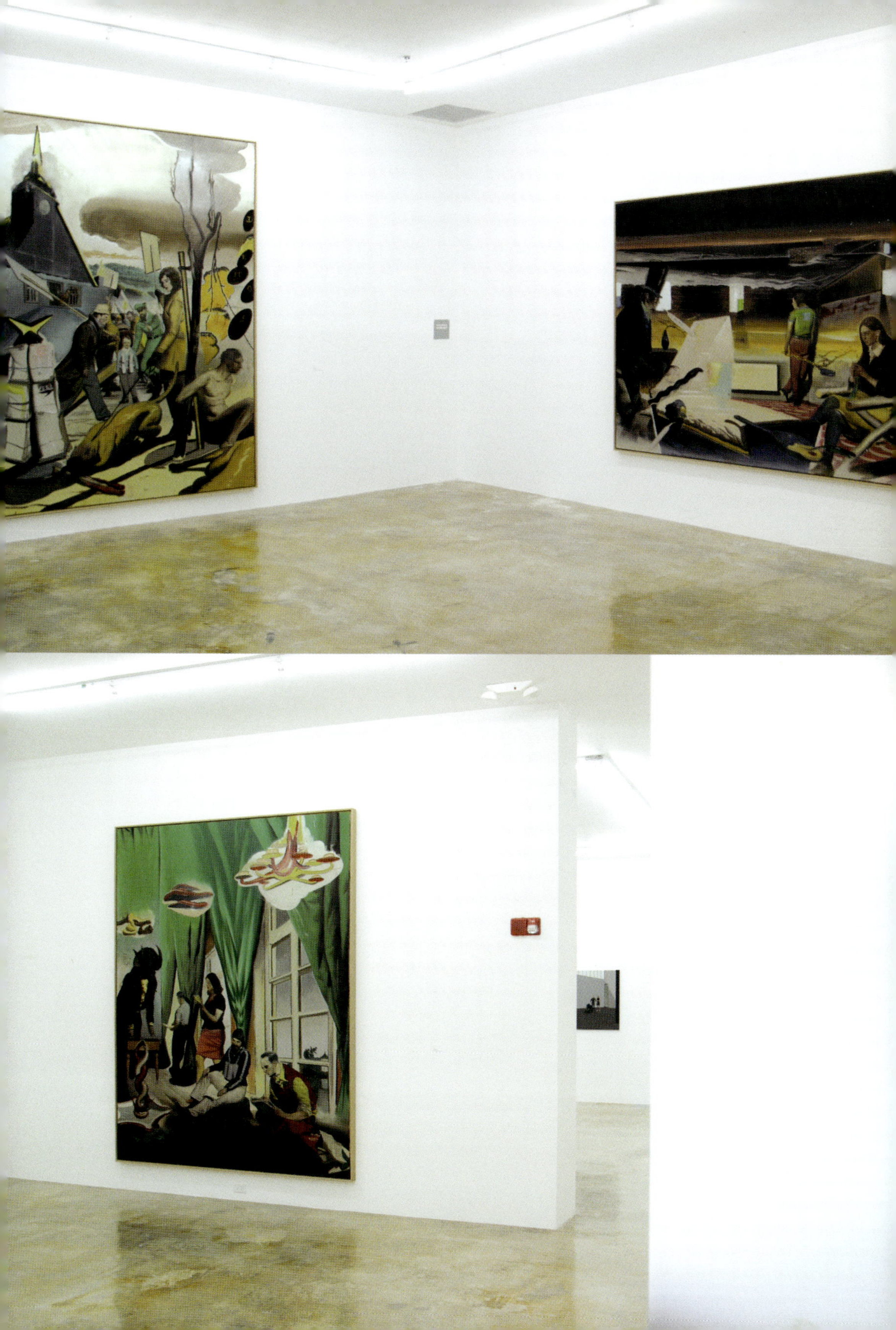

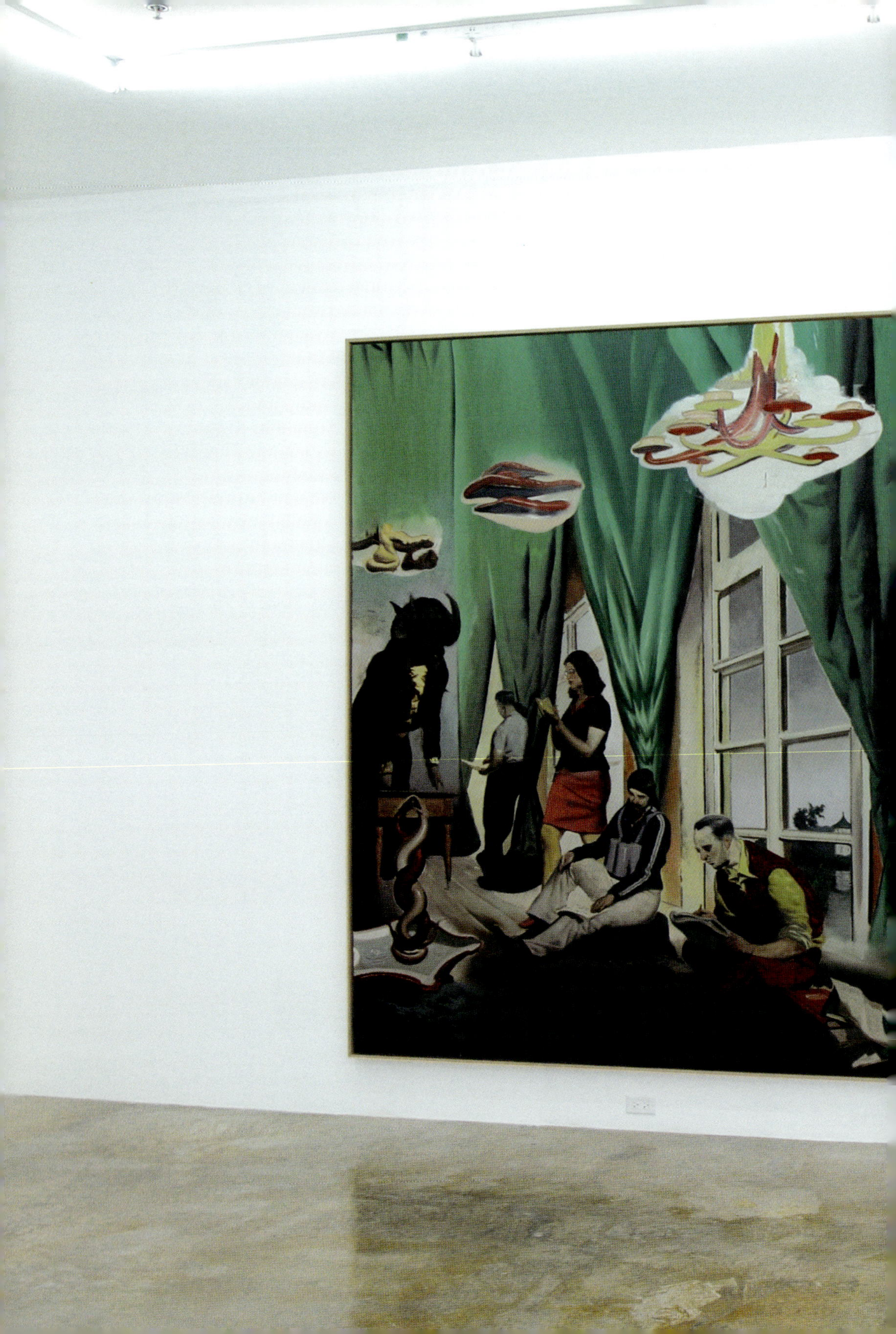

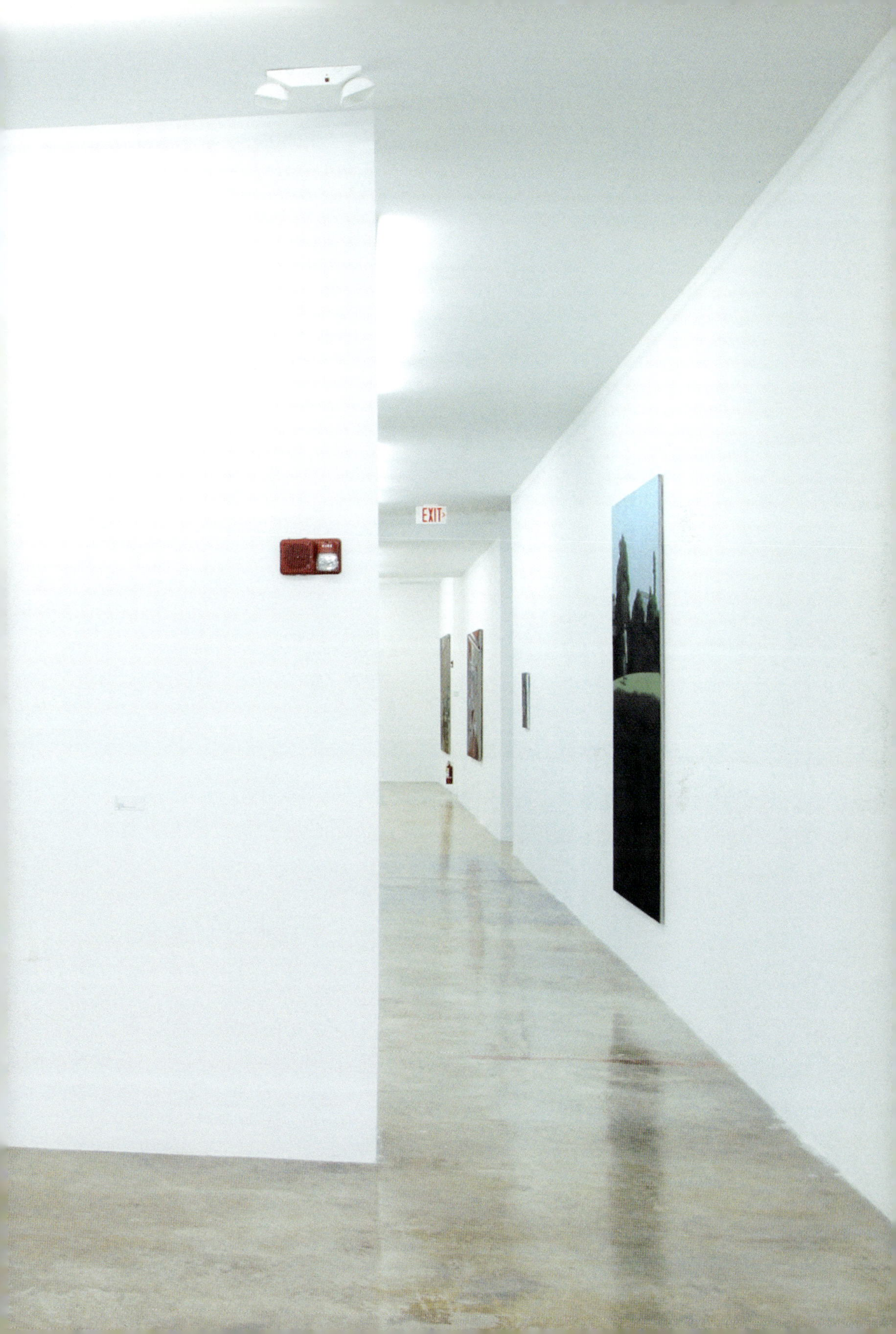
EXIT

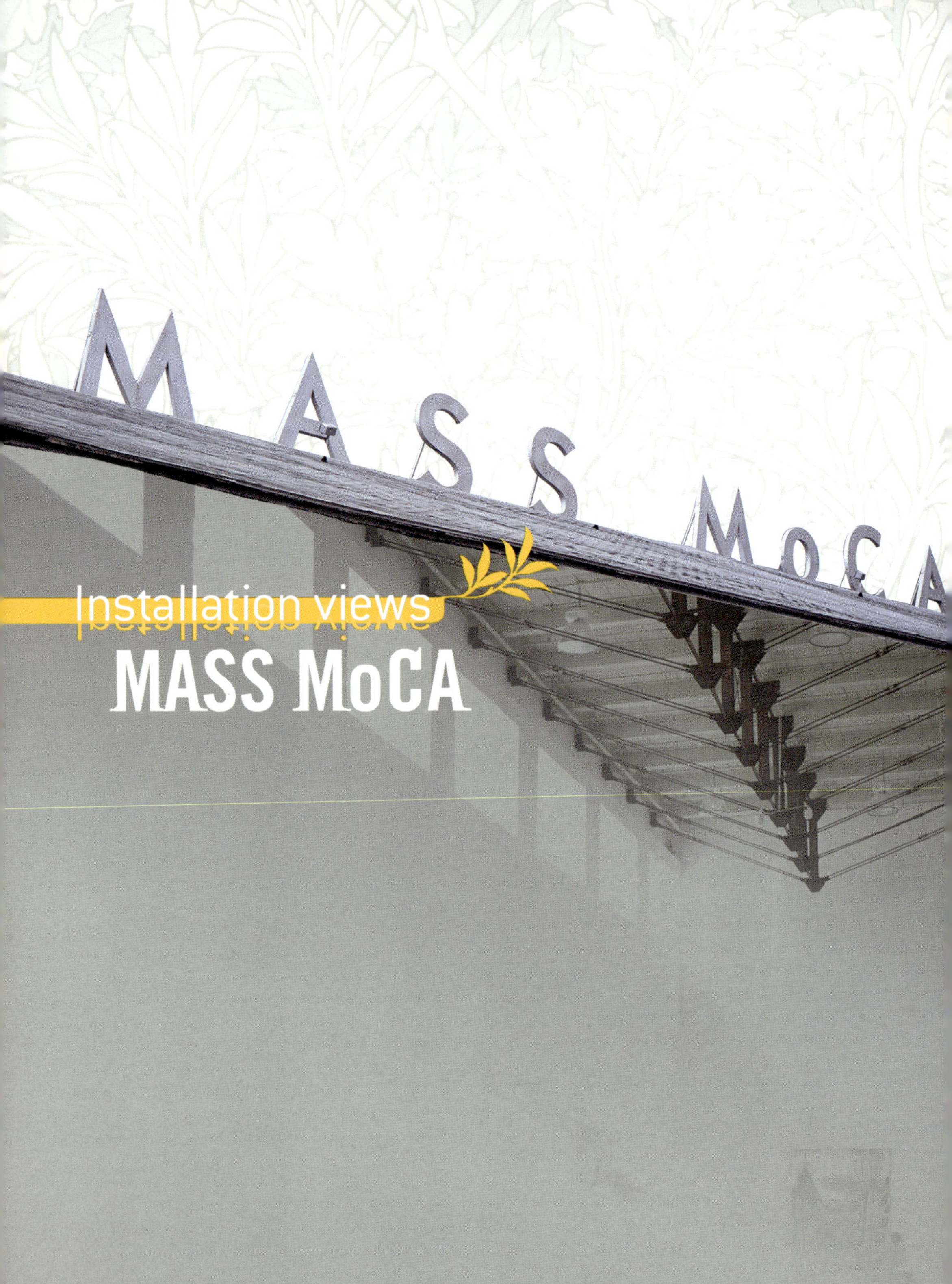

Installation views

MASS MoCA

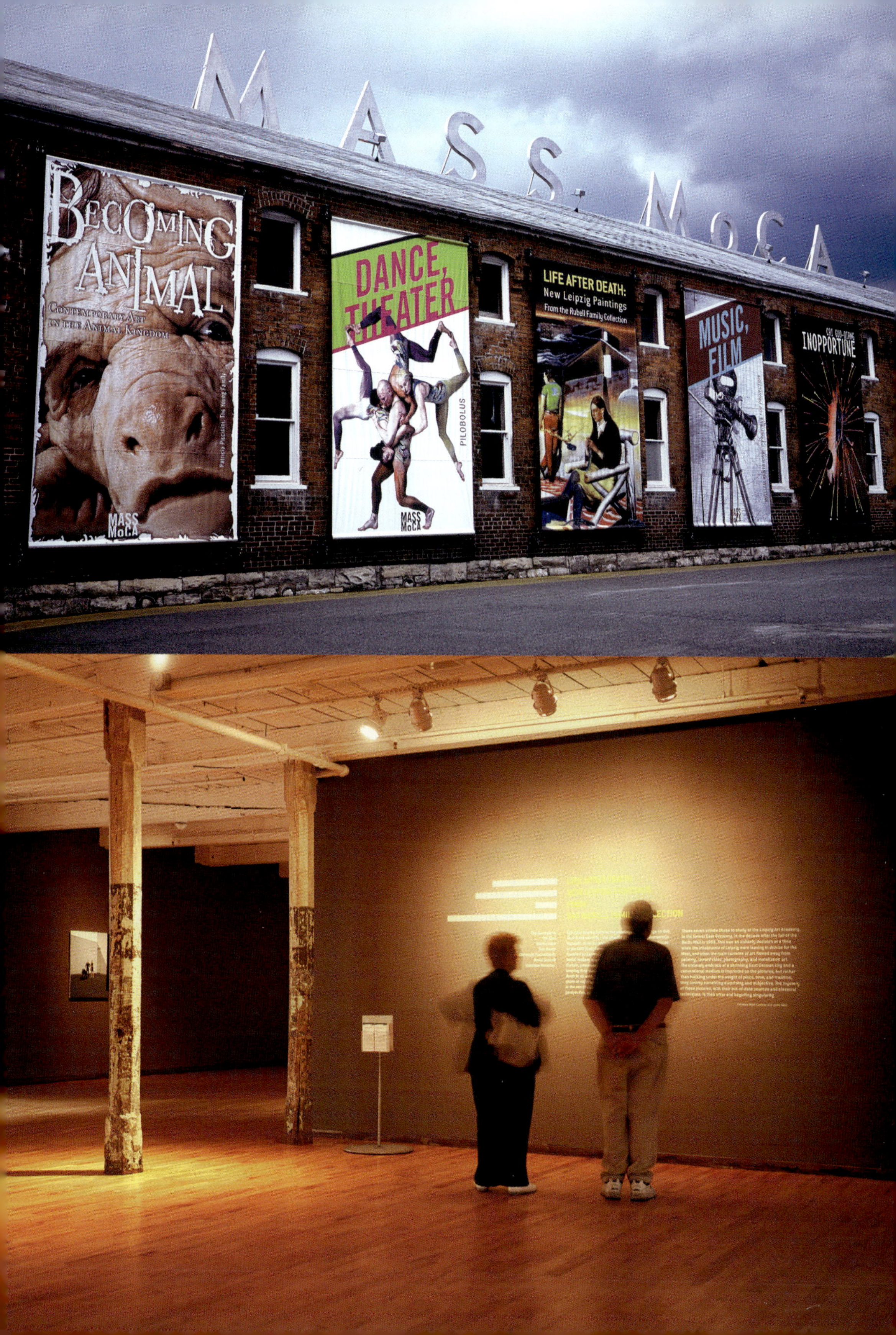
MASS MoCA
BECOMING ANIMAL
CONTEMPORARY ART IN THE ANIMAL KINGDOM
DANCE, THEATER
PILOBOLUS
LIFE AFTER DEATH:
New Leipzig Paintings
From the Rubell Family Collection
MUSIC, FILM
INOPPORTUNE

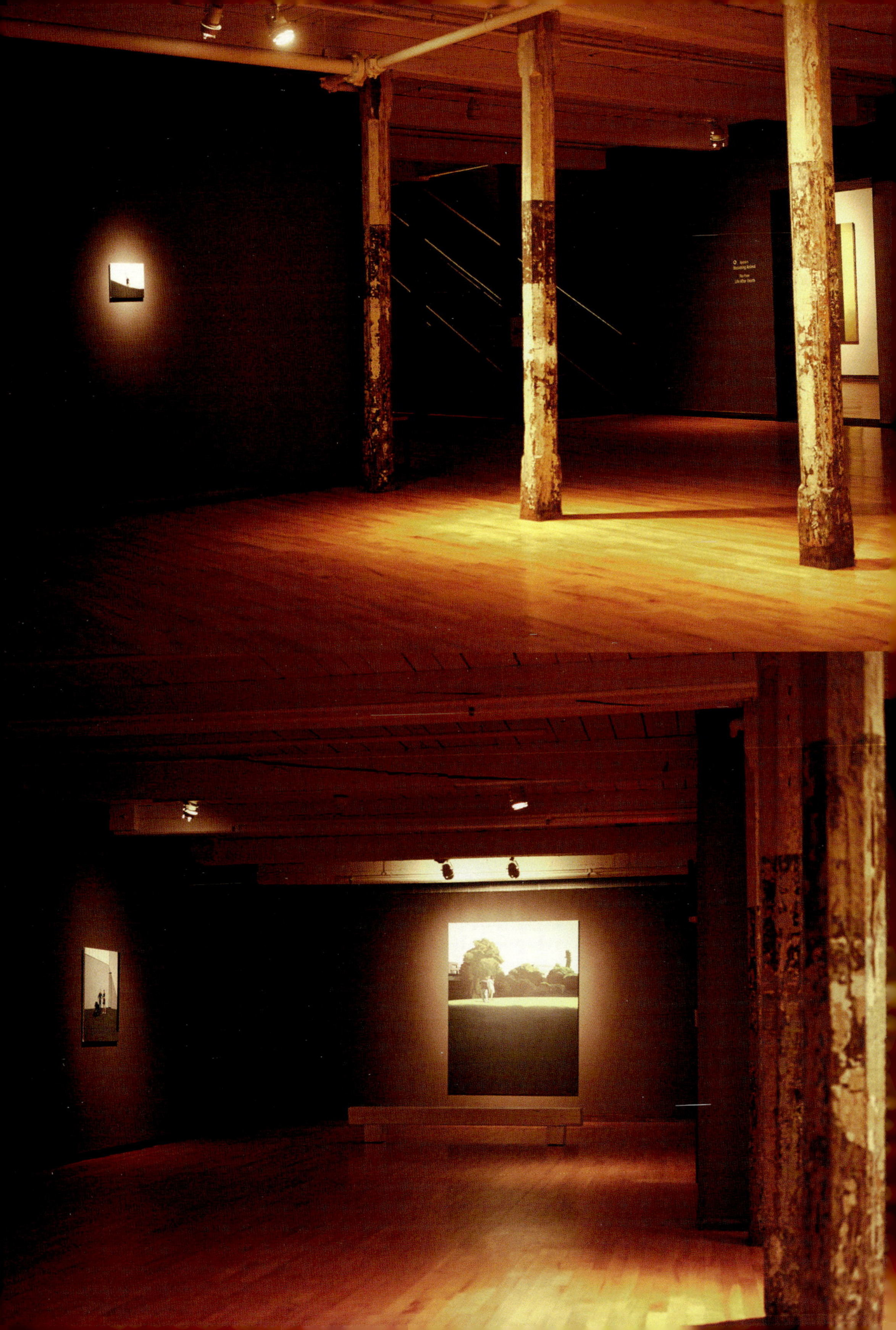

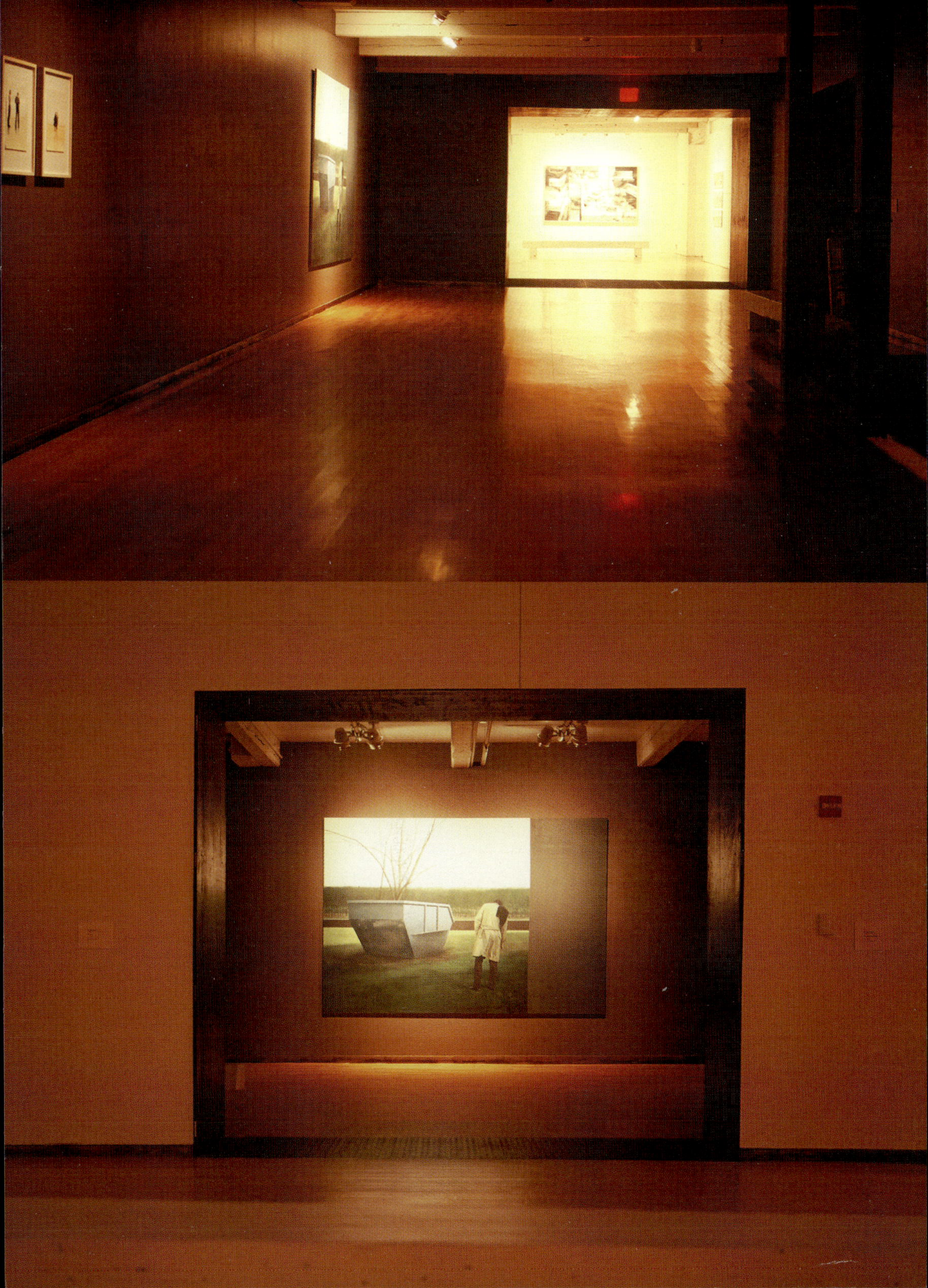

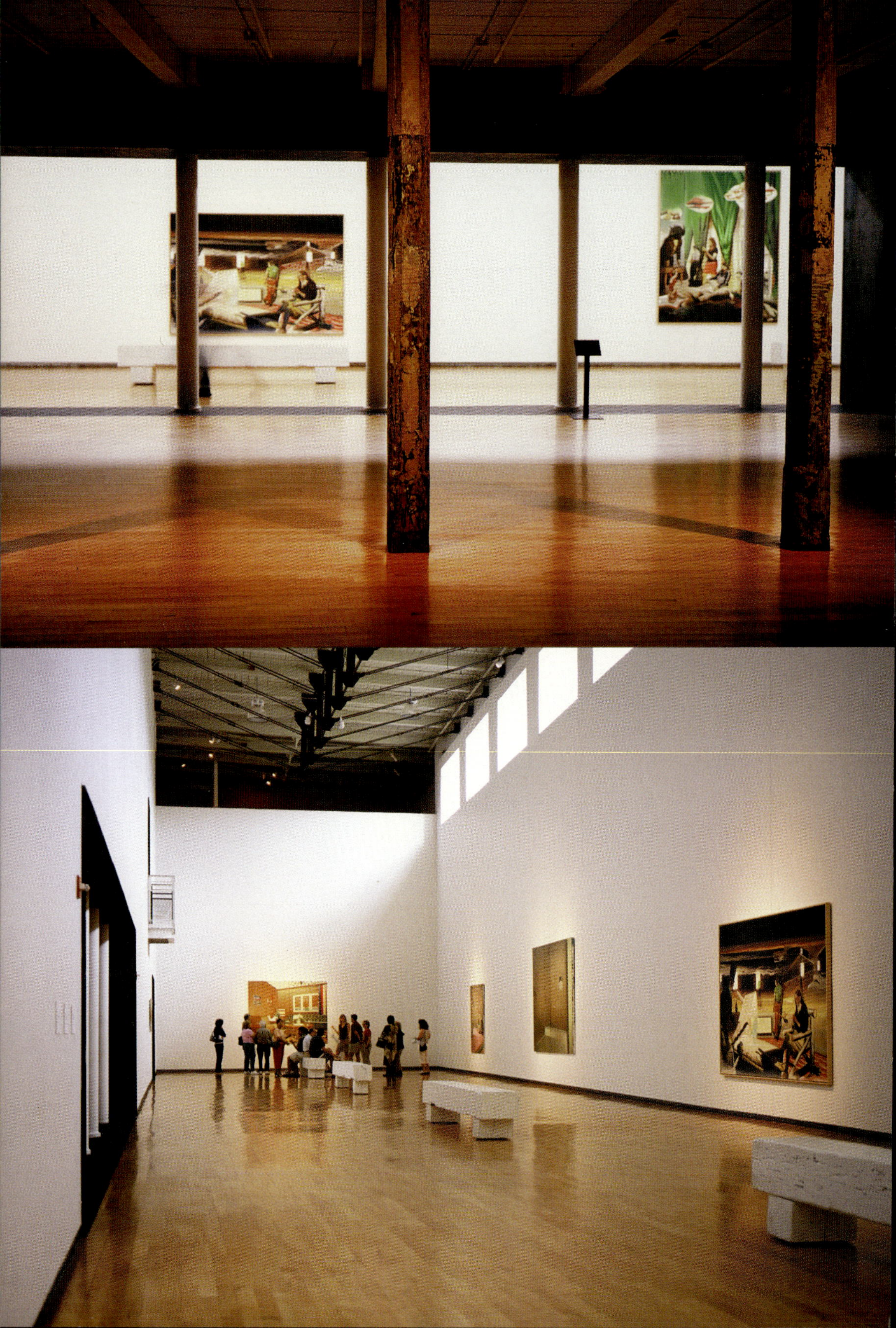

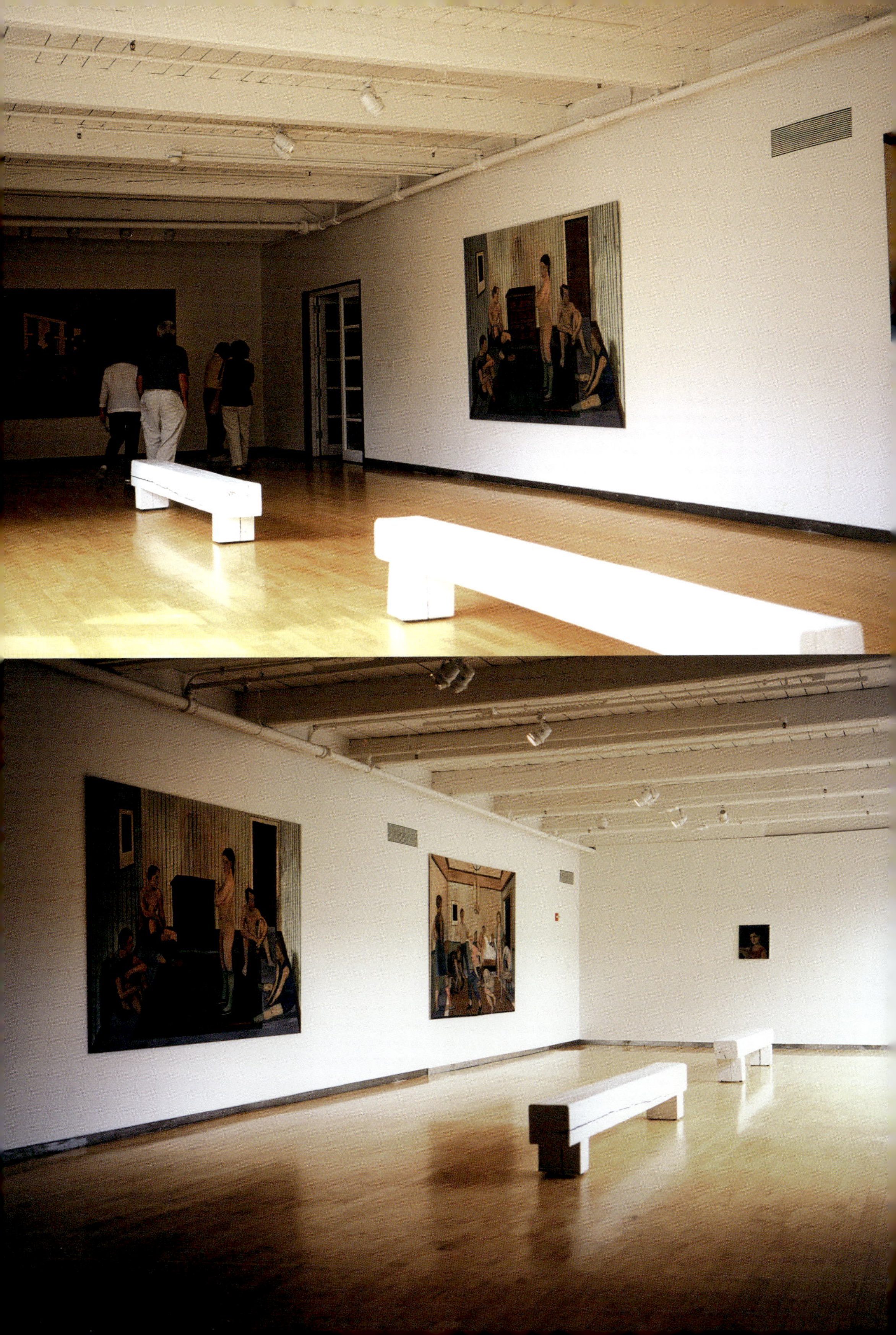

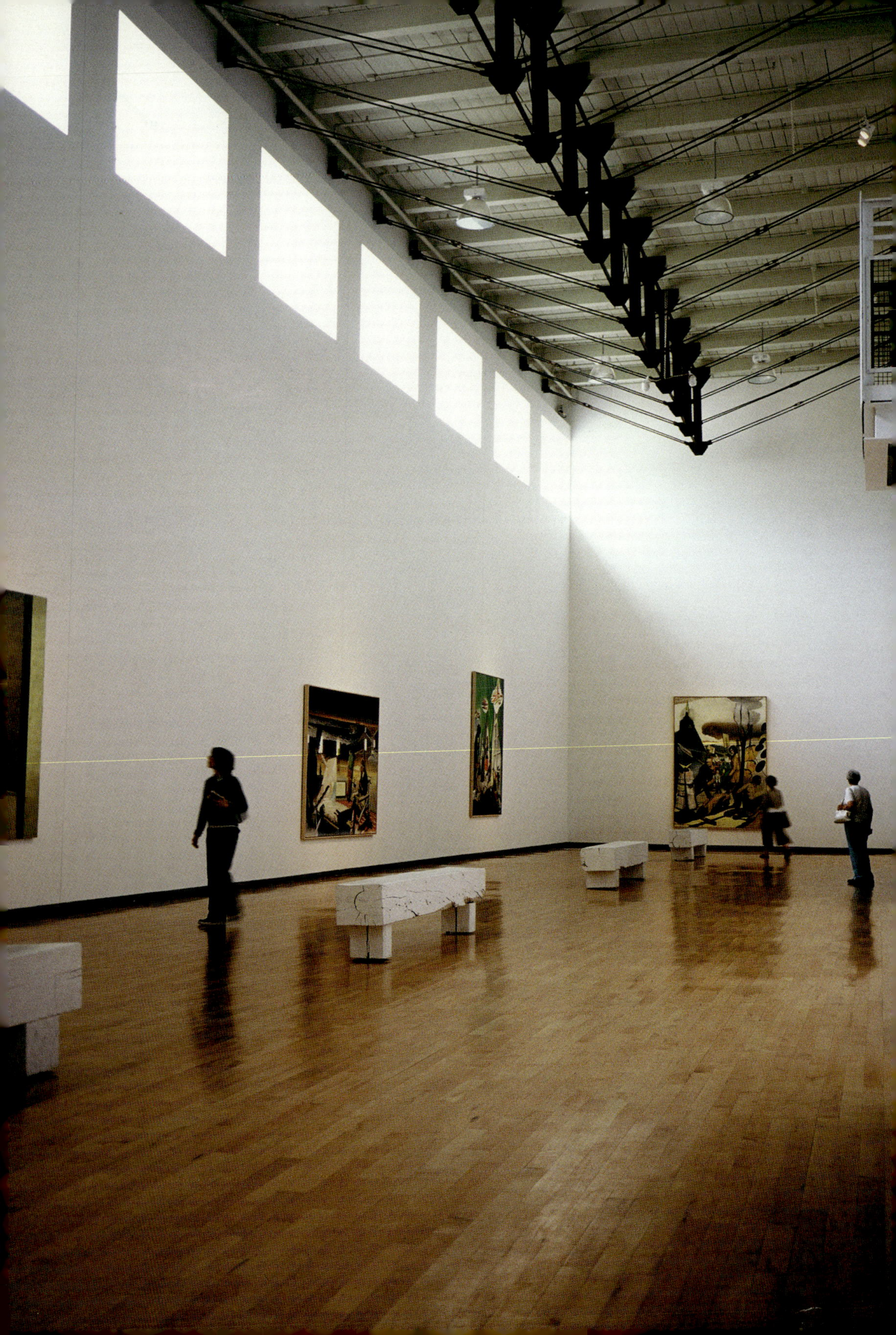

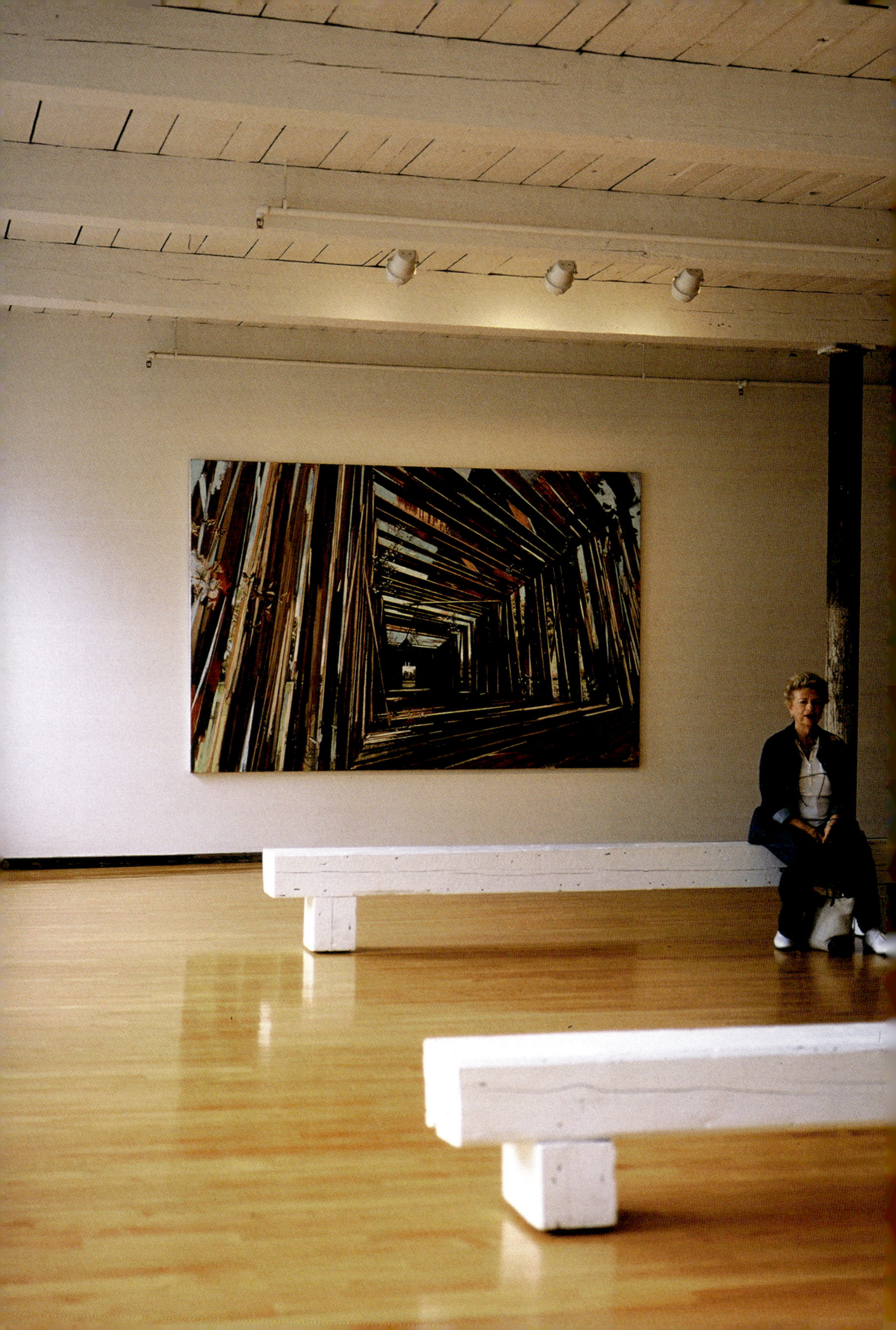

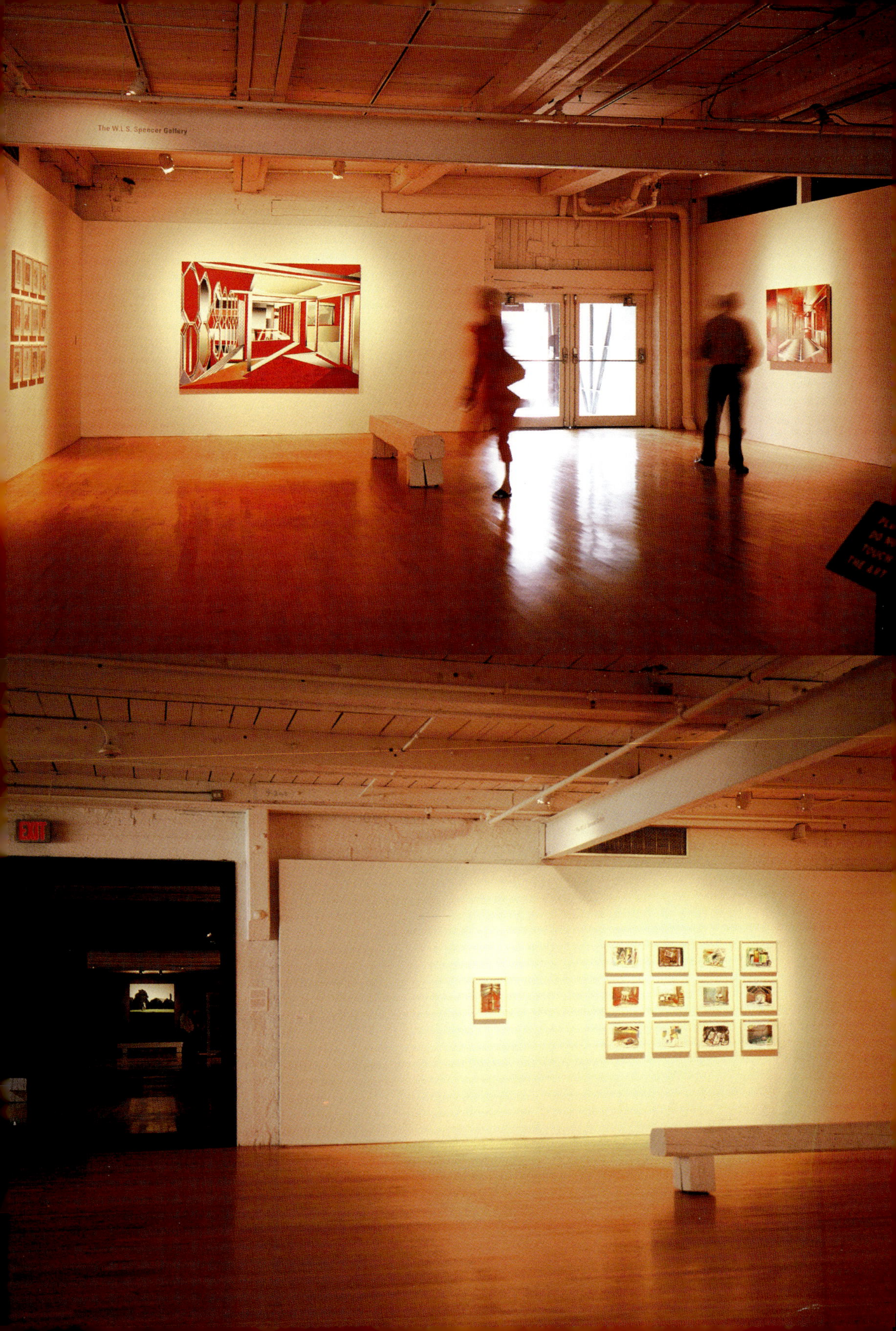
The W.L.S. Spencer Gallery
EXIT

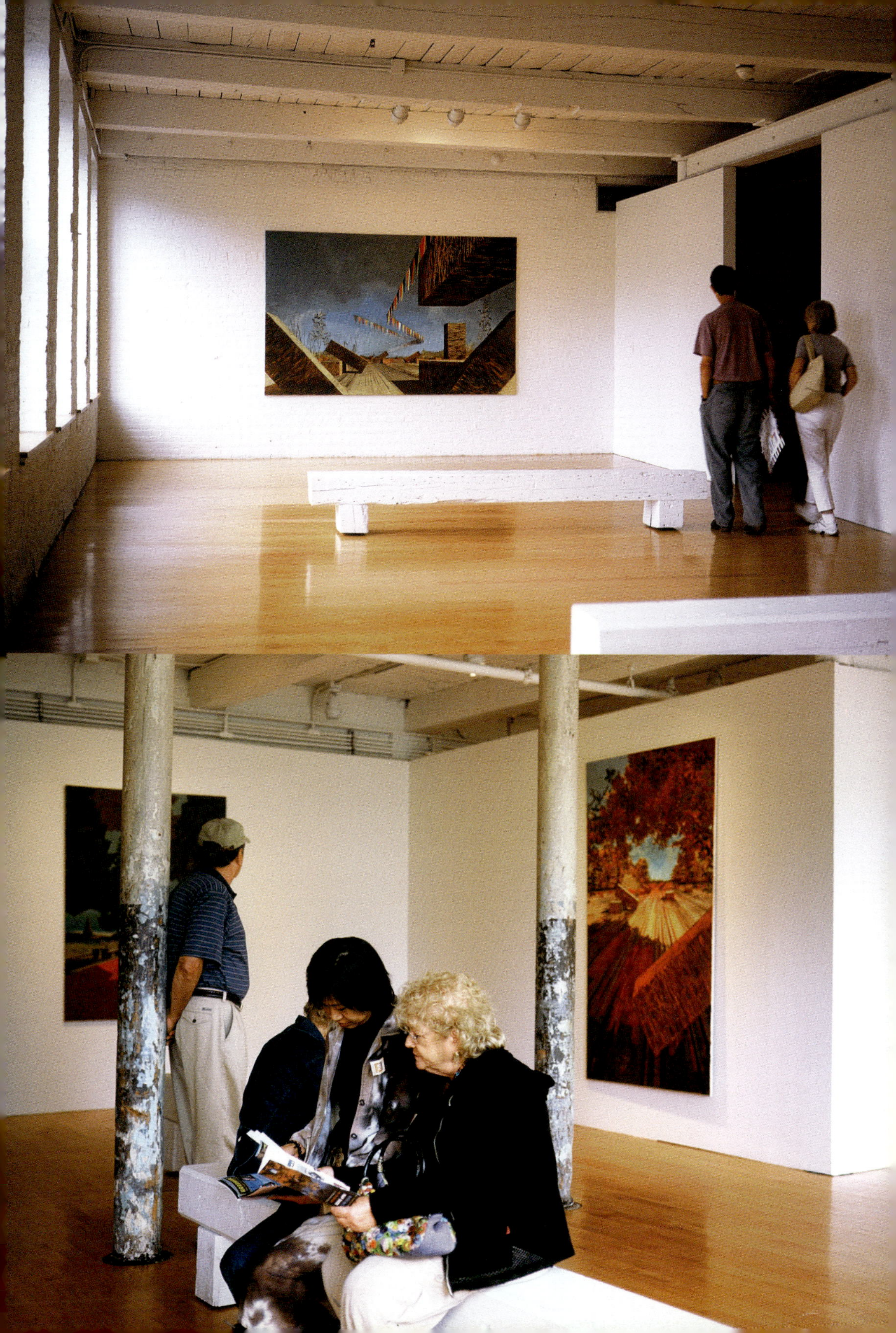

TILO BAUMGÄRTEL

1972
Born in Leipzig, Germany

Lives and works in Leipzig, Germany

Education

1998-2000

1991-1998

Solo Exhibitions

2006

2005

2004

2003

2002

2001

2000

Selected Bibliography

Charlesworth, J.J. "Coastal melancholy." Modern Painters (Summer 2003): 36-38.
Gisbourne, Mark. "Leipzig." Contemporary (No. 53-54, 2003): 40-45.
Herbert, Martin. "East International 2004." Art Monthly (September 2004): 28-30.
Koch, Ingrid. "Im Osten viel Neues." Weltkunst (June 2004): 45-48.
Macel, Christine. "In the East, Something New: Contemporary Painting in Germany." Art Press (No. 294, October 2003): 39-46.
Sommer, Tim. "Training mit Sift und Pinsel." ART: das Kunstmagazin (May 2003): 92-93.
Volk, Gregory. "Figuring the New Germany." Art in America (June/July 2005): 154-159, 197.

Group Exhibitions

2005

2004

2003

2002

2000

Meisterschüler (master student) in the class of Prof. Arno Rink, Hochschule für Grafik und Buchkunst, Leipzig, Germany

Painting, Hochschule für Grafik und Buchkunst, Leipzig, Germany

Wilkinson Gallery, London, England

Christian Ehrentraut, Berlin, Germany

Wilkinson Gallery, London, England

Galerie Kleindienst, Leipzig, Germany
Galerie LIGA, Berlin, Germany

Hydroplan, Museum der Bildenden Künste, Leipzig, Germany
Malerei und Zeichnungen, Galerie LIGA, Berlin, Germany
Ernst von Reutern Haus, Willinghausen, Germany

Kanalpatrouille 2, Galerie Kleindienst, Leipzig, Germany
Kanalpatrouille 1, Kunstverein Leipzig, Leipzig, Germany

Kunstraum b2, Leipzig, Germany
Eremia und Co., Galerie Kleindienst, Leipzig, Germany

From Leipzig: Works from the Ovitz Family Collection, Cleveland Museum of Art, Cleveland, OH (cat.)
Cold Hearts: Artists from Leipzig, Arario Gallery, Chungcheongnam-do, Korea
DAVID, MATTHES und ich, Kunstverein Bielefeld, Bielefeld, Germany; Kunstverein Nürnberg, Nürnberg, Germany
Life After Death: New Paintings from the Rubell Family Collection, MASS MoCA, North Adams, MA; traveling to SITE Santa Fe, Santa Fe, NM; Katzen Arts Center Museum, American University, Washington, DC; Frye Art Museum, Seattle, WA; Salt Lake Art Center, Salt Lake City, UT (cat.)

Northern Light: Leipzig in Miami, Rubell Family Collection, Miami, FL
EASTinternational 2004, Norwich School of Art and Design, Norwich, England
CLARA-PARK: Positions of Contemporary Painting from Leipzig, Marianne Boesky Gallery, New York, NY
Eastory, Galerie Suzanne Tarasieve, Paris, France

Sieben mal Malerei, Museum der Bildenden Künste, Leipzig, Germany; Galleri Nicolai Wallner, Copenhagen, Denmark (cat.)
Painting show, Anthony Wilkinson Gallery, London, England
FUTURE/Five artists from Germany, Sandroni.Rey Gallery, Los Angeles, CA
Malerei, Kunstforum Rheinhessen, Essenheim, Germany
LIGA - Junge Kunst aus Leipzig, Kunstverein Neustadt, Neustadt, Germany
Halbzeit, Galerie LIGA, Berlin, Germany

NEUER REALISMUS, Galerie Rothamel, Erfurt, Germany
Leipziger Lerchen, Kunstverein und Städtische Galerie im Kulturhof Flachsgasse, Speyer, Germany
Convoi, Metallgalerie, IG Metall, Frankfurt am Main, Germany; Kulturspeicher Oldenburg, Leipzig, Germany
Willkommen in Leipzig, Ausstellungsraum deLgt, Frankfurt am Main, Germany
5 aus 11, Galerie LIGA, Berlin, Germany

LIGA, Steibs Hof, Leipzig, Germany
Kunstraum b2, Leipzig, Germany

TIM EITEL

1971 Born in Leonberg, Germany

Lives and works in Berlin and Leipzig, Germany

Education 2001-2003

1997-2001

1994-1996

1993-1994

Solo Exhibitions 2005

2004

2003

2002

2000

Group Exhibitions 2005

2004

2003

2002

2001

Selected Bibliography

Baer, Patrick-Daniel. "Erste Wahl." SAX (December 2003).

"Brit-Art war gestern." Kultur-Kanal (August/September 2004): 1-3.

Czöppan, Gabi. "Unabhängiger Appetit auf „Krauts." Focus (December 12, 2004): 40-42.

Egan, Maura. "Neue School." The New York Times Style Magazine (Fall 2004): 126-128.

Einblick. "Tim Eitel Künstler." Die Tageszeitung (June 18, 2003): 27.

Farhall, Laura F. "Young Berliners." Lapiz (No. 199/200, January/February 2004).

"Frieder Burda Collection Opens." Flash Art (November/December 2004): 42.

Galloway, David. "The Eternal Reinvention of Painting." The International Herald Tribune (February 15, 2003).

Guth, Peter. "Kein Geheimniss, nichts Abgründiges." Leipziger Volkszeitung (December 23, 2003).

Harms, Ingeborg. "Kultur – Evolutionen." Vogue (October 2004): 212 – 220.

Heiland, Gert. "Lanze für die Malerei gebrochen." Wetzlarer Neue Zeitung (February 1, 2003).

Herbstreuth, Peter. "Tim Eitel in der Galerie Eigen+Art." Kunst-Bulletin (January 2004).

Illies, Florian. "Florian Illies plant seinen November." Kultur-Spiegel (November 2003): 4-5.

Kleinschmidt, Andreas und Knöfel, Ulrike. "Flamingos und Wildschweine." Spiegel (July, 2005): 160.

Krämer, Anja. "Flächenspiele." Lift Stuttgart (March 2005): 74.

Knöfel, Ulrike. "Siegeszug der Kraut Art." Deutsch Magazine pp.30-34.

Knack, Ingrid. "Figuren ruhen in sich, Landschaft wird zur Bühne." Backnanger Kreiszeitung (February 22, 2005).

Knack, Ingrid. "Zwischen fotografischem und malerischem Sehen." Backnanger Kreiszeitung (February 18, 2005).

Knack, Ingrid. "Shooting Star der Neuen Leipziger Schule in Backnang." Backnanger Kreiszeitung (January 29, 2005)

Koch, Ingrid. "Im Osten viel Neues." Weltkunst (No. 6, 2004): 45.

"Lauter Vertraute: in Tim Eitels Bildern trifft man Menschen, die man zu kennen vermeint." Stuttgarter Zeitung (February 18, 2005).

Leisten, Georg. "Melancholiker in Alltagsklamotten." Stuttgarter Zeitung (February 23, 2005): 31.

Liebs, Holger. "Krise? Welche Krise?." Süddeutsche Zeitung (January 20, 2004): 13.

Lledo, Elena. "Arte Joven en Berlin." Lapiz (January/February 2004): 156-167.

Maak, Niklas. "Im Land der hängenden Köpfe." FAZ (March 2005).

Maak, Niklas. "In einem anderen Land." Frankfurter Allgemeine Zeitung (January 16, 2003).

Macel, Christine. "In the East, Something New: Contemporary Painting in Germany." Art Press (No. 294, October 2003): 39-46.

Macel, Christine. "New Painting in Germany." Art Press (No. 294, October 2003): 41-46.

Mack, Gerhard and Hohenberg, Georg. "Die Stadt der Leiwandhelden." ART: das Kunstmagazin (December 2004): 34-45.

Meisterschüler (master student) in the class of Prof. Arno Rink, Hochschule für Grafik und Buchkunst, Leipzig, Germany

Painting, Hochschule für Grafik und Buchkunst, Leipzig, Germany

Fine arts, Burg Giebichtenstein, Halle, Germany

University of Stuttgart, Stuttgart, Germany

Saint Louis Art Museum, Saint Louis, MO
Kunstverein Göttingen, Göttingen, Germany
Terrain, Galerie der Stadt Backnang, Backnang, Germany (cat.)

Terrain, Museum zu Allerheiligen Schaffhausen, Schaffhausen
Switzerland; Crac Alsace – Centre Rhenan D'Art Contemporain, Altkirch, France (cat.)

Galerie EIGEN + ART, Leipzig, Germany

Künstlerhaus Bethanien, Berlin, Germany (cat.)
Galerie LIGA, Berlin, Germany

Frühjahrskollektion, Künstlergilde Ulm, Ulm, Germany

Prague Biennial, Prague, Czech Republic
New German Paintings, Carré d`Art – Musée D`Art Contemporain de Nimes, Nimes, France
From Leipzig: Works from the Ovitz Family Collection, Cleveland Museum of Art, Cleveland, OH (cat.)
Life After Death: New Paintings from the Rubell Family Collection, MASS MoCA, North Adams, MA; traveling to SITE Santa Fe, Santa Fe, NM; Katzen Arts Center Museum, American University, Washington, DC; Frye Art Museum, Seattle, WA; Salt Lake Art Center, Salt Lake City, UT (cat.)
Portrait, Galerie EIGEN + ART, Berlin, Germany

Not in New York: Emerging European Artists, Stefan Stux Gallery, New York, NY
Northern Light: Leipzig in Miami, Rubell Family Collection, Miami, FL
Funny Cuts, Staatsgalerie Stuttgart, Stuttgart, Germany
Contemporary Art from Germany, ECB, Frankfurt, Germany
Tim Eitel, David Schnell, Matthias Weischer, Galerie EIGEN + ART, Berlin, Germany

Marion Ermer-Preis, Oktogon Dresden, Dresden, Germany
Sommer bei EIGEN + ART, Galerie EIGEN + ART, Berlin, Germany
Groupshow, Sommer Contemporary Art, Tel Aviv, Israel
LIGA, Kunstverein Neustadt, Neustadt, Germany
Drei Positionen zur Malerei: Tim Eitel, Cornelius Völker, Matthias Weischer, Treptowers, Berlin, Germany (cat.)
Sieben mal Malerei, Museum der Bildenden Künste, Leipzig, Germany; Galleri Nicolai Wallner, Copenhagen, Denmark (cat.)
deutschemalereizweitausenddrei, Frankfurter Kunstverein, Frankfurt, Germany (cat.)

Galerie EIGEN + ART, Leipzig, Germany
6 aus 11, Galerie LIGA, Berlin, Germany

MenschenBilder, Galerie Rainer Wehr, Stuttgart, Germany

Selected Bibliography cont.

Meier, Philipp. "Lolita, Wolken, Seifenblasen." Neue Zürcher Zeitung (June 19, 2004).
Preuss, Sebastian. "Für mich steckt Gott in jeder Pflanze." Berliner Zeitung (December 1, 2004): 26.
Preuss, Sebastian. "Coole Träume von der blauen Blume." Berliner Zeitung (January 2, 2003).
Preuss, Sebastian. "Endstation Asien für die Hirschmenschen." Berliner Zeitung (September 29, 2004): 36.
Salzbrenner, Uwe. "Vom heiteren Zauber der Ordnung." Sächsische Zeitung (December 2003).
Schmidt, Johannes. "New Power, New Pictures." Flash Art International (November/December 2004): 78-83.
Schaernack, Christian. "Young German Art." u_spot (No. 3, 2004): 4.
Sommer, Tim. "Ausbruch ins Paradies." ART (No. 6, June 2004): 16.
Sorbello, Marina. "Domanda irrisolta: quale significato ha la pittura oggi?" Il Giornale Dell'Arte (May 2003).
Tannert, Christoph. "Agieren in der Etappe." Freitag 08 (February 2, 2005): 17.
"Tim Eitel." Le Monde Diplomatique (October 2003).
Tilmann, Christina. "Reif für den Pinsel." Tagesspiegel (January 24, 2003).
Villinger, Carina. "A League of Their Own." Art + Auction (June 11, 2004): 92-97.
Volk, Gregory. "Figuring the New Germany." Art in America (June/July 2005): 154-159, 197.
Wendland, Johannes. "Painted in Leipzig." Frankfurter Rundschau (April 1, 2003).
Wendland, Johannes. "Jenseits schneller Massenproduktion." Kunstzeitung (March 2003).
Werner, Lisa. "Zwischen Poesie und kühlem Intellekt." Art (December 11, 2003).
Werneburg, Brigitte. "Ein durchaus bekannter Vorgang." Die Tageszeitung (May 22, 2003).
Werneburg, Brigitte. "Definitiv nowtro." Die Tageszeitung (January 7, 2003).
Wesely, Kathrin. "Erbe der Romantiker." Südwest Presse (February, 2, 2005).
Wittneven, Katrin. "Hunger nach Trends." Der Tagesspiegel (April 10, 2004): 26.

MARTIN KOBE

1973
Born in Dresden, Germany

Lives and works in Leipzig, Germany

Education 2000-2003

1995-2000

Solo Exhibitions 2005

2004

2003

2002

Group Exhibitions 2005

2004

2003

2002

2001

2000

Selected Bibliography

Gisbourne, Mark. "Leipzig." Contemporary (No. 53-54, 2003): 40-45.
Koch, Ingrid. "Im Osten viel Neues." Weltkunst (June 2004): 45-48.
Macel, Christine. "In the East, Something New: Contemporary Painting in Germany." Art Press (No. 294, October 2003): 39-46.
Sommer, Tim. "Training mit Sift und Pinsel." ART: das Kunstmagazin (May 2003): 92-93.
Volk, Gregory. "Figuring the New Germany." Art in America (June/July 2005): 154-159, 197.

Meisterschüler (master student) in the class of Prof. Arno Rink, Hochschule für Grafik und Buchkunst, Leipzig, Germany

Painting, Hochschule für Grafik und Buchkunst, Leipzig, Germany

Christian Ehrentraut, Berlin, Germany
Loomings, Inside the White Cube, London, England

Galerie LIGA, Berlin, Germany
Wilkinson Gallery, London, England
Förderkoje, ARTCOLOGNE, Cologne, Germany

Kunstverein Leipzig, Leipzig, Germany
Malerei, Galerie LIGA, Berlin, Germany
Förderkoje, ARTCOLOGNE, Cologne, Germany

Martin Kobe – Malerei, Galerie Dogenhaus, Leipzig, Germany

Cold Hearts: Artists from Leipzig, Arario Gallery, Choonchungnam-do, Korea
Life After Death: New Paintings from the Rubell Family Collection, MASS MoCA, North Adams, MA; traveling to SITE Santa Fe, Santa Fe, NM; Katzen Arts Center Museum, American University, Washington, DC; Frye Art Museum, Seattle, WA; Salt Lake Art Center, Salt Lake City, UT (cat.)
From Leipzig, Cleveland Museum of Art, Cleveland, OH (cat.)

Northern Light: Leipzig in Miami, Rubell Family Collection, Miami, FL
East International, School of Art and Design, Norwich, England
Fehlfarben, Gemäldegalerie Neue Meister, Dresden, Germany
CLARA-PARK: Positions of Contemporary Painting from Leipzig, Marianne Boesky Gallery, New York, NY

LIGA - Junge Kunst aus Leipzig, Kunstverein Neustadt, Neustadt, Germany
Painting Show, Wilkinson Gallery, London, England
Sieben mal Malerei, Neuer Leipziger Kunstverein im Museum der Bildenden Künste, Leipzig, Germany; Galleri Nicolai Wallner, Copenhagen, Denmark (cat.)
Wild strawberries and favorite haunts, Suite 106, New York, NY

aus 11, Galerie LIGA, Berlin, Germany
Leipziger Lerchen, Kunstverein Speyer und Städtische Galerie Speyer im Kulturhof Flachsgasse, Speyer, Germany

Wildbahn, Bad Neuenahr, Germany

LIGA, Steibs Hof, Leipzig, Germany

NEO RAUCH

1960
Born in Leipzig, Germany

Lives and works in Leipzig, Germany

Education 1993-1998

1986-1990

1981-1986

Solo Exhibitions 2005

2004

2003

2002

2001

2000

1998

1997

1995

1994

1993

1991

1989

Selected Bibliography

Adams, Brooks. "Picabia the New Paradigm." Art in America (March 2003): 84-91.
Burton, Johanna. "Fabulism." Artforum (January 2004): 62.
Bush, Kate. "Cher Peintre, Lieber Maler, Dear Painter." Artforum (October 2002): 149.
Butler, Kate. "Neo Rauch." The New York Times (August 12, 2001).
Bourbon, Matthew. "Neo Rauch." NY ARTS (March 2000): 91-92.
Bylow, Christina. "Die probe deslebens." German Vogue (September 2004): 346.
"Carnegie International 2004-5." Flash Art (October 2004): 55.
Czöppan, Gabi. "Unabhängiger Appetit auf „Krauts." Focus (December 27, 2004): 40-42.
Egan, Maura. "Neue School." The New York Times Style Magazine (Fall 2004): 126-128.
Emsden, Christopher. "Bringing on the Best of the Biennale." Italy Daily (June 8, 2001): 3.
Fricke, Harald. "Neo Rauch, Galeris EIGEN + ART." Artforum (March 1999).
Galloway, David. "The New Look of Neo." ARTnews (December 2001): 110-111.
Gingeras, Alison M. "Neo Rauch: A Peristaltic Filtration System in the River of Time." Flash Art (November/ December 2002): 62-69.
Gioni, Massimiliano. "Neo Rauch: No Man's Land." Art Press (July/August 2002): 20-25.
Gioni, Massimiliano. "Euroland." Flash Art (October 2001): 69-72.
Girst, Thomas. "The Parallel Universe of Neo Rauch." Tema Celeste (Summer 2001): 60-63.
Grant, Daniel. "Rauch on the Rise." ARTnews (March 2005): 82.
Grieshaber, Kirsten. "Painter with a Vision that Translates." The New York Times (January 8, 2005): 9.
Grimes, Nancy. "New Rauch." ARTnews (June 2000): 144-145.
Goodbody, Bridget. "Fabulism." Art US (No.4 September/ October 2004): 42.
Gorsen, Peter. "Die Unterbrochene Scopfung." Feuilleton (October 11, 2004).
Halle, Howard. "Neo Rauch." Grand Street (Spring 2003): 116-121.
Halle, Howard. "Papering the House: MOMA Tries to Wrest a Zeitgeist from Drawing Now." Time Out New York (November 7-14, 2002): 81.
Halle, Howard. "Back to the Wall." Time Out New York (March 16, 2000): 81.
Heartney, Eleanor. "Neo Rauch at David Zwirner." Art in America (December 2002): 106-107.
Heiser, Jork. "Don't Ask." Frieze (No. 85, September 2004): 65.
Kalm, James. "Rot Kraut – or why New Yorkers don't get Neo Rauch." NY Arts (July/August 2002).
Kertess, Klaus: "Neo Rauch Works on Paper 2003 – 2004." Artforum International (December 2004): 191.
Kealy, Seamus. "Lieber Maler, male mir." Canadian Art International (Spring 2003).
Kimmelmann, Michael. "Neo Rauch: ‚Renegaten.'" The New York Times (May 27, 2005): 34.
Larkin, Anne. "Hunters and Collectors." Arco (No. 35, Spring 2005): 18-22.
Lewisohn, Cedar. "The Good, the Bad, and the Ugly." Flash Art (July/August 2001).
Johnson, Ken. "The Week Ahead: Art." The New York Times (May 2005): 23.
Johnson, Ken. "Pittsburgh Rounds Up Work Made in Novel Ways." The New York Times (November 4, 2004).

Assistant, Hochschule für Grafik und Buchkunst, Leipzig, Germany

Meisterschüler (master student) in the class of Prof. Bernhard Heisig, Hochschule für Grafik und Buchkunst, Leipzig, Germany

Painting, Hochschule für Grafik und Buchkunst, Leipzig, Germany

Neo Rauch: Renegaten, David Zwirner, New York, NY
Neo Rauch, Centro de Arte Contemporáneo, Malaga, Spain
Neo Rauch Works 1994-2000: The Leipziger Volkszeitung Collection, Honolulu Academy of Arts, Honolulu, HI

Neo Rauch, Albertina, Vienna, Austria
EASTinternational 2004, Norwich School of Art and Design, Norwich, England
Currents: Neo Rauch, Saint Louis Art Museum, Saint Louis, MI.

Neo Rauch, Bonnefantenmuseum, Maastricht, The Netherlands
Neo Rauch, David Zwirner, New York, NY
Neo Rauch, Galerie EIGEN+ART, Berlin, Germany

Neo Rauch - Sammlung Deutsche Bank, Mannheimer Kunstverein, Mannheim, Germany; Neues Museum Weserburg, Bremen, Germany; Deutsche Guggenheim, Berlin, Germany; Kunsthalle Zurich, Zurich, Switzerland; The Douglas Hyde Gallery, Dublin, Ireland (cat.)
Randgebiet, Haus der Kunst, Munich, Germany; Kunsthalle Zurich, Zurich, Switzerland (cat.)
Neo Rauch, International Culture Centre, Krakow, Poland

Randgebiet, Museum Galerie für Zeitgenössische Kunst, Leipzig, Germany (cat.)
Neo Rauch, Galerie EIGEN + ART, Leipzig, Germany
Neo Rauch, David Zwirner, New York, NY

Galerie EIGEN + ART, Berlin, Germany
Galerie der Stadt Backnang, Backnang, Germany (cat.)

Manöver, Galerie EIGEN + ART, Leipzig, Germany (cat.)
Museum der Bildenden Künste, Leipzig, Germany (cat.)

Galerie EIGEN + ART, Berlin, Germany
Dresdner Bank, Leipzig, Germany
Goethe House, New York, NY
Neo Rauch: Marineschule, Overbeck Gesellschaft, Lübeck, Germany (cat.)

Projekt Galerie, Kunstverein Elsterpark e.V., Leipzig, Germany

Galerie Alvensleben, Munich, Germany (cat.)
Galerie EIGEN + ART, Leipzig, Germany
Galerie VOXX, Chemnitz, Germany
nkabinettGalerie, Berlin, Germany

Galerie Schwind, Frankfurt am Main, Germany

Neo Rauch, Galerie am Thomaskirchhof, Leipzig, Germany (cat.)

Selected Bibliography cont.

Jones, Kristin M. "Neo Rauch." Frieze (June/August 2000): 116-117.
Leffingwell, Edward. "Report from São Paulo: the Extraterritorial Zone." Art in America (February 2005): 49-55.
Lamm, Elizabeth. "Out of the Cold." ArtReview (Vol. 2, No. 7, July/August 2004): 54-57.
Macel, Christine. "In the East, Something New: Contemporary Painting in Germany." Art Press (No. 294, October 2003): 39-46.
Mack, Gerhard. "Mit den Waffen des Malers." Art: Das Kunstmagazin (January 2001): 12-23.
Madoff, Steven Henry. "Neo's Realism." Talk (October 2001): 66.
Mason, Christopher. "She Can't Be Bought." New York Magazine (March 7, 2005): 32.
"Miami Beach in December: Cool Stuff." Art in America (December 2004).
Mosler, Paul. "Die Posetische Kraft des Suchenden." Leipziger Volkszeitung (February 2005): 8.
Naves, Mario. "Neo Rauch's Fraught Narratives Confound Easy Explanation." The New York Observer (May 23, 2005): 18.
Puvogel, Renate. "Neo Rauch, Among the Workers." Bonnefanten Magazine (Summer 2002): 48-57.
Replinger, Mercedes. "Interrogating Painting Part I." arco (Spring 2005): 27-31.
Rubiro, Sergio. "Neo Rauch, Escenografías del fracaso." EXIT Express (October 2004): 11.
Ruth, Ingeborg. "Ohne Risiken und Nebenwirkungen." Berliner Zeitung (December 12, 1999): 13.
Rosenberg, Karen. "Neo Rauch: Renegaten." New York (May 2005): 75.
Ostrow, Saul. "Strategic Images: From Leipzig at Cleveland Museum of Art." Angle (Vol. 2, No. 19, March/April 2005): 12-13.
Schjeldahl, Peter. "Critic's Notebook Realism and Rauch." The New Yorker (June 2005): 28.
Schjeldahl, Peter. "The Drawing Board." The New Yorker (November 4, 2002): 102-103.
Scott, Andrea K. "Neo Expressionism." Edifice Rex (March 8, 2000).
Shearing, Graham. "The 54th Carnegie International." Angle (Vol. 2, No. 17, November/December 2004): 4-5.
Siegel, Katy. "2004 Carnegie International." Artforum (January 2005): 175.
Smith, Roberta. "Neo Rauch." The New York Times (April 26, 2002): E33.
Smith, Roberta. "Retreat from the Wild Shores of Abstraction." The New York Times (October 18, 2002): E31–E33.
Smith, Roberta. "More Space for Young Artist." The New York Times (February 19, 1999).
Sonkin, Rebecca. "Neo Rauch." Art & Auction (December 2002): 122-123.
Skarf, Shayna. "Judgment Day." Time Out New York (May 2-9, 2002): 64.
Stevens, Mark. "Out of Line." New York Metro (December 16, 2002): 63-64.
Tuymans, Luc. "What the Painters Say." Art Press (July/August 2002): 37-46.
Tully, Judd. "Frieze Frames Hirst Coup." Art and Auction (December 2004).
Utter, Douglas, Max. "Reviews: Cleveland." Art Papers (May/June 2005): 50.
Volk, Gregory. "Figuring the New Germany." Art in America (June/July 2005): 154-159, 197.
Volk, Gregory. "Report from Pittsburg. Let's Get Metaphysical." Art in America (March 2005): 62-69.
Wilkinson, Jeanne. "Neo Rauch." Review (March 2000): 26.
Winter, Peter. "Von Wahnmobeln, Wahnturmen und Wahnkindern." Frankfurter Allgemeine Zeitung (December 15, 1999): 16-17.
Worth, Alexi. "Neo Rauch/David Zwirner." ArtForum (September 2002).

Group Exhibitions

2005

2004

2003

2002

2001

2000

Almost, Robert Miller Gallery, New York, NY
Cold Hearts: Artists from Leipzig, Arario Gallery, Choongchungnam-do, Korea
Contemporary Voices: Works from the UBS Art Collection, Museum of Modern Art, New York, NY
Every Picture Tells a Story: The Narrative Impulse in Modern and Contemporary Art, Galerie St. Etienne, New York, NY
Generation X, Kunstmuseum Wolfsgurg, Wolfsburg, Germany
Life After Death: New Paintings from the Rubell Family Collection, MASS MoCA, North Adams, MA; traveling to SITE Santa Fe, Santa Fe, NM; Katzen Arts Center Museum, American University, Washington, DC; Frye Art Museum, Seattle, WA; Salt Lake Art Center, Salt Lake City, UT (cat.)
Portrait, Galerie EIGEN + ART, Berlin, Germany
Symbolic Space: The Intersection of Art & Architecture Through the Use of Metaphor, Hudson Valley Center for Contemporary Art, Peekskill, NY
From Leipzig, Cleveland Museum of Art, Cleveland, OH (cat.)
On Paper III, Carnegie Museum of Art, Pittsburgh, PA

Northern Light: Leipzig in Miami, Rubell Family Collection, Miami, FL
Disparities & Deformations: Our Grotesque, SITE Sante Fe International Biennial, Santa Fe, NM (cat.)
Perspectives @ 25: A Quarter Century of New Art in Houston, Contemporary Arts Museum Houston, Houston, TX (cat.)
Carnegie International, Carnegie Museum of Art, Pittsburgh, PA
Ice Hot: Recent Paintings from the Scharpff Collection, Staatsgalerie Stuttgart, Stuttgart, Germany
Treasure Island: 10 Years Collection Kunstmuseum, Kunstmuseum Wolfsburg, Wolfsburg, Germany
Fabulism, Joslyn Art Museum, Omaha, NE (cat.)
26th Bienal de São Paulo, São Paulo, Brazil (cat.)

Ice Hot: Recent Paintings from the Scharpff Collection, Hamburger Kunsthalle, Hamburg, Germany
Dear Painter, Paint Me, Schrin Kunstalle Frankfurt, Frankfurt, Germany
Crosscurrents at Century's End: Selections from the Neuberger Berman Art Collection, Henry Art Gallery, University of Washington, Seattle, WA; Norton Museum of Art, West Palm Beach, FL; Tampa Museum of Art, Tampa, FL; Chicago Cultural Center, Chicago, IL (cat.)
For the Record: Drawing Contemporary Life, Vancouver Art Gallery, Vancouver, BC, Canada (cat.)
Outlook, Technopolis, Benaki Museum and Athens School of Fine Arts, Athens, Greece (cat.)
Sommer bei EIGEN + ART, Galerie EIGEN + ART, Berlin, Germany
Berlin-Moscow/Moscow-Berlin 1950-2000, Martin Gropius-Bau, Berlin, Germany; Neuen Tretjakow Galerie, Moscow, Russia
Europe Exists, Macedonian Museum of Contemporary Art, Thessaloniki, Greece
Die Erfindung der Vergangenheit, Pinakothek der Moderne, Munich, Germany
Monuments of Melancholy, Kunstmuseum Wolfsburg, Wolfsburg, Germany
Social Strategies: Redefining Social Realism, Univeristy Art Museum, University of California, Santa Barbara, CA; University Galleries, Illinois State University, Normal, IL; DePauw University Art Gallery, Greencastle, IN (cat)

Drawing Now: Eight Propositions, Museum of Modern Art, New York, NY
Dear Painter, Paint Me, Centre Georges Pompidou, Paris; Kunsthalle Wien, Vienna, Austria; Schrin Kunstalle Frankfurt, Germany
Mare Balticum, National Museum of Denmark, Copenhagen, Denmark
Painting on the Move, Kunstmuseum Basel, Basel, Switzerland
Pertaining to Painting, Contemporary Arts Museum, Houston, TX; Austin Museum of Art, Austin, TX

La Biennale di Venezia, Venice, Italy
Collection Deutsche Bank, Kunstverein Mannheim, Mannheim, Germany; Neues Museum Weserburg, Bremen, Germany; Douglas Hyde Gallery, Dublin, Ireland; International Culture Centre, Krakow, Poland
The Mystery of Painting, Sammlung Goetz, Munich, Germany
EU, Stephen Friedman Gallery, London, England
Wirklichkeit in der zeitgenossischen Malerei, Stadtische Galerie Delmenhorst, Delmenhorst, Germany
Squatters, Museu Serralves, Porto, Portugal; Witte de With, Rotterdam, The Netherlands

Premio Michetti, Museo Michetti di Francavilla al Mare, Italy
Contemporary German Art, The Last Thirty Years/Thirty Artists from Germany, Goethe Institute, Germany; Bombay, Bangalore, Calcutta, India
Salon, The Delfina Studio Trust, London, England

Group Exhibitions cont. 1999

1998

1997

1996

1995

1994

1993

1992

1991

1990

1988

fter the Wall, Moderna Museet, Stockholm
erman Open, Kunstmuseum Wolfsburg, Wolfsburg, Germany
e Golden Age, Institute of Contemporary Arts, London, England
hildren of Berlin, P.S.1, Long Island City, NY
rawing and Painting, Galerie EIGEN + ART, Berlin, Germany
alerei, INIT Kunst-Halle, Berlin, Germany

e Macht des Alters - Strategien der Meisterschaft, Deutsches Historisches Museum Berlin, Berlin, Germany; Kunstmuseum Bonn, Bonn, Germany; Deutsches Hygiene Museum, Dresden, Germany
ansmission, Espace des Arts, Chalon-sur-Saône, France

gural. Figürlich. Figurativ., Bankhaus Trinkhaus & Burkhardt, Düsseldorf, Germany
ontemporary Art at Deutsche Bank, Deutsche Bank, London, England
erleihung des Kunstpreises der Leipziger Volkszeitung 1997, Leipzig, Germany
G Deutsche Gesellschaft fur Christliche Kunst, Munich, Germany
ust und Last, Germanisches Nationalmuseum, Nürnberg, Germany; Museum der Bildenden Künste, Leipzig, Germany (cat.)
eed for Speed, Grazer Kunstverein, Graz, Austria (cat.)
tale Module; Gegenwartskunst aus Sachsen, Städtische Galerie "e.o.plauen"; Kunsthaus Dresden, Dresden, Germany; Kunstverein Ludwigshafen, Ludwigshafen, Germany

er Blick ins 21ste, Kunstverein Düsseldorf, Düsseldorf, Germany

alerie Alvensleben, Munich, Germany
oethe House, New York, NY

echsische Kunstausstellung, Dresden, Germany

ipziger Jahresausstellung, Leipzig, Germany
instler traumen Berlin, Marstall, Berlin, Germany
esdner Bank, Frankfurt, Germany

r Harz, Galerie am Kraftwerk/ Dependance Specks Hof, Leipzig, Germany
lerie Alvensleben, Munich, Germany
ipziger Sezession, Krochhochhaus, Germany
nge Künstler aus Leipzig, BASF, Ludwigshafen, Germany
flex Ost-West, Potsdam, Germany
NTA Preis, Norris Halle, Nürnberg, Germany (cat.)

s Gewitter (with Klaus Killich), Galerie am Kraftwerk Leipzig, Germany
oße Kunstausstellung NRW, Düsseldorf, Germany
lerie Utermann, Dortmund, Germany

lerie Maerz (with Roland Borchers and Gerhard Petri), Linz, Austria
oße Kunstausstellung NRW, Düsseldorf, Germany
89 Große Kunstausstellung NRW, Düsseldorf, Germany (cat.)
ischenspiele, Künstlerhaus Bethanien, West Berlin, Germany (cat.)
nge Künstler der DDR und Kubas, East Berlin; Havana, Cuba

Kunstausstellung der DDR, Dresden, Germany (cat.)
uerwerbungen des Ludwig-Institut für Kunst der DDR, Ludwig-Institut Oberhausen, Oberhausen Germany
eiten aus vier Kunsthochschulen Leipzig, Warsaw, Vienna, Berlin, Hofer Gesellschaft, Bahnhof Westend, West-Berlin, Germany
pziger Secession, Krochhochhaus, Leipzig, Germany
86 Junge Künstler im Bezirk Leipzig, Staatliches Lindenau- Museum, Altenburg, Germany

CHRISTOPH RUCKHÄBERLE

1972
Born in Pfaffenhofen, Germany

Lives and works in Leipzig, Germany

Education

2000-2002

1995-2002

1991-1993

Solo Exhibitions

2005

2004

2003

2002

2001

Selected Bibliography

"Die Stadt der Leinwandhelden." ART: das Kunstmagazin (December 2004): 35-45.
Egan, Maura. "Neue School." The New York Times Style Magazine (Fall 2004): 126-128.
Johnson, Daniela. "EAST International." Flash Art (October 2004): 65.
Macel, Christine. "In the East, Something New: Contemporary Painting in Germany." Art Press (No. 294, October 2003): 39-46.
Marsh, Andrew. "Christoph Ruckhäberle: Sutton Lane." Flash Art (January/February 2005): 120.
Price, Matt. "Mixed Paint: Christoph Ruckhäberle." Flash Art (November/December 2004): 95.
Ribas, Joao. "Debut: Christoph Ruckhäberle." Art Review (September 2004): 102.
Schmidt, Johannes. "New Power, New Pictures." Flash Art (November/December 2004): 78-83.
Villinger, Carina. "A League of Their Own." Art + Auction (June 11, 2004): 92-97.
Volk, Gregory. "Figuring the New Germany." Art in America (June/July 2005): 154-159, 197.

Group Exhibitions

2005

2004

2003

2002

2001

2000

Meisterschüler (master student) in the class of Prof. Arno Rink, Hochschule für Grafik und Buchkunst, Leipzig, Germany

Painting, Hochschule für Grafik und Buchkunst, Leipzig, Germany

Animation studies, California Institute of the Arts, Valencia, CA

Galerie Kleindienst Leipzig, Germany
Nye Eventyr, Galleri Nicolai Wallner, Copenhagen, Denmark

Zach Feuer/LFL Gallery, New York, NY
Sutton Lane, London, England
Galleri Nicolai Wallner, Copenhagen, Denmark

Malerei, Galerie LIGA, Berlin, Germany

Malerei, Galerie LIGA, Berlin, Germany
Malerei, Galerie Kleindienst, Leipzig, Germany (cat.)

Malerei, Galerie Kleindienst, Leipzig, Germany

Cold Hearts: Artists from Leipzig, Arario Gallery, Choongchungnam-do, Korea
Dresden-Leipzig School, Prague Biennial, Prague, Czech Republic
Neo-Con, Gavin Brown's Enterprise at Passerby, New York, NY
From Leipzig: Works from the Ovitz Family Collection, The Cleveland Museum of Art, Cleveland, OH (cat.)
Life After Death: New Paintings from the Rubell Family Collection, MASS MoCA, North Adams, MA; traveling to SITE Santa Fe, Santa Fe, NM; Katzen Arts Center Museum, American University, Washington, DC; Frye Art Museum, Seattle, WA; Salt Lake Art Center, Salt Lake City, UT (cat.)
Reflection, Part II, Sutton Lane, London, England
Baby-Shower, Galleri Nicolai Wallner, Copenhagen, Denmark

Northern Light: Leipzig in Miami, Rubell Family Collection, Miami, FL
The New Leipzig School of Painting, Contemporary Art Museum, Baltimore, MD
East International, Norwich School of Art and Design, Norwich, England
CLARA-PARK: Positions of Contemporary Painting from Leipzig, Marianne Boesky Gallery, New York, NY
Grasland, Wassermann Galerie, Munich, Germany
Lazarus Effect, Prague Biennial, Prague, Czech Republic
Sieben mal Malerei, Museum der Bildenden Künste, Leipzig, Germany; Galleri Nicolai Wallner, Copenhagen, Denmark (cat.)
Halbzeit, LIGA, Berlin, Germany

Wunschbilder, Museum der Bildenden Künste, Leipzig, Germany
Convoi, Metallgalerie, IG Metall, Frankfurt am Main, Germany; Kulturspeicher Oldenburg, Leipzig, Germany
Willkommen in Leipzig, Ausstellungsraum de Ligt, Ausstellungshalle Schulstrasse, Frankfurt am Main, Germany
Zweidimensionale, Kunsthalle der Sparkasse, Leipzig, Germany
Junge Kunst Aus Leipzig, Kunstverein Sulzfeld, Leipzig, Germany
6 aus 11, Galerie LIGA, Berlin, Germany
Leipziger Lerchen, Kunstverein Speyer und Städtische Galerie Speyer im Kulturhof Flachsgasse, Speyer, Germany

Junge Malerei, Galerie Binz & Krämer, Cologne, Germany
Arte Saxonia, Kuppelhalle der Dresdner Bank, Leipzig, Germany
Leipziger Maler, Kunstverein Galerie Markt Bruckmühl, Leipzig, Germany

LIGA, Steibs Hof, Leipzig, Germany
Junge Kunst, Galerie Kleindienst, Leipzig, Germany

DAVID SCHNELL

1971
Born in Bergisch Gladbach, Germany

Lives and works in Leipzig, Germany

Education

2000-2002

1995-2002

Solo Exhibitions

2004

2003

2002

2001

Group Exhibitions

2005

2004

2003

2002

2001

2000

Selected Bibliography

De Ligt, Natalie. "David Schnell." Bdap (No. 18, Summer 2005).
Dreckmann, Claus. "Leben in Leipzig, malen für die Welt." Bunte (March 2005): 89-90.
Gerd, Held. "Der fordernde Gott." FAZ (January 2005).
Glasser, Ronald J. "We are not Immune." Harper's Magazine (July 2004): 34.
Kleinschmidt, Andreas und Knöfel, Ulrike. "Flamingos und Wildschweine." Spiegel (July 2005): 160.
Hafner, Hans-Jürgen. "David, Matthes und ich." Kunstforum International (No. 175, May 2005): 336-338.
Maak, Nils. "Les mystères de l' école de Leipzig." Le Journal des Arts (January 21, 2005).
Macel, Christine. "In the East, Something New: Contemporary Painting in Germany." Art Press (No. 294, October 2003): 39-46.
Mack, Gerhard und Hohenberg, Georg. "Die Stadt der Leinwandhelden." Art (No. 12, December 2004): 34-45.
"Mission erfüllt in Berlin." Sächsische Zeitung (September 26, 2004): 17.
Michael, Meinhard. "Landschaft mit Zuchtstempel." Leipziger Volkszeitung (January 2005).
Mustroph, Tom. "Konstruktivistisch real." Neues Deutschland (December 12, 2004).
Nüchterlein, Birgit. "Praktische Hilfe für das Leben nach dem Studium." Nürnberger Nachrichten (November 2005).
Preuss, Sebastian. "Endstation Asien für die Hirschmenschen." Berliner Zeitung (September 23, 2004): 36.
Schmidt, Johannes. "New Power, New Pictures." Flash Art (November/December 2004): 78-83.
Tannert, Christoph. "Agieren in der Etappe." Freitag 08 (February 25, 2005): 17.
Villinger, Carina. "A League of Their Own." Art + Auction (June 11, 2004): 92-97.
Volk, Gregory. "Figuring the New Germany." Art in America (June/July 2005): 154-159, 197.
Wittneven, Katrin. "Die Wellenreiter." Der Tagesspiegel (November 27, 2004): 33.

Meisterschüler (master student) in the class of Prof. Arno Rink, Hochschule für Grafik und Buchkunst, Leipzig, Germany

Painting, Hochschule für Grafik und Buchkunst, Leipzig, Germany

Galerie LIGA, Berlin, Germany

Sandroni. Rei Venice, CA

Wandertag, Galerie LIGA, Berlin, Germany
New German Landscape, Gallery Rhodes + Mann, London, England
David Schnell / Malerei, Galerie Kleindienst, Leipzig, Germany

Galerie Kleindienst, Leipzig, Germany

Life After Death: New Paintings from the Rubell Family Collection, MASS MoCA, North Adams, MA; traveling to SITE Santa Fe, Santa Fe, NM; Katzen Arts Center Museum, American University, Washington, DC; Frye Art Museum, Seattle, WA; Salt Lake Art Center, Salt Lake City, UT (cat.)
Portrait, Galerie EIGEN + ART, Berlin, Germany
Kunstverein Nürnberg, Nürnberg, Germany (cat.)
Kunstverein Göttingen, Göttingen, Germany

Northern Light: Leipzig in Miami, Rubell Family Collection, Miami, FL
Tim Eitel, David Schnell, Matthias Weischer, Galerie EIGEN + ART, Berlin, Germany

Future/Five Artists from Germany, Sandroni. Rey Gallery, Los Angeles, CA
Sieben mal Malerei, Neuer Leipziger Kunstverein im Museum der Bildenden Künste, Leipzig, Germany; Galleri Nicolai Wallner, Copenhagen, Denmark (cat.)
Halbzeit, Galerie LIGA, Berlin, Germany

Leipziger Lerchen, Kunstverein Speyer und Städtische Galerie Speyer im Kulturhof Flachsgasse, Leipzig, Germany
5 x 5 Junge Kunst aus Sachsen, Neue Sächsische Galerie, Chemnitz, Germany
3 aus Leipzig, Kunstverein Sulzfeld, Sulzfeld, Germany
5 aus 11, Galerie LIGA, Berlin, Germany
Convoi, Metallgalerie, IG Metall, Frankfurt am Main, Germany; Kulturspeicher Oldenburg, Leipzig, Germany
Willkommen in Leipzig, Ausstellungsraum de Ligt, Frankfurt am Main, Germany
Wunschbilder, Museum der Bildenden Künste, Leipzig, Germany

Junge Malerei, Galerie Binz & Krämer, Cologne, Germany
Leipziger Maler, Kunstverein Galerie Markt Bruckmühl, Leipzig, Germany

Junge Kunst, Galerie Kleindienst, Leipzig, Germany
Diplomausstellung Waldwege, HGB Leipzig, Leipzig, Germany
LIGA, Steibs Hof, Leipzig, Germany

MATTHIAS WEISCHER

1973
Born in Elte, Germany

Lives and works in Leipzig, Germany

Education
2000-2003
1995-2001

Solo Exhibitions
2004
2003
2002
2001

Selected Bibliography

"Arts Sans Frontières, Le Mentorat Rolex 2e cycle." La Revue des Moutres (2004): 75.
Beßling, Rainer. "Matthias Weischer." Artists Kunstmagazin (April 2004): 28-31.
Bergmann, Rudij. "Geordnete Unordung." Frankfurter Rundschau (September 2004).
Bergmann Rudij. "Hinter der Popfassade." Frankfurter Rundschau (May 2004).
"Czech Republic – The Prague Biennale." The Art Newspaper (May 2005): 9.
Christmann, Holger. "Der Meisterschüler." Art (No. 7, 2004): 118.
Dreckmann, Claus. "Leben in Leipzig, malen für die Welt." Bunte (March 2005): 89-90.
Egan, Maura. "Neue School." The New York Times Style Magazine (Fall 2004): 126-128.
Farhall, Laura F. "Young Berliners." Lapiz (January/February 2004).
"Genf: Rolex Mentor und Meisterschüler Initiative." Kunst Bulletin (September 2004): 70.
Hochstein, Christine. "Spannendes Rennen Kopf an Kopf." Leipziger Volkszeitung (May 2005): 10.
Hochstein, Christine. "Interieur als Psychogramm." Leipziger Volkszeitung (May 2005): 10.
Hafner, Hans-Jürgen "David, Matthes und ich." Kunstforum International (No. 175, May 2005): 336 – 338.
Karcher, Eva. "Exklusives Lehrjahr." Vogue Deutsch (November 2004): 326.
Lledo, Elena. "Arte Joven en Berlin." Lapiz (January/February 2004): 156-167.
Maak, Niklas. "Les mystères de l` ècole de Leipzig." Le Journal des Arts (January 2005).
Maak, Niklas. "Mit Dekor: Matthias Weischer in Bremen."
Frankfurter Allgemeine Zeitung (September 2004): 41.
Macel, Christine. "In the East, Something New: Contemporary Painting in Germany." Art Press (No. 294, October 2003): 39-46.
Mack, Gerhard and Georg Hohenberg. "Die Stadt der Leinwandhelden." ART: das Kunstmagazin (December 2004): 34-45.
"Matthias Weischer." Monopol (August/September 2004).
"Mission erfüllt in Berlin." Sächsische Zeitung (September 2004): 17.
Mustroph, Tom. "Konstruktivistisch real." Neues Deutschland (December 14, 2004).
Petiz, Joana. "Boas ideias." Oindependente (August 2004).
Pfeffer, Susanne. "Matthias Weischer." bdap (No. 18, Summer 2005).
Preuss, Sebastian. "Endstation Asien für die Hirschmenschen." Berliner Zeitung (September 2004): 36.
Preuss, Sebastian. "Design oder Nichtsein." Berliner Zeitung (September 2004): 34.
Pupat, Hendrik. "Kunst als einsamer Dialog." LVZ (January 2005).
Schmidt, Johannes. "New Power, New Pictures." Flash Art International (November/December 2004): 78-83.
Selldorf, Annabelle. "Die Typisch deutsche Gründlichkeit tut der Qualität sehr gut." AD (October 2004): 56.
Tannert, Christoph. "Agieren in der Etappe." Freitag 08 (February 2005): 17.
Villinger, Carina. "A League of Their Own." Art + Auction (June 2004): 92.
Volk, Gregory. "Figuring the New Germany." Art in America (June/July 2005): 154-159, 197.
Wiensowski, Ingeborg. "Ostige Räume." Kultur Spiegel (December 2004): 32.

Group Exhibitions
2005
2004
2003
2002
2001
2000

Meisterschüler (master student) in the class of Prof. S. Gille, Hochschule für Grafik und Buchkunst, Leipzig, Germany

Painting, Hochschule für Grafik und Buchkunst, Leipzig, Germany

Simultan, Künstlerhaus Bremen, Bremen, Germany (cat.)

3 Zimmer, Diele, Bad, Galerie LIGA, Berlin, Germany

Räumen, Kunsthaus Essen, Essen, Germany (cat.)

Matthias Weischer. Malerei, Galerie Kleindienst, Leipzig, Germany
Antrittsausstellung, Kabinett der Galerie im Kunsthaus Essen, Essen, Germany

The Experience of Art, 51st Venice Biennial, Padiglione Italia, Venice, Italy
Prague Biennial, Prague, Czech Republic
Cold Hearts: Artists from Leipzig, Arario Gallery, Choongchungnam-do, Korea
From Leipzig: Works from the Ovitz Family Collection, Cleveland Museum of Art, Cleveland, OH (cat.)
Life After Death: New Paintings from the Rubell Family Collection, MASS MoCA, North Adams, MA; traveling to SITE Santa Fe, Santa Fe, NM; Katzen Arts Center Museum, American University, Washington, DC; Frye Art Museum, Seattle, WA; Salt Lake Art Center, Salt Lake City, UT (cat.)
Portrait, Galerie EIGEN + ART, Berlin, Germany
DAVID, MATTHES und ich, Kunstverein Nürnberg, Nürnberg, Germany; Kunstverein Bielefeld, Bielefeld, Germany (cat.)

Northern Light: Leipzig in Miami, Rubell Family Collection, Miami, FL
CLARA-PARK: Positions of Contemporary Painting from Leipzig, Marianne Boesky Gallery, New York, NY
Direkte Malerei, Kunsthalle Mannheim, Mannheim, Germany
Leipzig in Hamburg, Museum der bildenden Künste Leipzig at Produzentengalerie, Hamburg, Germany
Matthias Weischer, David Schnell, Tim Eitel, Galerie EIGEN + ART, Berlin, Germany

Sieben mal Malerei, Neuer Leipziger Kunstverein im Museum der Bildenden Künste, Leipzig, Germany (cat.)
Drei Positionen zur Malerei: Tim Eitel, Cornelius Völker, Matthias Weischer, Treptowers, Berlin, Germany (cat.)
Wilkinson Gallery, London, England

5 aus 11, Galerie LIGA, Berlin, Germany
Leipziger Lerchen, Kunstverein Speyer und Städtische Galerie Speyer im Kulturhof Flachsgasse, Speyer, Germany
Junge Malerie, Kunstverein Sulzfeld, Sulzfeld, Germany
Galerie EIGEN + ART, Leipzig, Germany

Szenenwechsel XX, Museum für Moderne Kunst, Frankfurt am Main, Germany
At Home, Kunstverein Lindau, Lindau, Germany

okal, Galerie EIGEN + ART, Leipzig, Germany
LIGA, Steibs Hof, Leipzig, Germany

Exhibition Checklist

Tilo Baumgärtel
Die Pause (The Pause), 2004
Coal on paper
62 1/2 x 102 in. (158.8 x 259 cm)
TB1
pp **33**, *34*, *35*, 113

Tim Eitel
Verweis (Reference), 2003
Watercolor on paper
12 x 9 in. (30.5 x 22.8 cm)
TE1
pp **37**, 104, 105, 113

Tim Eitel
Bomberjacke (Bomber Jacket), 2003
Watercolor on paper
12 5/8 x 9 3/8 in. (32.2 x 23.7 cm)
TE2
pp **38**, 104, 105, 113

Tim Eitel
Kleine Anhöhe (Little Hill), 2003
Oil and acrylic on canvas
9 1/2 x 9 1/2 in. (24 x 24 cm)
TE3
pp **39**, 104, 106, 112

Tim Eitel
Film, 2003
Oil and acrylic on canvas
94 1/2 x 70 7/8 in. (240 x 180 cm)
TE4
pp **40**, 95, 102, 105, 109, 112, 117

Tim Eitel
Leerer Raum (Empty Room), 2004
Oil and acrylic on canvas
35 1/2 x 27 1/2 in. (90 x 70 cm)
TE5
pp **41**, 104, 105, 107, 111, 112

Tim Eitel
Container, 2004
Oil on canvas
82 3/4 x 118 1/8 in. (210 x 300 cm)
TE6
pp **42**, **43**, 104, 105, 113

Martin Kobe
Untitled, 2003
Acrylic on canvas
64 3/4 x 90 5/8 in. (164.5 x 230 cm)
MK1
pp **45**, *46*, *47*, 95, 98, 99, 100, 101, 109, 117

Martin Kobe
Untitled, 2005
Acrylic on canvas
34 x 58 in. (85 x 145 cm)
MK2
pp **48**, **49**, 117

Neo Rauch
Das Neue (The New), 2003
Oil on canvas
82 1/2 x 118 1/4 in. (209.5 x 300 cm)
NR1
pp **51**, *52*, *53*, 106, 107, 111, 114, 115

Neo Rauch
Demos (Demonstrations), 2004
Oil on canvas
118 1/8 x 82 3/4 in. (300 x 210 cm)
NR2
pp **54**, 106, 107, 115

Neo Rauch
Diktat (Dictation), 2004
Oil on canvas
106 x 82 1/2 in. (269 x 209.5 cm)
NR3
pp **55**, 106, 107, 108, 114, 115

Christoph Ruckhäberle
Frau mit Perlenkette (Woman with Pearl Necklace), 2002
Oil on canvas
20 1/2 x 17 3/4 in. (52 x 45 cm)
CR1
pp **57**, 95, 100, 101, 102, 109, 116

Christoph Ruckhäberle
Theater, 2003
Oil on canvas
74 3/4 x 110 1/4 in. (190 x 280 cm)
CR2
pp **58**, 100, 101, 116

Christoph Ruckhäberle
Komodie (Comedy), 2003
Oil on canvas
75 x 110 1/4 in. (190 x 280 cm)
CR3
pp **59**, 100, 116

Christoph Ruckhäberle
Suite, 2003
Oil on canvas
75 x 110 1/4 in. (190.5 x 280 cm)
CR4
pp **60**, **61**, 101, 116

Bold – Plates / Italic – Details / Standard – Installations

David Schnell
Park, 2000
Tempera on canvas
70 3/4 x 51 1/4 in. (179.5 x 130 cm)
DS1
pp **63**, 103, 119

David Schnell
Ballen (Bales), 2003
Oil on canvas
71 x 110 1/4 in. (180.5 x 280 cm)
DS2
pp **64**, **65**, 102, 103, 119

David Schnell
Durchblick (Vista) , 2004
Oil on linen
90 1/2 x 49 1/8 in. (230 x 125 cm)
DS3
pp *66*, **67**, 102, 119

David Schnell
Bretter (Planks), 2005
Oil on canvas
78 3/4 x 118 1/8 in. (200 x 300 cm)
DS4
pp **68**, **69**, 118

Matthias Weischer
KO, 2003
Oil on canvas
29 1/2 x 33 1/2 in. (75 x 85 cm)
MW1
pp **71**, 96, 98, 114

Matthias Weischer
Chair, 2003
Oil on canvas
75 x 67 in. (190.5 x 170 cm)
MW2
pp *72*, **73**, 97, 98, 114

Matthias Weischer
Zweiteilig (Bisected), 2003
Oil on canvas
92 1/2 x 119 7/8 in. (235 x 304.5 cm)
MW3
pp **74**, **75**, 96, 97, 112, 114, 115

Matthias Weischer
St. Ludgerus, 2004
Oil on linen
78 3/4 x 99 in. (300 x 251.5 cm)
MW4
pp **76**, **77**, 95, 98, 99, 100, 101, 109, 114

Matthias Weischer
Untitled, WV 100, 2004
Graphite on Paper
9 3/4 x 10 1/2 in. (24.8 x 26.7 cm)
MW5
pp **78**

Matthias Weischer
Untitled, WV 241, 2004
Graphite on Paper
7 5/16 x 9 13/16 in. (18.5 x 25 cm)
MW6
pp **79**

Matthias Weischer
Untitled, WV 282, 2004
Graphite on Paper
8 1/4 x 11 13/16 in. (21 x 30 cm)
MW7
pp **79**

Matthias Weischer
Untitled, WV 360, 2005
Graphite on Paper
7 7/8 x 11 1/4 in. (20 x 28.5 cm)
MW8
pp **79**

Matthias Weischer
Untitled, WV 361, 2005
Graphite on Paper
8 1/4 x 11 5/8 in. (21 x 29.5 cm)
MW9
pp **79**

Matthias Weischer
Untitled, WV 369, 2005
Graphite on Paper
7 11/16 x 11 1/2 in. (19,5 x 28.3 cm)
MW10
pp **80**

Matthias Weischer
Untitled, WV 376, 2005
Graphite on Paper
11 3/4 x 8 1/4 in. (19.6 x 28.2 cm)
MW11
pp **80**

Matthias Weischer
Untitled, WV 377, 2005
Graphite on Paper
11 3/4 x 8 1/4 in. (29.8 x 21 cm)
MW12
pp **81**

Matthias Weischer
Untitled, WV 397, 2005
Graphite on Paper
8 1/4 x 11 3/4 in. (21 x 29.8 cm)
MW13
pp **82**

Matthias Weischer
Untitled, WV 398, 2005
Graphite on Paper
7 11/16 x 11 1/4 in. (19.5 x 28.5 cm)
MW14
pp **82**

Matthias Weischer
Untitled, WV 403, 2005
Graphite on Paper
8 x 11 3/8 in. (20.3 x 29 cm)
MW15
pp **82**

Matthias Weischer
Untitled, WV 408, 2005
Graphite on Paper
8 5/16 x 11 3/4 in. (21.1 x 29.8 cm)
MW16
pp **82**

Matthias Weischer
Untitled, WV 409, 2005
Graphite on Paper
8 1/4 x 11 5/8 in. (21 x 29.5 cm)
MW17
pp **83**

Matthias Weischer
Untitled, WV 411, 2005
Graphite on Paper
8 x 11 3/8 in. (20.2 x 29 cm)
MW18
pp **83**

Matthias Weischer
Untitled, WV 416, 2005
Graphite on Paper
8 1/4 x 7 3/4 in. (21 x 29.8 cm)
MW19
pp **83**

Matthias Weischer
Untitled, WV 418, 2005
Graphite on Paper
7 9/16 x 11 1/8 in. (19.2 x 28.2 cm)
MW20
pp **83**

Bold – Plates / Italic – Details / Standard – Installations

Matthias Weischer
Untitled, WV 419, 2005
Graphite on Paper
11 1/4 x 7 3/8 in. (28.5 x 18.9 cm)
MW21
pp **84**

Matthias Weischer
Untitled, WV 420, 2005
Graphite on Paper
8 1/4 x 11 3/4 in. (21 x 29.8 cm)
MW22
pp **85**

Matthias Weischer
Untitled, WV 421, 2005
Graphite on Paper
8 1/4 x 11 3/4 in. (21 x 29.8 cm)
MW23
pp **85**

Matthias Weischer
Untitled, WV 422, 2005
Graphite on Paper
8 1/4 x 11 3/4 in. (21 x 29.8 cm)
MW24
pp **85**

Matthias Weischer
Untitled, WV 423, 2005
Graphite on Paper
8 1/4 x 11 3/4 in. (21 x 29.8 cm)
MW25
pp **85**

Matthias Weischer
Untitled, WV 424, 2005
Graphite on Paper
8 1/4 x 11 5/8 in. (21 x 29.5cm)
MW26
pp **86**

Matthias Weischer
Untitled, WV 432, 2005
Graphite on Paper
8 1/4 x 11 3/4 in. (21 x 29.8 cm)
MW27
pp **86**

Matthias Weischer
Untitled, WV 433, 2005
Graphite on Paper
7 11/16 x 11 7/16 in. (19.5 x 29.4 cm)
MW28
pp **86**

Matthias Weischer
Untitled, WV 436, 2005
Graphite on Paper
8 1/4 x 11 3/4 in. (21 x 29.8 cm)
MW29
pp **87**

Matthias Weischer
Untitled, WV 510, 2005
Oil pastel and graphite on paper
8 1/4 x 11 5/8 in. (21 x 29.5 cm)
MW30
pp **88**, 117

Matthias Weischer
Untitled, WV 512, 2005
Oil pastel and graphite on paper
11 5/8 x 8 1/4 in. (29.5 x 21 cm)
MW31
pp **89**, 117

Matthias Weischer
Untitled, WV 514, 2005
Oil pastel and graphite on paper
8 1/4 x 11 5/8 in. (21 x 29.5 cm)
MW32
pp **90**, 117

Matthias Weischer
Untitled, WV 518, 2005
Oil pastel and graphite on paper
8 1/4 x 11 5/8 in. (21 x 29.5 cm)
MW33
pp **90**, 117

Matthias Weischer
Untitled, WV 520, 2005
Oil pastel and graphite on paper
8 1/4 x 11 5/8 in. (21 x 29.5 cm)
MW34
pp **90**, 117

Matthias Weischer
Untitled, WV 521, 2005
Oil pastel and graphite on paper
8 1/4 x 11 5/8 in. (21 x 29.5 cm)
MW35
pp **90**, 117

Matthias Weischer
Untitled, WV 523, 2005
Oil pastel and graphite on paper
8 1/4 x 11 5/8 in. (21 x 29.5 cm)
MW36
pp **91**, 117

Matthias Weischer
Untitled, WV 524, 2005
Oil pastel and graphite on paper
8 1/4 x 11 5/8 in. (21 x 29.5 cm)
MW37
pp **91**, 117

Matthias Weischer
Untitled, WV 525, 2005
Oil pastel and graphite on paper
8 1/4 x 11 5/8 in. (21 x 29.5 cm)
MW38
pp **91**, 117

Matthias Weischer
Untitled, WV 526, 2005
Oil pastel and graphite on paper
8 1/4 x 11 5/8 in. (21 x 29.5 cm)
MW39
pp **91**, 117

Matthias Weischer
Untitled, WV 530, 2005
Oil pastel and graphite on paper
8 1/4 x 11 5/8 in. (21 x 29.5 cm)
MW40
pp **92**, 117

Matthias Weischer
Untitled, WV 531, 2005
Oil pastel and graphite on paper
8 1/4 x 11 5/8 in. (21 x 29.5 cm)
MW41
pp **92**, 117

Matthias Weischer
Untitled, WV 534, 2005
Oil pastel and graphite on paper
8 1/4 x 11 5/8 in. (21 x 29.5 cm)
MW42
pp **92**, 117

Bold – Plates / Italic – Details / Standard – Installations

Rubell Family Collection

The Rubell Family Collection is one of the leading collections of contemporary art in the world and includes a research library with over 30,000 volumes. Exhibited in a converted 45,000 square-foot former D.E.A. confiscated-goods warehouse, it is a permanent museum of the Rubells' extensive collection of work dating from the 1960s to the present. Open to the public since 1996, the Collection features rotating exhibitions of work by such prominent artists as Maurizio Cattelan, Keith Haring, Damien Hirst, Anselm Kiefer, Jeff Koons, Paul McCarthy, Takashi Murakami, Charles Ray, David Salle, Julian Schnabel, Gregor Schneider, and Cindy Sherman. The Collection began soon after Don and Mera Rubell were married in 1964. At a relatively young age, their son, Jason and their daughter, Jennifer, joined their parents in expanding the Collection. In fact, Jason began his own personal art collection at the age of fourteen, initially financed by stringing tennis rackets after school.

Mark Coetzee has been the director and curator of the Rubell Family Collection since 2000. He is originally from Cape Town, South Africa, where he set up the Fine Art Cabinet, a not-for-profit space, where he curated over 60 exhibitions. Coetzee has published extensively on art, writing for journals such as the Mail and Guardian, Revue Noire and the Sunday Independent. He has published over 30 monograph catalogues on various artists. He has received various grants and awards for his work from foundations such as: Harry Crossley Foundation, the Maggie Laubscher Foundation, the Ruth Prowse Foundation, the Irma Stern Foundation, Montague White Trust and the W.K. Kellogg Foundation. He has also been recognized for his research and curatorial achievements by grants from the National Arts Council of South Africa as well as the Human Sciences Research Council. His latest publication is "Not Afraid" by Phaidon Press.

Laura Steward Heon is the director and curator of SITE Santa Fe, a non-profit contemporary art space located in Santa Fe, New Mexico, known internationally for its international biennial exhibitions, as well as for its contemporary art programming. Appointed to the position in April 2005, she came to SITE from MASS MoCA, one of the world's largest centers for contemporary visual and performing arts, where she was founding curator. She organized the majority of exhibitions at MASS MoCA since it opened in 1999 and wrote most of its catalogues. A graduate of Harvard Univeristy and the Williams/Clark Graduate Program in the History of Art, and prior to her post at MASS MoCA, Heon worked in the Department of Prints and Drawings at the Philadelphia Museum of Art. Her exhibitions have received several important awards, including an AICA prize for best installation for Ann Hamilton: corpus. She has taught art history at Williams College and Bennington College.

Thanks

The Staff at the Rubell Family Collection: Registrar, Juan Valadez; Designer, Jung Kim; Building Manager, Paul Thyssen; Bookstore Manager, Paul Gaeta; Curatorial Assistant, Maria Jiminez; Chief Preparator, Richard Kern; Interns: Valeria Duarte, Izabel Galliera and Kerstin Niemann; Assistant, Natasha Lopez De Victoria; Proofreader and Text Editing, Elizabeth Martinez; Documentation, Kerra Quarles; Accounting, Liliana Zarif; Controller, Sheila Kirschenbaum; Volunteer, Matthew Snitzer.

All the staff at MASS MoCA especially: Exhibition Coordinator, Larry Smallwood; Director of Art Fabrication and Installation, Richard Criddle and his crew; Interns, Molly O'Rourke and Liza Statton; Public Relations, Katherine Myers.

Christian Ehrentraut and Gerd Harry Lybke

David Zwirner, New York, NY; Galerie Binz+Kramer, Cologne, Germany; Galerie EIGEN+ART, Berlin and Leipzig, Germany; Galerie Kleindienst, Leipzig, Germany; Galleri Nicolai Wallner, Copenhagen, Denmark; Marianne Boesky Gallery, New York, NY; Sandroni Rey, Los Angeles, CA; Sommer Contemporary Art, Tel Aviv, Israel; White Cube, London, England; Wilkinson Gallery, London, England; Zach Feuer Gallery (LFL), New York, NY

$30.00
ISBN 0-9716341-4-9
53000>
EAN
9 780971 634145